MONEY. SEX. BEER. GOD.

BY JOHN CROWDER

Sons of Thunder Ministries & Publications
Portland, Oregon

Money.Sex.Beer.God. by John Crowder
Published by Sons of Thunder Ministries & Publications
P.O. Box 40
Marylhurst, OR 97036

www.thenewmystics.com
Phone: **1-877-343-3245**
Email: info@thenewmystics.org

Library of Congress Catalog Number: 2016903904
International Standard Book Number: 0977082660

Printed in the United States of America

Special acknowledgments to Pierre and Johane Morin, Lily Crowder and Brandon Tripp for your contributions to editing.

9 8 7 6 5 4 3 2 1

Dedicated to G.G.E.
Your fellowship has been an inspiration.
*Utinam decidat Dominus mihi testiculos,
si umquam fidem fallam.*

In memory of
Marvin and John Crowder Sr.
who showed me from an early age the humor of life …
and Rosalyn Parker for whom I carry on our
lineage of circus people.

CONTENTS

{ INTRODUCTION ... Pg. 7 }

MONEY. 23

SEX. 69

BEER. 133

GOD. 185

The Life of the Party

In the beginning, God opened His mouth and out spilled galaxies, sea horses, pineapples, beaches, little girls, cinnamon trees and the laws of physics. He was enthralled by the whole bonanza and took a day off to admire the artistry of His craftsmanship. The Father, Son and Spirit had orchestrated a grand jamboree of lightning bolts, barracudas and plum blossoms, replete with Vivaldi, Chopin and Led Zeppelin guitar riffs. The *eternality* of her Creator's delight was echoed in the blueprint of creation's design, in untold billions of unique human fingerprints and infinitudes of unmatched snowflakes – each a distinct Picasso, falling unseen from human eyes in the blistery heights of the Himalayas.

He called the whole thing *good*. From Him came wine to drink, money to blow and rollicking genitals for frisking about and carrying on this whole business of creating. It was all a big, lavish bash engineered to reflect His eternal gladness.

God is pro pleasure. Mankind was created to dwell in the bliss of God's presence in Eden. Eden literally means *pleasure* or *voluptuous living*. [1] Humanity was not designed for depression, toil and the curse of a fallen world. Deep within, humanity longs for the ultimate satisfaction for which we were made – to drink of those rivers of pleasure flowing from His side forevermore (Ps. 36:8, Gen. 2:10).

There is something innate within us that resonates with the truth we were made *for the fun of it*. Religionists wrongly attribute the desire for pleasure to the *sinful nature*. Yet the sinful nature was that fallen Adamic delusion that we could find ultimate satisfaction outside of God.

Christians have often viewed the heathen world chasing after gratification and thus concluded that the pursuit of happiness is inherently *wrong*. Furthermore it is often stated that the believer should attempt to crucify and kill off his appetite for pleasure. But the heathen also have

---

[1] James Strong, *Exhaustive Concordance of the Bible* (Nashville: Abingdon, 1890), Entry H5727 from *adan or ednah* "pleasure."

7

noses on their faces. Does that mean we should cut off our noses because the pagans have them? No there is a God-shaped hole in the heart of *every* man that cannot be quenched with lesser loves. The church, seeing the epicurean chase for sensual fulfillment all around them, has attacked the longing for happiness itself. Any number of legalisms and attempts to suppress our God-given yearnings only cause a perversion of those appetites and cause sin to increase (Rom. 5:20).

"But be sure that human feelings can never be completely stifled. If they are forbidden their normal course, like a river they will cut another channel through the life and flow out to curse and ruin and destroy," writes A.W. Tozer.[2]

People unknowingly pursue materialism, substance abuse and promiscuity in a misguided chase to recapture this lost sense of satisfaction that only the presence of God can provide – something man inherently remembers from the garden. Sin offers any number of momentary indulgences which are followed by devastation to health and homes, ending in broken families, poverty, suicide and destruction for future generations. There are countless billboards offering the promise of satisfaction in this world, but if you are going to be a real *hedonist* – a true pleasure seeker – you must inevitably embrace Jesus. He is the fountainhead of all delight. "*Christ arrived as the high priest of the bliss that was to be ...*" (Heb. 9:11, MOF[3]).

Surely all our fountains are in Him. Christ alone can satisfy the eternal thirst of mankind. But a Pandora's Box of confusion opens up, laying waste to our lives in this question: *does our embrace of Christ mean a complete disconnect from the delight of this world around us?* We have recognized that He is transcendent above creation. But we have missed the reality that He is immanent and tangible *within* and *through* His creation! So often (for fear of abuse or idolatry) the church has encouraged us to radically *forsake* the earthly bounties of this planet.

In rightly warning us to reject (in fact *hate)* the perverse, fallen *worldly system* we inherited in Adam's fall, Jesus never exhorted us to spurn

---

[2] A.W. Tozer, *That Incredible Christi*an (Harrisburg, Pa.: Christian Publications, 1964), 50-52.

[3] James Moffatt, *The Bible: James Moffatt Translation* (San Francisco: Harper Collins, 1922/1994).

the world itself ... the very thing we are *in but not of* is the very thing the Trinity so adamantly loves and sought to redeem (John 3:16).

Religion Hates Materiality

The humanity of Jesus is a litmus test for orthodoxy. It tells us that God finds this material world to be worthwhile – valuable enough to permanently unite Himself with it in the incarnation. Religion has always built a business on attacking the natural, physical world. Starve yourself silly with fasting, because God hates food. Do not drink. Stay single. Take a vow of poverty. No drums in the worship band. Do not enjoy *anything.*

Religion never wants you to figure out that creation is good and to be relished in God's presence. Fr. Robert Capon writes, "To be sure, God remains the greatest good, but, for all that, the world is still good in itself. Indeed, since He does not need it, its whole reason for being must lie in its own goodness. He has no use for it; only delight. ... The world is no disposable ladder to heaven. Earth is not convenient; it is good; it is, by God's design, our lawful love."[4]

In recognizing that Christ is our ultimate delight (in principle), still we have unwittingly divorced Him from the world around us. He must be distant. Our fragmented minds have attempted to partition God off from our natural, earthy existence. A massive fracture exists between our spirituality and our daily life. While mouthing the words "God is good" we foster a lingering suspicion that He is not *authentically* good. Perhaps He is good in that sort of spooky, inhuman way that divine beings must be. But there is this lingering sense of "otherness" to God. He is not *good* by our own earthy definition of the word (perhaps "good for us" like cough medicine, but not in a relatable ecstatic sense of gummy bears and waterslides). While theoretically we recognize a need for Him, there is still a contorted view that God is intrinsically *against our humanity.* Lurking in our theological closet is the idea that He is both *distant* and *against our happiness.*

This *otherness* of God is bolstered by innumerable religious fears that He is the supreme Ego who cannot be supplicated. He demands retribution and sits far away aloof and non-sympathetic to our day-to-day

---

[4] Fr. Robert Capon, *Supper of the Lamb: A Culinary Reflection* (New York: Doubleday & Co., 1969).

affairs. We project our own fears, condemnation and human hatred onto our image of Him, essentially inventing a caricatured entity of *G.O.D. Inc.*, which is a distant spectre of a deity who cannot possibly relate to our real-time joys of living. *Don't make me come down there!*

The Distant God

It is our fallen minds that have contrived a division between God and ourselves. We cannot fathom a God who is, in more ways than not, radically *similar* to us. A God who is human. A God whose image and likeness is the core of our very being – when playing hockey, eating ice cream or watching Clint Eastwood movies. We have invented an ethereal, unrelatable deity who cannot possibly empathize with our temporal needs and wants because He is essentially *unnatural* ... a disembodied, incorporeal spook. Sitting on a sterile white cloud, unconcerned with the trivial cares of our lives. When we fell away from God, we wrongly assumed that He fell away from us.

We have been highly confused about who He is. No wonder we have wanted distance. In Adam, we ran and hid in the bushes, expecting Mr. Happy to obliterate us. Over several millennia, that same fallen Adamic mind gradually worked up a systematic theology (a theory of God) that said: *God is over there, and I am over here.* The foundational doctrine of the fall of Adam is the idea of *separation from God.* This idea was profoundly developed and flourished in early Greek philosophy, which has influenced and permeated Christendom in the Western world for nearly 2,000 years.

But the gospel is not about separation. It is about *union.*

The incarnation is a monumental shift in how we must view reality. God has come close. Heaven and earth are reconciled in the incarnation. God and man find their union in the flesh and blood person of Jesus Christ. Heaven and earth have been permanently rewired in the person of Christ. This union somehow always existed (even when we were sinners), as it cosmically stands outside the limitations of time and space. Long before little baby Jesus was born in Bethlehem's manger, His death mystically pre-dated the foundation of the world! (Rev. 13:8, 1 Pet. 1:20) You were always *in Him*, even before you fell in Adam.

10

In a very real sense, there never was a separation between heaven and earth – except in the enmity of our own minds caused by sin (Col. 1:21-22). We have been obsessed with a separation that does not exist from His perspective. A separation He has dealt with once and for all – even before it happened. Yes, separation was very "real" from our perspective. Isaiah 59 tells us that our sins "separated us" from God. It blinded us to the actuality of His love and nearness. As the chapter continues, "Like the blind we grope along the wall, feeling our way like people without eyes" (Isa. 59:10). It blinded us to His glory, but sin never veritably "removed" God from us. Isaiah says this glory completely fills heaven and earth (Isa. 6:3). Indeed sin caused us to pull away, fleeing from intimacy, relationship and vulnerability. But there is no rock we could hide under, no bush that is not aflame with His presence. David said, "If I make my bed in hell, there you are!" (Ps. 139:8). Sin had two radically different effects upon man and God. For man, sin caused us to run away from Him. For God, sin caused Him to run toward us. And this God-to-human movement was consummated in the incarnation, life, death and resurrection of Jesus (something He had always fore-ordained from the dawn of time, before we ever fell away).

The New Testament never tells us that Jesus died to "reconcile God back to us," as if God had ever pulled back from us disgusted by our failings. No the scriptures clearly state that Christ died to "reconcile *us* back to God" (2 Cor. 5:18-19, Col. 1:20, Rom. 5:10, Eph. 2:16). The gospel is concerned with pulling *us* back – waking *us* up to the reality that we were never abandoned. The cross was not about God being *paid off* so the Father could love us. It was about repairing our corrupted state! We were the ones that needed the fix. It was about destroying our old, fallen delusional nature (a nature that was never the *authentic you)*. God was always present and *for us*, even when we slipped into the idiocy that we could run and exist apart from Mr. Existence Himself. He has always unconditionally loved us.

> In that day you will **realize** that I am in my Father, and you are in me, and I am in you (John 14:20).

There is never a time when Jesus was not in the Father. Never a time when we were not "in Him." The problem has been a lack of *realization* – a lack of *faith*.

MONEY. SEX. BEER. GOD.

What is Gnostic Dualism?

Bad theology produces bad worldviews. And such worldviews have caused all sorts of destruction throughout the centuries. The incarnation flies in the face of the Greek *dualism* that has shaped many of our ideas about theology, science, politics and life itself. Dualism is a term you will want to remember.

Dualism claims there is a separation between "natural world" and "spiritual world." Visible and invisible. Mind versus matter. Spirit substance versus material container ... and most prominently, the idea that God is separate from man. This stuff infected the ideas of the early Church from the beginning.

The dualistic concept that God is distant from us is the source of our problems. And the full-blown blossoming of dualism always results in *Gnosticism*. *Gnosticism* is the ancient heresy with which I intend to have a four-round cage match in this book. Every church the apostle Paul planted fell into one of two errors: either legalism or *Gnosticism*. Just because it is a 2,000-year-old idea does not mean the church ever kicked it to the curb. Gnosticism begins with this extreme dualistic idea that the material world is divorced from the spiritual world. But Gnosticism steps further.

Gnosticism is the concept that the material world is *evil*.

This is the core concept of religion. Killing off the natural, in order to become spiritual. The first Gnostics could not even believe Jesus came in the flesh, because His natural body would have been evil. They said He was just a "spirit being." No way could God have stepped into our stinky, sullied tangible skin! So the apostle John warned us anyone claiming Christ did not come in the flesh is of the *antichrist*. Gnosticism is the bread and butter of religion: the *spirit of the antichrist*.

> *By this you know the Spirit of God: every spirit that confesses that Jesus Christ has come in the flesh is from God, and every spirit that does not confess Jesus is not from God. This is the spirit of the antichrist, which you heard was coming and now is*

in the world already (1 John 4:2-3, ESV[5]).

For many deceivers have gone out into the world, those who do not confess the coming of Jesus Christ in the flesh. Such a one is the deceiver and the antichrist (2 John 1:7, ESV).

Jesus ate, drank, sweat, farted and laughed with His buddies. He made tables and drank wine. He fully incorporated the human life into the Godhead. St. Gregory Nazianzen said, "The unassumed is the un-redeemed."[6] Jesus stepped in and fully assumed a complete humanity in order to completely redeem our entire human existence from dark-ness, uniting our material existence to God. He experienced our full range of human emotion, thought, feeling and corporeal life. But Gnos-ticism holds to the premise that we must reject everything that is natu-ral and earthy. We must beat up our bodies to gain spiritual benefit. This is why religion loves practices like fasting and asceticism (extreme self denial). Anything physically pleasurable is considered wrong.

This vilification of the natural world manifests in a thousand ways in religion today. Money, wine and music are considered evil. Procreate with your wife; but do not *enjoy* it, because physical pleasure is wrong! You are not even allowed to wear comfortable clothes to many churches – *you cannot be comfortable and spiritual at the same time.*

In the following pages, I will offer a basic understanding of how Gnostic dualism has foundationally skewed Western thought and theology for centuries. On one side you have the spirit/idea/thought/unseen realm. On the other side you have the natural/physical/material world.

Gnosticism by strict definition was originally a cultic sect with a number of specific strange ideas. But over time, theologians have tended to use the term "Gnosticism" more loosely to define any system of belief that considers the material world evil. This fundamental anti-physical-world philosophy has spawned countless heresies throughout the church age. While we will look at a number of different nuanced beliefs throughout the book, I will be simply using the looser, broader definition of Gnosticism for convenience.

---

[5] *The English Standard Version Bible: Containing the Old and New Testa-ments with Apocrypha* (Oxford: Oxford University Press, 2009).

[6] Gregory of Nazianzus, *Epistle* 101.7

Christ in the Flesh

One specific, nuanced variant of the "against the body" ideology of Gnosticism is the heresy of *Docetism.*

Docetism is the direct belief that Christ did not physically come in the flesh. He was just a spiritual being – a ghost or a spectre. For the Gnostic Docetist, Jesus could not have assumed material flesh, because real-world meat and bone are corrupt.

Gnosticism is the anti-anointing, anti-anointed-one spirit. It rejects the very bridging of God and man in the incarnation. It directly throws salvation back upon ourselves by forcing us to escape our own bodies with the goal of becoming a disembodied spirit.

The apostle John goes beyond saying that Jesus became a *human.* He clarifies that Jesus actually became *flesh* (Greek: sarx). He sat around the campfire and laughed with the boys. He had body odor. He wept; He rejoiced; He became indignant. He had the full scope of an emotional life. If He cut His finger in Joseph's carpenter shop, it was still the blood of the Lamb, but it left a stain on the table nonetheless.

For the Gnostic, spiritual growth is all about escaping the "lower nature" or the physical container of the material body. The goal is to escape our own humanity. For the Gnostic, the body itself is evil. Again, this is why all material world pleasure is considered wicked by religionists.

Our anti-material view of God is the very thing that has caused us to perceive of Him as a brutal taskmaster – the grumpy school marm who does not want us to enjoy life. But this religious rejection of the goodness and pleasure of natural living is an *anti-gospel* masquerade of false "holiness." The Bible never once tells us the antichrist is one specific person we need to one day beware like the fictional end-time yarns of Tim LaHaye. *Religion* is the antichrist spirit. But we do not think religion is *that* bad. "It's not like murder or pornography or rape ... It's just religion! Shows up to church every Sunday." We think of religion as the white witch of the east ... not as wicked as outright carnality. But religion is the very anti-incarnation that seeks to impose a division between God and humanity and get you climbing an endless hill of redundant works to bridge a non-existent gap that can never be breached with God. It replaces the finished work of Christ by throwing salvation back upon your lap to kill of your natural self and appetites, scaling an unseen spiritual ladder. In actuality, those God-given appetites are not bad. They are merely in need of proper, biblical direction.

Wait … did you say *biblical?* This Gnostic lens has even caused us to view the *Bible itself* as anti-pleasure. Let us be honest; most of the world does not think to jump for joy when it is *Bible reading time*. This is only because we have been indoctrinated to view scripture through this same dualistic lens that pits our spirituality against a happy life.

An Incarnational Lens

If all of Paul's churches succumbed to legalism or Gnosticism, rest assured these are still our two biggest struggles today. Dualistic thinking causes untold harm to how we relate to the planet around us. Ninety-nine percent of folks (even many atheists), would believe, "It's more spiritual to go to church than to play baseball." You *are* the church; and when you play baseball, you are the church playing ball. The world is a sanctuary, burning with the glory of God. The work of the church is not merely preaching, evangelism and singing hymns. The work of the church is farming, coffee roasting, manufacturing, sailing, baking and brewing single malt scotch.

Let us face it: there are a few areas of our lives the church has been quite reluctant to baptize. In the next few sections we will chat up a storm about the stuff your pastor never wants to talk about but you want to hear about: *money, sex and beer*.

After all, that is really why you bought the book.

So yes we need to deal with the fundamental way that *we think* (repent! The Greek word *metanoia* means *change your mind)* about the relation between our spiritual and natural lives. Booze, cash and coitus tend to clash with spirituality in the minds of most churchgoers. God is no less in the bedroom or the bar than He is at the altar. Dropping our schizophrenia opens us up to such a place of wholeness and harmony … it settles the unrequited tempests of both addiction, as well as misplaced self-denial. The concept of our union with God is not just *thought about*. It must be lived. While the final *God* section of the book offers a radical, necessary theological overhaul; in the bulk of these pages we will aim to crack a glass of cabernet and talk real life.

I began this section by saying that God is pro pleasure. His presence is pure ecstasy and the thing we crave at our deepest level. This in no way ever precludes the rock solid fact that God also gives us *natural pleasures!* He never expected that the only time you are ever allowed to experience happiness is when you get a goose bump and fall backward in a foot-stomping Holy Ghost meeting. God made boobs and gold and India Pale Ales. He made tropical beaches, espresso, pheromones, fatty foods and carbohydrates.

The truth lies not in the eradication of appetites and desires, but directing them toward their biblical outlets. We are to *consider ourselves dead to sin* (Col. 3:5), and realize that our truest longings are satisfied in God alone. Therefore we can appreciate those good things of life with which He graces us in a wholesome balance. Glorifying God through our partaking without confusing the gifts for the Giver.

The Bible as Pleasure Manual

Somehow the sacred texts of scripture have been so abused by our dualistic minds, we have failed to see their whole purpose. The Bible is not an arbitrary rulebook designed to quench our fun. In fact, the scriptures are all about *enhancing our pleasure*. The point was never to enforce haphazard regulations against anything that is enjoyable. In fact, just the opposite is true.

For starters, the New Testament commends us ultimately to true love. Yes there are guidelines and exhortations against sin involved — but that is because sin does not produce ultimate joy and satisfaction. If you get *love* right, you are not going to go wrong with the material world. You are not going to slip into idolatry. You will not be a hoarder; you will be a giver. You will not idolize sexual immorality but will love and honor your spouse (or your future spouse if you are single). You are free to eat but you will share your bread with the hungry – which is the essence of what Isaiah says fasting is all about. You will drink a big pint of suds, but you will also buy a beer for your neighbor and not be an overindulging swine to the detriment of yourself, friends and society.

16

Ultimately, only love will satisfy. Furthermore, when Christ – Mr. Love Himself – is given His place, then the scriptures find their place. Otherwise you are looking at an impossible, conflicted list of hair cutting patterns and genital mutilations. Scripture is the means of grace by which we see Him. Yet when improperly handled, it becomes the very object of biblio-idolatry that blinds us to the Author Himself. In other words, when I read Leviticus, I should no longer see a big legalistic finger pointing at me, condemning me for my failure at upholding the law. Instead, I must see every scripture pointing me to Jesus Christ and His finished work. He is the ultimate Word of God and the lens through which I read every other text. With this perspective, even reading Leviticus now cheers me up!

To say that scripture is "all about Jesus" does not flippantly mean that moral guidelines no longer have application to my life. But moral rules are not "steps" to holiness. Our holiness and identity is found in Jesus alone. Only in grasping our identities as a new creation in Him, can we see that morality exhortations are helpful directives to live according to who we *already* are in Him.

A Gracious View of Morality

In the New Testament we find freedom from the law of sin and death – freedom from ceremonial and legal regulations of the Mosaic codes that were never intended to fix up our problems anyway. The law highlighted our need for grace. But the apostles did not leave it there. "Okay kids, now that you're free from the requirements of the law, just go poke around in the dark and try your damnedest to figure out a way to live that works best for you." No. Surely whom the Son sets free is free indeed. We are children of liberty. But only a deadbeat father would let his kids run loose without providing direction on how their lives should be most successfully spent and satisfactorily lived. The Abba of Jesus is our Abba, and He wants the best for us. He guides and counsels us. Living ethically is not about averting His anger. Biblical ethics are precepts that show us what happy, loving, selfless, abundant living looks like.

Again: freedom from the law does not mean the scriptures are no longer applicable to us today in terms of guiding how we should live! In the New Testament, the apostles have extracted for us the very *spirit* of right living that was even shadowed in the Old Testament law. Peter,

MONEY. SEX. BEER. GOD.

Paul and John dismiss the redundant Old Covenant regulations on what to eat and what to wear and hundreds of eccentric commands that were only shadows pointing to Christ. They were external trappings that had no real moral value. Symbolic rules that would be meaningless once the True Substance, which is Jesus, had appeared.

But there are many moral guidelines – even in the ancient law – which are timeless (Don't shoot people. Don't milk the milkman.). And the apostles (men directly commissioned by Christ Himself to teach us), by divine inspiration tell us what guidelines spell out the essence of neighborly love, and therefore carry over into this new era of grace. Circumcision is irrelevant they say. Paul tells us clipping the end of your tallywhacker is pointless; but he also tells us not to stick it into someone you are not married to, because that goes against the *spirit of the law*, which is love. True love – on that level – is not to be confused with mere lust. So tallywhacker usage is confined to a committed, monogamous, married relationship where sex is designed to give us the deepest, lasting fulfillment the way God intended.

In other words, New Testament moral guidelines are veritably *recipes for satisfaction*. Not prohibitions to quench your party. They are parameters to aim you toward the fullness of life in this world according to God's design. We are so ready to settle for the quick fix of sin that brings long-term brokenness. But God – the great Master of the party – knows what will bring you the deepest, lasting satisfaction. Can you trust Him to know what is best for you?

The church is in the habit of either making up its own stupid rules, or ignoring the guidance we have already been given in the epistles. In the name of "freedom" we often feel we can make better decisions for ourselves than what the New Testament moral guidelines prescribe. The end game is always going to be a lesser enjoyment and diminished glory than if we listened to the One who sees the end from the beginning. God will still love us if we forge an unbiblical path. Love is not performance based. But why settle for less?

Part of the problem is that most people see the scriptures as a homogenous book of restrictions. They do not know the difference between old and new covenants. Between law and grace. Between a life of regulation and a life of relational communion in the Spirit. They do not know that Jesus perfected us, and therefore we are not on a

18

treadmill of performance to avert God's wrath or clean ourselves up. The average Christian may grasp the basic concept that Old Covenant rules do not make you holy (forfeiting shellfish or pork chops does not fix your heart). However, the problem is that these same Christians often *do* think that the New Covenant moral standards – mostly found in Paul's letters – constitute a sort of *New Testament law*. Furthermore, they think New Covenant morality is a *road to perfection*, rather than a picture of what the outworking of our holiness should look like.

Paul did not offer moral guidelines as a way to purify you or make you acceptable to God. "Husbands honor your wives. Parents don't exasperate your children ... Do these things and you will *become* holy." No! That is the exact opposite of what Paul said. He always starts with the indicative ("You are already holy thanks to Jesus") and then moves to the imperative action ("Now since you are holy, start acting like it!").

> *For you have died and your life is hidden with Christ in God. ... Therefore consider the members of your earthly body as dead to immorality* (Col. 3:3,5, NASB[7])

Paul always starts with identity, and out of that flows our action. Change of lifestyle is presented as a *fruit* of recognizing our gift of holiness, not a surcharge to purchase it. *You are a good boy. So act like it.*

Knowing moral guidelines are not formulas for "getting right" with God takes performance out of the equation. I can now see God already loves and accepts me regardless. So why does He tell me to live a certain way? Because only in walking in this God-given design am I going to experience all of the deep joys and divine happiness He has intended. I can live a life of true charity and be a blessing to others in my family, community and society. And thanks to Jesus, I am free from the sinful propensities that once ruled me. My old nature died with Him.

Filtering Pleasures Through the Word

If we feel that biblical morality is an impersonal, one-size-fits-all blanket regimen that feels restrictive, we have missed the point. God speaks to us about living life in ways that apply to everyone – principles that ap-

---

[7] *New American Standard Bible* (La Habra, Ca.: The Lockman Foundation, 1977).

ply to all that is intrinsically human. If we *feel differently* than what we find in scripture, it does not mean our emotional longings are wrong – but they are sometimes misplaced due to our lack of understanding. You may *feel* that you want to shag your girlfriend, but trust that God knows best when He says to first put a ring on it.

The Lord wants the best for your life on this planet. Despite Old Covenant legalisms, even our Hebrew forefathers understood this. Hebrew thought was not infected with Greek dualisms we now have in modern Christianity. In many ways, they knew God was a celebrationist more than we do today! The patriarchs did not dissect a difference between their physical and spiritual lives – they considered much of what the church now calls evil to be a gift. You did not see Jews taking *vows of celibacy* because they thought sex was evil. Wine was a blessing. And when have you known a Jewish brother to take a *vow of poverty?*

Ironically, in many ways, even Judaism was less restrictive than the legalisms many fundamentalist preachers impose on their flocks today!

Only in the biblical model do natural world pleasures serve us, rather than destroy us. We are made to enjoy life's delectations. *The key is that we filter those pleasures through the word.* The scriptures serve as a guide to keep us from going into the ditch. For instance, alcohol is a gift. But we are warned away from overindulgence and encouraged to use moderation. A few drams of 16-year Lagavulin never hurt anyone. But drink a whole bottle Jack Daniels everyday and you are going to end up in a gutter, lose your job and get a divorce. That is not pleasurable. See, contrary to popular opinion, the scriptures are *pro-pleasure* at their core. God wants you prospering in healthy, faithful relationships, enjoying the cornucopia of life without killing yourself.

When the Lord is priority and His presence takes centrality in our lives, only then does everything begin to make sense. When He becomes our overindulgence, we are not prone to glut ourselves on lesser loves which may in fact require moderation. Jonathan Edwards once wrote, "There is no such thing as excess in our taking of this spiritual food. There is no such virtue as temperance in spiritual feasting."[8]

---

[8] Jonathan Edwards, "The Spiritual Blessings of the Gospel Represented by a Feast," in *The Works of Jonathan Edwards*, vol. 17, *Sermons and Discourses*,

There is no moderation in feasting on Him. As our satisfaction is found in the Word, *Christ Himself*, then all other creaturely delights serve us appropriately, rather than becoming slave masters that will never scratch our infinite itch. So let us relish Him above all, and learn the appropriate biblical prescription for the created gifts He has bestowed.

How I love the scriptures! A fixed, yet living point of reference: God's words, which point us to *The Word,* enabling us to see Him present, through and within the wonder of the created order.

Greek and Roman Gnosticism

Before we fully dive into those biblical prescriptions for money, hooch and nookie, we should define something important. I want to explain the distinction between two types of Gnostic thinking. These are two ditches on the same road that we often veer into with earthly gifts. These two forms of Gnosticism are *Greek and Roman.* Both consider the material world to be evil, but they respond to that belief differently.

The Greek Gnostic *rejects the world*, moving heavily into asceticism (total abstinence). Fasting is big for the Greek Gnostic. Because it is all about starving off the physical man in order to attain the spiritual. Money is obviously considered evil (Jesus never knocked money by the way, only the idolatry of it), so Greek Gnosticism embraces a love of poverty *(which is also a root of all kinds of evil).* For centuries our Catholic brothers have seen poverty as a virtue and committed their lives to it! And who is the guy that all Christians agree to hate? The prosperity preaching televangelist of course. No matter his motives, he is an easy target because God wants us poor, broke and depressed.

Then there is sex. What an area of confusion! Ever since the early church, it was taught that sex is sinful and our bodies are dirty (hence the age-old vow of celibacy and a two-millennia-old misconstruction of Paul's teachings on singleness being better than marriage).

Obviously uptight Christians demonize alcohol. The list goes on: music, dancing, playing cards, corncob pipes, etc. Physical world gifts that the Greek Gnostic rejects as sinful.

1723-1729, ed. Kenneth P. Minkema (New Haven, Conn.: Yale University Press, 1996), 286.

MONEY. SEX. BEER. GOD.

But what about the *other* version of Gnosticism?

Remember, the *Roman* version of Gnosticism also views the material world as intrinsically evil. However the Roman Gnostic approaches it differently. Rather than taking the ascetic route of fasting and self-denial, the Roman Gnostic figures, "We're all messed up and locked into this fallen physical world. There's nothing we can do about it anyway ... so let's have an orgy!" The Roman Gnostic turns to licentiousness and overindulgence as he figures his escape from the "evil world" is impossible. He can do anything he wants; and in a sense, because everything is "sinful," then nothing is truly considered "sinful" at all.

So Gnostic thought can take one of two paths: a strict, Greek austerity or a careless, Roman free-for-all. Paul, in his preaching of the scandalous grace of the cross, was often accused of teaching "license to sin;" and thus his adversaries leveled a charge that he was teaching Roman Gnosticism. But grace is freedom *from* sin, not freedom *to* sin!

In Christianity today, you see both of these manifestations. Either strict denial of all "wine, women and song" or else a loose, careless, antinomian living. Interestingly, Jesus warned us of two types of bad yeast – the leaven of the Pharisees and the leaven of Herod (Mark 8:15). One represents religious abstinence and the other represents worldly excess. But Christ Himself is the true leaven of heaven (Matt. 13:33), worked throughout the entire dough of our humanity so we experience unity and wholeness between our earthly and spiritual lives. We can enjoy luxuries of life in a non-idolatrous way when Christ is our center.

Again, the ancient Hebraic mind always understood God gives the delights of this world as a gift to be received with thanksgiving. We may enjoy the world without being worldly when we take in life *through the word!* God only puts moral parameters on our earthly delights for the benefit of ultimate goodness. Gnosticism has duped us into thinking the scriptures are anti-fun. Anti-earth. Anti-life. But in reality, the New Testament moral guidelines have always been about enhancing and sustaining our holistic joy! A joy that is intrinsically from God, sourced in God and organically connected to our life in the Spirit – the source of all satisfaction. A refreshing, right understanding of scripture directs us into the full, satisfying abundant life God has always intended for us *in this world and the next!*

MONEY.

How Filthy is Lucre?

There is nothing quite like the combo topics of God and money to ruffle people's feathers. This is what I have learned about Christians over the years: If you do not get offended at the gospel of grace, you will get offended at miracles. If you do not get offended at miracles, you will absolutely get offended over money. My hope is to graciously challenge the Gnostic, poverty mentality that grips so many hearts and minds in today's church and thus bring a touch of freedom in this area.

Money is a huge subject. It plays a massive role in our lives. Whether they have it or not, money consumes the *thought life* of almost everyone: concern over bills, how much stuff costs, how much to work, how much to pay. While folks brood over it continually, they rarely ever integrate this area of their life with their spirituality. Some get offended if their pastor talks about it in church, yet money is all they think about the rest of the week. There is a sharp dualistic division in our mind between moolah and God stuff. It is a taboo subject in Christianity.

I have found that in some of the most ecstatic, glorious moments in our meetings – when waves of refreshing are washing over the people – the moment you suggest receiving an offering, everyone suddenly seizes up and prepares for exploitation! They forget the glory they are experiencing and jump right into fearful silence or outright criticism. They should have expected the money-grubbing preacher to strike at some point. But generosity and giving are such an intoxicating part of our new nature. The exchange of currency is literally a tangible demonstration and expression of love. The church has a lot of work to do in this area in terms of renewing the mind. Both expecting more and giving more. We are created for success in life. People set a low bar for themselves by divorcing this world's economy from their spirituality.

Revelation is needed. And that is what we aim to unpackage here. One of the most life-changing gifts of God I have experienced is liberation from divisive thinking about money. People have formulated such strong views on the topic that it is very difficult to discuss money in a thorough manner in church, without having your motives questioned.

There is a high level of distrust when you put the words "preacher" and "money" in the same sentence. Whether that is from manipulation and abuse we have experienced or just general stereotype, nevertheless it is where most people stand. Fortunately in a book like this, where I am not fishing for a tithe or offering, you can lay your strong opinions aside for a moment and hear me out. Depending on your church background, there are trigger terms you will read that might frustrate you: *sowing, reaping, prosperity, etc.* I would encourage you to keep an open mind.

Prosperity Gospel?

It is mind-boggling to see how certain Reformed evangelicals typecast and pigeonhole every charismatic Christian on the planet with a gross caricature. Anyone who believes in physical healing or any other New Testament charismata is lumped together under the hackneyed idea of a late-night TV preacher selling miracle cures. And anyone who believes God could potentially extend His hand with monetary blessing is demonized with cliché terms such as "Word of Faith" or "prosperity gospel." Some of the most vocal bigots among them assume every charismatic is necessarily an idolater of cash.

Whatever your opinions on the so-called "prosperity gospel" (a loaded term) I should point out that:

A) Stereotypes are never helpful in getting at the truth of a matter.
B) Why listen to a broke preacher teach about money?

That is a big statement, considering that lot of people see poverty as a virtue. As a matter of fact, to take holy orders in the Catholic Church you have to make a lifelong pact with poverty. Sounds like shaking hands over a business deal with the devil.

For all the religious harping you hear against materialism, Jesus baptized the material world by stepping into a material body. And for all the droning you hear against financial prosperity, know that it is usually a bunch of pious pap to justify people's own stinginess or lack of success in this area. Prosperity is not a problem, *greed* is. If we do not learn to separate those two things and get unlocked from broad-brush critical views, chances are we are going to struggle. We must be teachable.

If I am sick – the last thing I should do is knock healing ministry.

24

If I am broke – I should not knock biblical financial advice.

Often the people who bash prosperity do not have two nickels to rub together to help the poor, while offering their unsolicited opinions on how much *other* Christian churches and preachers should give. There is a hypocritical mantra in many evangelical churches that tells us to give funds, yet we are told it is inherently wrong to generate those funds. Many Christians are told not to even pursue wealth, because money is considered *evil*. Are you going to help starving AIDS orphans in Africa by taking a vow of poverty? It is ridiculous as taking a vow of sickness – but then again, some of the saints of the church even did that! They begged God for cancers and tumors just to humble themselves. Absolute religious idiocy. In fact, the curse of poverty is solemnly viewed as a virtue in the church! Why even attempt to liberate the poor from poverty if being broke is a spiritually elevated state?

Jesus never said one negative thing about money. He only knocked the idolatry of it. He knows that you have need of cornflakes and Dolce & Gabbana sunglasses. But He says put your priorities right – put first the kingdom – and all this stuff will be added to you.

> *So do not worry, saying, 'What shall we eat?' or 'What shall we drink?' or 'What shall we wear?' For the pagans run after all these things, and your heavenly Father knows that you need them. But seek first his kingdom and his righteousness, and all these things will be given to you as well* (Matt. 6:31-33, NIV[1])

Funny how poverty pushers conveniently remove the last part of that final verse "all these things will be given to you as well." The problem is an endemic Gnostic mindset that has vilified money simply because it is a natural, material world commodity.

I Love Money

But is money the root of all evil? No the Bible says, "the *love of money* is the root of all kinds of *evil*" (1 Tim. 6:10). As with any natural world gift the issue is giving it the inappropriate place in our lives.

For most Christians, the *love of money* is a term bearing very subjec-

---

[1] *The Holy Bible, New International Version* (Grand Rapids: The Zondervan Corporation, 1973, 1978, 1984). International Bible Society.

tive definitions. Let me be very clear about something:

I love money!

Don't you? Of course you do. If you are already angry about that statement, thinking piously of yourself, "Well Mr. Crowder, *I surely do not love money!*" Then that just makes you a money-loving liar. If you have no desire whatsoever in your life for money, then why on God's green earth do you even work? Why do you have a bank account? Why do you have a house? A car? Wear clothes?

In saying that I *love* money, I am not talking about the idolatrous *love* Paul exhorts Timothy against. No, I am saying that I love what money can accomplish. I love that I can rescue five-year-old boys from whorehouses in India. I love that I have coin to rescue six-year-old girls from brothels and feed them, clothe them, educate them and give them a loving home. I love that I can be bread to the hungry, feet to the lame and a father to the fatherless. I can make the widow's heart sing.

We are so hesitant to talk about cash in church, that we even make up silly *Christianese* names for it:

Finances
Resources
Provision
Seed

Why can we not just call it "M O N E Y?" Before we go a step further, I would encourage you to reach into your wallet and pull out a nice, crisp bill. Take a good long look at it. Turn it over. Inspect it. Sniff it. Is it evil? Does it have a heart? A mind? A soul? I am pretty sure that upon close investigation that you will find it is just a piece of paper. It is *amoral.*

Now if Adolph Hitler owned the bill in your hand, what would it be used for? *Evil.* If Mother Theresa owned the bill in your hand, what would it be used for? *Good.* Money is simply a tool that will be employed for usage according to the heart of its owner. Thank God for it.

I love a lot of things in a *storge* type of way (Greek for a fondness, familiarity type of "love"). I love my dog. My smoking jacket. My sweatpants that still fit me. But I do not *idolize* those things. I do not *philia* money (Greek for human *friendship love*) by elevating it to the degree I would sell out my fellow man. I do not *eros* money (Greek for *romantic love*), because I have never once made out with it. And I surely do not *agape* money (Greek for *divine love*), because I do not bow the knee to it.

For centuries, the church chock full of Gnosticism, has vilified something God never said one negative thing about. It has rejected the incarnational reality that we are not only allowed but commanded to thrive and multiply in this physical world. Our Jewish brothers have always understood that money – material wealth – was considered a blessing from God. It is only Greek pagan philosophy with its dualisms that have subconsciously caused us to settle for far less in this life than we could achieve and accomplish by bringing in more bacon.

Expect More

How often have you heard some pious soul utter the prayer, "Lord, I don't ask for much. Just help me cover my house note and my car payment, and I won't bother you for anything else." As selfless as this supplication may sound, it is actually selfish self-centeredness. Just wanting to squeak by with my own petty needs covered. God wants us to dream bigger. To dream His dreams. He wants us thinking about nations. He has created us to be resource providers for the poor. He wants to expand our vision beyond ourselves. *A good man leaves an inheritance to his children's children* (Prov. 13:2). How about expecting and achieving more in life: putting your kids through college, funding unwed mothers, sending out missionaries or actually making some kind of difference for the gospel?

If some or all of these types of things are not in our hearts, chances are we are already idolaters focused on our own needs. In the name of stewardship, many people think it is godly to cut as many corners as possible, clipping coupons, cooking with generic brand flour – being thrifty with our tight-wadded, clammy hands. But this crumb-snatching mentality is a faithless, inefficient and godless way to view life. What if we worried not about lack, but what we would do with overabundance? Conceiving not of new ways to save, but entrepreneurial ideas to generate more wealth, take risks, invest and pioneer new sources of income? Brooding and mulling over redundant ways to ration out the few pennies we have erases God from the picture. I do not suggest waste, but rather abandoning a Great Depression, spendthrift outlook.

Years ago, I wrestled with this same poverty mentality. I would comb through the cell phone bill every month to make sure there were no hidden charges and I was not being billed for any extraneous calls I did not make. The more we are consumed and constantly thinking about money – whether we actually have any or not – the more idolatrous we are. It is a fruit of worry and fear (and by the way, worry and fear are sins that are widely accepted in the Christian world). One day, I felt the Lord was encouraging me to "not even think about money anymore." In other words, stop being obsessed and anxious about it all the time. From that point forward, I did a radical thing. I stopped balancing my checkbook altogether. Sure I occasionally take a look at the bank account. And obviously I must reconcile all the line items at the end of the year for tax purposes. But as for the day-to-day concern over my financial well being, I just let it go. Money comes in. Money goes out. I stopped stressing. So what if milk costs $10 a gallon? Just buy the milk. Your Father knows you need milk. So what if gas costs $10 a gallon? You need gas. Just buy it. Your Father knows you have need of these things. Would you like to be liberated from constant anxiety over money? What is stopping you? Paradoxically if I ever find myself stressing about money, I have learned to act in the *opposite spirit* – it is the perfect time to give some away!

Here is a startling conclusion I have reached. The Lord would absolutely love it if we were all millionaires. I am not talking about fueling your greed. I am talking about making us resource centers for the nations. When we pray, "Let it be on earth as it is in heaven," we are not asking for the Sahara to come down from the sky. If we have a problem with wealth, we are surely going to despise heaven. I believe a primary reason He lovingly does not entrust us with more cash is because He cannot *trust us* with more cash. If we are not faithful with the little, how can we be entrusted with more? In our greed, we would likely kill ourselves with millions if we do not learn the joy and freedom of generosity, which is the very frequency of our new creation hearts. More than filling our bank accounts, the Lord's primary concern is for us to realize the freedom of giving – a condition of the heart.

The fact is, whether we are rich or broke, we can still struggle with idolatry or a poverty mentality. In fact, someone could be a millionaire, when in all actuality the Lord longs to entrust him with billions. But perhaps they have not learned generosity or how to hold things open-handedly. It is His tangible grace in our lives that we often do not move into financial abundance in our immaturity.

Is Money God's Blessing?

Let me be clear up front that the amount of money we have is not an indicator of our spirituality. This is a common misconception leveled by anti-prosperity critics, that we associate money itself with God's blessings. God's blessings are primarily intangibles – peace, joy, charity – but this is not to relegate away the physical world gifts. We are also blessed in tangible ways: with family, friends … and yes, with cold-hard stacks of dead presidents. This does not mean money itself is a standalone indicator of God's blessing. It does not mean that the child digging through the garbage dump of Indonesia is any less loved by God than Donald Trump. One's stock portfolio is not at all the gauge of their spirituality. But if we make the grossly inaccurate statement that money is altogether *not* a gift from God, then we should stop thanking Him for it and stop saying grace before our meals. His gifts are often given indiscriminately. It is for us to recognize their source and use them accordingly for His glory. If "stuff" can never be considered a gift of God, please stop being appreciative of it.

Yes, the general principle is that God would love to give us more income. He would love to bankroll us, and yet Providence often holds back if we would not steward it correctly or kill ourselves with it through self-centeredness. Many fat cats do indeed harm themselves with it (neither is this a sign of God's hatred of the rich). But to think God would not want to bless us with more cheddar is itself a wicked doctrine. We must know His heart is to overflow through us in tangible ways to feed the hungry and liberate the oppressed. Even here, we do not want a fickle, indeterminate view of God who haphazardly blesses one over another based on performance. Performance is clearly an issue, but not in earning God's approval. There are simply real-life economic principles involved that should not be over-spiritualized. We do not just lie on the couch, introspectively "getting our hearts right" so that we can be financial conduits of God's blessing. There are practical realities such as: going to college, pursuing career, working diligently, investing wisely and using the God-given tools you already have at hand to prosper. Nevertheless, without an underpinning view that God *wills* our success in this life, many young people are afraid to take risks like borrowing school loans or pursuing any "secular" career that is not directly related to our churchy definition of *ministry*.

The Gnostic assumption that the accumulation of wealth is inherently wicked is not a biblical principle. But the view has driven a bad hermeneutical approach to reading scripture, even among academic scholars. The *a priori* preconceived idea that money is bad has led many to assume Jesus' admonition to the rich young ruler in Matthew 19 is a command for *everyone* to adopt. The rich young ruler asked Jesus, "Teacher, what good thing must I do to get eternal life?" (Matt. 19:16) Anyone with a fundamental revelation of the gospel of grace knows that we can *do nothing* to be saved. God saves us single-handedly apart from our works. This was the underlying point Jesus is driving home in this passage. Jesus is essentially telling the kid that, if he plans to save himself by doing good, then he must *follow the law.* Impossible. But Mr. Moneybags thought he was doing a good job of that, so Jesus further shows the impossibility of saving himself by zeroing right in on his favorite idol. *Okay kid, go sell everything you have and give it to the poor.* The whole point of this passage is that you cannot do enough good to get saved. "Only God is good" (verse 17) and "with man this is impossible, but with God all things are possible" (verse 26).

The passage highlights that only God Himself – not our good works or charity – is the sole source of salvation. But Jesus personally tailors a recipe for salvation for this young fellow which He knows will be impossible to fulfill. He goes after the kid's idol to highlight his need for a new heart and the grace that only Christ can afford.

A Command to Generate Wealth

Jesus is not making a blanket statement that all Christians of every shape and size should empty their bank accounts in order to go to heaven. Yes, the Lord surely takes His standard swipe at greed. But in another passage, Christ points out another form of wickedness ... the sin of *not making money!*

In Matthew 25, we find the parable of the servants who were given cash (talents) to invest in the master's absence. Some invested wisely, doubling their initial principal. But another servant buried his talents and refused to pursue any risks to generate even more income with it.

"The master was furious. 'That's a terrible way to live! It's criminal to live cautiously like that! If you knew I was after the best, why did you do less than the least? The least you could have done would have been to invest the sum with the bankers, where at least I would have gotten a little interest. Take the thousand and give it to the one who risked the most. And get rid of this "play-it-safe" who won't go out on a limb. Throw him out into utter darkness'" (Matt. 25: 26-30, MSG[2])

Now I will not spend time deconstructing your fears that poor investment strategies will send you to hell. That is not my point. Nevertheless, it is a solemn wake-up call to those with cowardice to stop penny pinching and take financial risks. Wise use of talents is not the housewife reusing coffee filters to save a nickel at the grocery store. That is a false sense of stewardship. Dream bigger. Start thinking in bigger denominations. I often wonder if, for most Christians, their greatest fear is not of failure but a fear of success. It takes so little effort to manage a meager portion. But what if we got out of our comfort zone and started shooting for the stars? If your vision in life is something you can accomplish in your own strength and by your own means, then it is not God's vision for you. As bizarre as it may sound, what if our biggest *fear* is not rejection, but complete acceptance by God? Scared of the abundance that entails. How prepared are you to steward millions? We prefer the safety of mediocrity we have known.

I often see among Christians what I would call the *George Müller complex*. Müller was a remarkable man of faith who cared for more than 10,000 orphans in his life. However, he is often known for living day-to-day in such a way that he did not know where the next meal would come from, until baskets of bread would miraculously appear on his doorstep by suppertime. In no way would I belittle such charity and risk. Nevertheless, a common mindset has been hatched in many minds that God only provides for us *at the last moment*, right before we need a thing.

Often, the Lord may indeed stretch our faith with these types of scenar-

---

[2] Eugene Peterson, *The Message* (Colorado Springs: NavPress Publishing Group, 2005 ed.).

ios. Very often people want to take short-term mission trips with us, but they do not have the cash to afford the entire thing. Many times, we have seen the ones who actually take the *baby step* of faith, who submit their trip application and initial deposit (without even having the final amount yet in their account) see incredible miracles. At the last moment, they are given thousands of dollars, air miles for travel, etc. In fact, we have seen people take the initial faith-act of signing up, and afterward their bosses cover the whole thing and give them a paid vacation. On our last mission trip to the Middle East, three of our team members even received multi-thousand-dollar raises at their work the moment they returned home!

Mediocrity vs. Abundance

So yes, there is a principle in which our faith is grown day-to-day, hand-to-mouth and stretched to begin walking in a direction God calls us; and at times we do not see the provision until the instant that we need it. But there is also a dark side to this mentality if we begin lowering our expectations in life to believe God only has a paycheck-to-paycheck existence for us. What if "He who gives you power to get wealth" is okay with a bit more cushion in our bank accounts (Deut. 8:18)? What if there is *more than enough*? Leftovers. Abundance. Is it so bad to elevate our expectancies? How much is too much?

Many times we settle for a survival mentality, rather than a thriving mentality. We may feel the Lord is good enough to rescue us from abject destitution. Yet we think the best He can do (or all He *wants* to do) is to pull us out of debt into a place of mediocrity. One of my favorite passages from the Psalms about the poor tells us that God does not simply lift them out of poverty ... but He lifts them all the way to royalty.

> *He lifts the poor from the dust and the needy from the garbage dump. He sets them among princes, even the princes of his own people!* (Psalm 113:7-8, NLT[3])

This is where many believers who staunchly oppose a concept of "prosperity" begin to offer some compromise. *Okay, God wants to*

---

[3] *New Living Translation* (Wheaton: Tyndale House Publishers, 1996, 2004, 2007).

32

bless us to some degree ... but you can't take that too far. How far is too far when it comes to God's financial favor? I cannot think of another area besides money in which the church has such a rubber ruler, subjective moral standard.

How much is *too extravagant?* For one person, they think it is too wasteful to take their wife out on a date night and a movie. For another person, it is godly to drive a Hyundai, but it is too extravagant to drive a Lincoln. Imagine if you were an African living on a dollar a day and your only mode of transport was a bicycle. Is it okay for an American to have a Hyundai, but not an African? For an African to go from bike to Hyundai would be more extreme than for an American to go from Hyundai to Lamborghini.

The term *too extravagant* is radically subjective. Is it "too much" to expect enough money to send your kid to college? But he should expect community trade school, not Harvard, because that is *too much* (after all, he should hope to change someone's tires, not change the world).

I am sure the citizens of Congo would consider air conditioning an extravagance, but most Christians in Texas would not be accused of materialism simply because they have A/C in both the house and the car. If you have central heat and air in many countries, that makes you a *one-percenter.* For one person, he is not sure God is willing for him to own his own home – it is more spiritual to rent. But to own *two houses?* That is surely over the top. How many bedrooms are too many? One for each kid, or must they double up (maybe quadruple up)? Could we trust God for an extra bedroom for guests? Is it allowable to own a dozen properties and live off the real estate investment? *Careful, don't be a hoarder!* Or is it more spiritual to break a sweat and break your back everyday working on a factory assembly line? After all, the Bible says strife and toil are fruits of the Spirit right?

Diligence vs. Strife

There is an incalculable level of idiocy and misplaced religious zeal in the helm in countless pulpits, wherein the curse of human strife has replaced wisdom. I heard an angry preacher shouting the other day, "Men you should live exhausted! You should go to bed tired and wrung out every night without a drop of energy left! There should be no free time left in your schedule – you should be working harder!" Hard work is admirable. There is undeniable blessing on diligent hands. But not at the expense of wisdom, using your God-given brain and living out of a center of rest and trust in the gospel. The Bible says more about rest than it does faith! In fact, rest is the flavor of faith (Heb. 4). Faith is trusting in God. If human striving is involved, it ceases to be faith.

But we are taught that bending our backs in hardship for a few peanuts is more admirable than using wisdom and understanding. We were designed, like Adam, for *garden works*. Where our vocation and our play are intertwined. Please do not think I suggest that bankers are more spiritual or enlightened than auto mechanics. Maybe you love working on cars; you are great at it, and that is your calling. In fact, Paul says, "make it your ambition to lead a quiet life: You should mind your own business and *work with your hands"* (1 Thess. 4:11). But this is not an overarching directive that we cannot have Christian professors, architects or mathematicians. Even a mechanic uses wisdom. You can try to pound off a lug nut with a crowbar, or you can use a pneumatic drill. As a matter of fact you can open your own shop, hire some employees and only get your hands greasy on the fun projects like restoring your favorite classic cars. Diligence is not the same as working *hard.* Work smarter not harder.

The point is we have been told to limit our dreams. There is a glass ceiling placed upon success, all in the name of fear of avarice. Greed is merely a counterfeit for the God-given desire for success and accomplishment that is placed in the heart of every man. There is absolutely nothing wrong with your desire to achieve great things. When this is rooted and founded in the love of God – and bolstered by a love for your fellow man – never let religionists limit your success. I do not watch Christian television, but recently everyone was in an uproar because Creflo Dollar wanted a $60 million airplane. I could care less if he wants a $500 billion submarine. I do not have a clue whether the jet is warranted or not, but why do we feel a knee-jerk pressure to weigh in and measure this stuff in self-righteous criticism? Mostly it boils down to jealousy I suppose – a symptom of greed and comparison.

Garden Works

Adam lived in a place of abundance. He owned *all* the real estate. There was a river called Pishon in Genesis 2 flowing from the Garden of Eden. The scriptures simply tell us, "The gold is right there." Imagine Adam walking along, "Oh look! More of that shiny stuff." No big deal. The earth was literally spitting its treasures at Adam's feet. Adam was a centrifuge for blessing. A money magnet. Everything was easy and effortless. Sure he had a career, tending the Garden of Pleasure, but I am sure that he loved his job. Just like Tarzan, swinging through the trees. There was no toil. No striving or sweat.

We are often confounded in choosing a career path, or finding our calling. I would argue that it was not until after Adam's fall that mankind's work and play became separate things. We are all created to work (studies have shown that after three months of no work, psychological issues can set in). The problem is that our work and play have been divorced. Now we work in order to afford play time, and we play in order to escape work. God created us to thoroughly enjoy our occupation. What is the one thing in the world you would do with your time, even if you did not get paid for it? There is a good chance that your calling is somehow associated with that – and there is a way to get paid for it. Less striving, more fruitfulness.

It was not until after the fall that everything became inverted. Adam's eyes fell from God to the earth. When God was his focus and priority, the earth placed baskets of gold on his doorstep everyday. He slid into all the best parking spots. Everything was easy for Adam. But when his eyes shifted from God and he came under the slave master of sin, everything changed. It seems the earth also fell away from Adam.

Proverbs says, *"Cast but a glance at riches*, and they are gone, for they will surely sprout wings and fly off to the sky like an eagle" (Prov. 23:5, NIV).

When Adam's eyes moved from God (as well as the open-handedness and generosity that would entail from prioritizing a higher source) and he came under the curse, everything went backward. Instead of his provision appearing effortlessly without strife, now Adam was hunched over digging in the furrows by the sweat of his brow among the thorns and the thistles. Paradoxically, as Adam's eyes dropped to the ground beneath him, to the *stuff,* that is when the stuff sprouted wings and flew away and was hard to come by. The book of Job speaks of the earth swallowing up its gold.

Thank God the story did not end with Adam's fall. Jesus Christ stepped into our Adamic humanity. He bore those very thorns and thistles on His own sweaty brow and reversed not only the curse of poverty itself, but destroyed sin and the fall in His own broken body – rescuing us from the power of darkness and bringing us into His glorious light.

Holding Lightly

There is a principle here. When we hold natural things lightly (like money) with our eyes focused on God in generosity, we prosper. But when we are obsessed with idols – anxious, toiling, digging for them – we lose even that which we have. Understand there is nothing inherently wrong with producing. The issue is the emphasis and priority of our heart. Amounts are subjective and meaningless. We can make exponentially more money yet be far less focused on it than the man who obsessively struggles at earning every dime but has nothing.

The pre-fallen Adam walked in what could be defined as *favor*. Favor is the unearned, unmerited blessing of God. You could call it *grace*. One moment of God's favor is worth more than a lifetime of striving self-effort. It is much better to have favor – with greenbacks clinging to you like a magnet – than to be striving for every advancement in life. Planet earth became frustrated at Adam's fall (Rom. 8:20). What was at the core of the planet's frustration? What dynamics are at play by which we no longer see the effortless favor of Eden all around us?

I understand that Christians do not believe in sowing and reaping (as a preacher dependent upon the generosity of the people, I can attest this is a verified fact); nevertheless, the earth itself *does* believe in sowing and reaping. We see in Romans 8 that the earth has a *voice*. It is mystically groaning for the sons of God to wake up to the revelation of their identity as sons. Here the earth is in a position of longing and frustration. Even though church folks dismiss "sowing and reaping" as a televangelism ploy to ratchet open their pockets, well the earth views it quite differently. We have viewed sowing through the legalistic lens of karma or law – we have viewed it as a legal duty. But the earth on the other hand views it as it was truly intended ... as a built-in system of blessing beyond comprehension. The earth recognizes that you put seed into the ground and almost magically, it multiplies. We are talking about exponential growth that outpaces the stock market! It is rare to find a high-cap stock or bond that multiplies over a few months like a kernel to an ear of corn or wheat. Sowing and reaping is like a built in slot machine. Moreover, it is like the loosest slot in Las Vegas. Imagine there was a slot on the Vegas Strip wherein every single time you fed it cash you won the jackpot. You would be an absolute idiot not to shove every last buck you had into it!

The earth recognizes this. As in the garden, where the river laid its treasures at Adam's feet, the earth loves to sow into the sons of God. But the earth knows better than to sow into the slaves of sin. You do not want to reap that whirlwind. So why is the earth frustrated? *The earth is frustrated because it lost its inheritance.* Yes we tend the earth, but the earth is also here to serve us. I am sorry if this seems too mystical – if you are appalled at my giving the earth a voice or equating Christian generosity to a trip to Vegas. But sowing and reaping is just a mechanical principle that is set into place by God whether we like it or not. When we begin to catch a revelation that sowing and reaping is a joy that is intrinsically woven into the fabric of reality *for us* and for our prosperity – it begins to shift our paradigms on generosity dramatically.

Grace Giving

The concept of *sowing and reaping* is quite misunderstood from many angles. But for all our harping against abuse and manipulation, we cannot deny that it is a solid, Pauline New Covenant principle (and scripture is clear that Paul is talking about cold, hard cash). Thank God for the Word of Faith movement that recovered this biblical concept in the twentieth century. Yes there has been legalism, avarice and gross misapplication of it on many levels. But the overwhelming prejudice in the evangelical and charismatic world today is solidly *against* the Pauline doctrine (if not in theory then in practice). While our evangelical brothers think every charismatic Christian service is a TBN fund-raising marathon with people just throwing their money at the altars, any real-life charismatic can tell you that fear and stinginess cuts across all denominational lines.

The real question is: how do we view sowing and reaping through a lens of grace and the finished work of the cross? If it is transactional, as if we are buying a blessing, does that not invalidate the free gift of grace in Jesus? Over the past several years there has been an international awakening to the message of grace, as countless people have been freed from legalism and religious bondage. Nevertheless, the concept of a *grace movement* entails a big conglomerate host of different preachers that often teach polar opposite things. The term "grace preacher" really irritates me in fact. Nobody has a complete angle on grace, and often teachers are just spinning out oddball side doctrines that are not really gracious at all.

One such *grace teacher* who has a bit of traction in some circles has gone so far as to dualistically allegorize all of the New Testament admonitions about sowing and reaping. He says that Jesus is the Seed that was sown, so we do not sow anymore. On the surface this sounds very gracious and Christocentric, but it is quite ridiculous. This is like saying God is love, so we do not love anymore! The issue for a grace believer is not *giving versus not giving*. The difference we must see is *law giving versus grace giving*.

We cannot relegate Paul's sowing doctrine to spiritual metaphor. Admittedly at times Paul worked with his own hands to fund his ministry. But at other times, Paul was adamantly bold in his collections. He told one church to prepare their gifts a *year in advance*. For the poor in Jerusalem he literally sent Titus on an offering tour! (2 Cor. 8) "Okay boys, get ready. We're coming to town to pass the plate. We'll back up the wagon, load up your savings and leave." How offensive is that? People get upset at itinerate ministers blowing through town receiving offerings. In this case, cash was the sole purpose of Paul's visit!

So if this is in the New Covenant, how do we see giving through the lens of grace? In Luke 11 Jesus rebukes the Pharisees who meticulously give a tenth of their spices, mint and cumin … imagine the law giver with a razor blade clinically cutting 10 percent of his powders like lines of cocaine, "Oops, that's one grain too many!" We've all been there before, whipping out our scientific calculators and calculating our tithe down to the 58th decimal point. "I'm feeling generous this month, Lord. I'm going to round up that last nickel in your favor." Legalistically and anal retentively we gave 10 percent under the law. And the law giver's motive is usually duty, obligation and *fear of the devourer* if he does not meet God's command. The law giver is also trying to earn something. Trying to climb into a blessing.

The grace giver, on the other hand, splatters generosity all over the walls! He knows that he is a resource provider to the nations! We are not trying to climb into something. Ephesians 1:18 says you have al-

38

ready obtained an inheritance! He says you already have *everything*. What would happen if we were to give out of our identity, as if we were already loaded? As if we had already won the lottery – if we are already kings? The law giver is trying to reach the finish line, but the grace giver contributes as if he has already arrived.

How would you give if you were already rich? We gauge our assets based on what the bank account statement says. But what if we started prophetically sowing as if we were already at a different level of income? Maybe then we would start to see the bank account align with the truth of the resources God says we already have from His perspective. Sow where you want to go. Give like you are already there.

All is Grace

Although we commonly use the word "offering," giving is more of a *response* to Christ's self-giving offering on the cross. It is aligning with the new creation heart that thrives on and enjoys generosity. And when we live according to design, we manifest accordingly. The new covenant giver literally gets *intoxicated* on it. Righteous earthly economies that are not based on corruption have the natural ramification of prospering citizens. In the same way, there are built-in spiritual ramifications to how we live our personal financial lives.

From a grace perspective, everything is a gift. Imagine hypothetically you pull out your wallet and gave the whole thing to God. Let me ask: how much have you ever given God? Think about it ... Here is the answer: *nothing*. Where did the contents of your wallet come from anyway? "My job at Home Depot?" you may say. No. *He gives seed to the sower* (2 Cor. 9:10). It is all from Him. Did you pay for the air you breathed working at Home Depot? No it is all a gift (If you were striving at your job, that's your fault. Do not blame Him).

See there is nothing we give that did not already come from Him. This is grace. He puts the seed in your hand. This is not transactional karma. To the New Covenant grace giver, He says, "Now watch this ... Trust me with it. Sow that seed into my glory." We respond, "But Lord, I don't want to be presumptuous." Do not worry, He responds, "You've never been presumptuous in this area in your life!" If our sweaty white knuckles ever become unclenched and we drop it in there, suddenly it multiplies! Is it not interesting that even religious skinflints never actually *regret* an offering? Sure, it is pure torture wrenching it from your wallet to the offering basket, but once you have done it, you always feel good and know that you set yourself up for a return.

Sowing for the New Covenant believer is always an exercise in trust. It is not buying favor. It is like an investment. If you could take a time capsule back to 1982 you would be insane not to invest all your cash in Apple or Microsoft stock, because retrospectively you know it is a sure bet. In our act of trusting God with our stuff, we see Him multiply it. In fact, with sowing you are not truly *giving away* anything. You are putting *your* seed in the ground, so that it grows and comes back to *you*. But our doubts stifle us. The offering plate passes by; we constrict with agony, and we guiltily drop in a little tip. God is not a maitre d' that He should be tipped. It is like walking by Santa Claus ringing the Salvation Army kettle in front of the supermarket at Christmas and we guiltily throw in a few bucks so we do not feel like Uncle Scrooge. That's a tip.

A Cosmic Principle

When we get beyond our orphan mentalities, we start giving at a level that is beyond us. But this takes a revelatory understanding that sowing and reaping is a rock solid principle woven into God's design of the universe. You do not break the law of gravity. If you step off a building, you will only illustrate it. Jesus says if we cannot believe in earthly principles, we will have a difficult time grasping heavenly principles (John 3:12). Sowing is just a principle of nature itself. Consider that the richest billionaires of the world – Warren Buffett, Bill Gates – these guys give away billions of dollars, and they also bring in billions of dollars. This is not just about a tax write-off. Maybe they call it karma. Maybe they call it philanthropy. Maybe they call it "what goes around comes around." But nevertheless the principle of sowing and reaping is at work. If an unbelieving farmer plants a row of beans, do the beans not grow because he is an unbeliever? Of course they grow! It is just a natural principle, whether the guy is a Christian or not. Sowing and reaping is ingrained in the fabric of reality.

But the religious poverty mentality needs to see the outcome before it can trust. A few times I have heard someone say, "Brother if I ever win the lottery, I'm going to give you _____!" As if this was the pinnacle of his good will and intention. But I say, "Try giving me _____ now and see if you don't win the lottery!" Faith comes before the manifestation.

People have so many hang ups catching the revelation that sowing and reaping is a biblical fact. So we can hardly sever a few hundred bucks from our pockets. How ever can we begin to trust God with thousands, tens of thousands or hundreds of thousands? We are ingrained with a stuck mentality, and it is much easier to question the motives of the minister who encourages your charity than to actually try giving. *My pappy was poor. My grand pappy was poor. I'm going to be poor.* We just settle. But the cycle breaks when we learn to trust. As a minister, cynics regularly question my motives, "He just wants our money!" I often put their minds at easy by clarifying my motives. "Yes, I'll take *all* your money!" But it is not so I can buy hair plugs and liposuction. I know what I want to do with the cash. I want to rescue orphans from the sex trade. Preach the gospel to the poor. I want to break the fangs of the wicked and snatch the victims from their teeth!

Even if I went to Tahiti every weekend on the offering till, that is still irrelevant when it comes to the heart of the giver. Giving is between you and God. You would still be blessed regardless of the motive of the minister (just as the early church determined that baptisms and sacraments were still valid, despite the motives of the minister performing them). Often in our stinginess we shift blame. I am not saying that sowing is a *magical formula*, but it is a rock solid principle. And yes, we should be led of the Spirit in it. But for all of our fear of presumption that we might be giving too much, hands down the usual problem is that we do not recognize His leading when He is prompting us to *higher* amounts than we are comfortable with! As for presumption, it is always better to err on the side of risk than cowardice.

From the Trailer

Before we go much further, I should give you a bit of my own personal history. As a product of the 1980s I remember quite clearly the televangelism debacles of that decade. I remember the uproar over Jim Baker's alleged air-conditioned doghouse and the mascara streaked tears of Tammy Faye pleading for donations. For people of my generation, you just do not bring up the subject of money and ministry in the same breath. There is an innate distrust of preachers. Most ministers have cowed to this fear of misperception long ago, and rarely breach the subject of money with their parishioners without a dozen disclaimers about "not wanting any of you to feel uncomfortable."

MONEY. SEX. BEER. GOD.

So it was only natural that I should harbor the common critique that preachers are hungry for filthy lucre. Although I was a faithful legalistic tither, I was very critical when it came to ministers asking for money. I even owned a Benny Hinn mockumentary video. Every time Benny said something, his animated eyeballs popped out with dollar signs.

This was my mindset, over a decade ago, when I realized the Lord was calling me into full time ministry. At the time I had a lot of potential. I was moving in a number of spiritual gifts. I was healing the sick. I could prophesy. I even had quite a bit of revelation brewing inside of me that needed to get out to the world. But there was one small hiccup ...

I was absolutely broke.

At the time I was living in a trailer in Alaska. Loads of ministry potential. But the one thing holding me back – the one cork in the bottle that was preventing all of my gifts from being released – was money. If you do not have dough, the thing is never getting off the ground.

Do you have a vision from the Lord? Something He has called you to do? Maybe it is missions, business, government, art, media or whatever. Do you need some cash to make it happen? Let me encourage you that if you have a vision but you do not have the cash – get hold of some revelation! Start sowing kamikaze. Get addicted to generosity and watch how your whole perspective turns upside down! It is not just about a new mindset – until you physically reach in your pocket and start giving like it, chances are you have not really changed your mind!

Anyway – I did not have that perspective. As I said, I was a regimented tithe payer, but that never helped me out much in my singlewide (By the way, do not take this as a slam if you live in a trailer. Consider my poor predicament ... I was in a *refrigerated* trailer in Alaska!). I was preaching for free and leading local small groups, but I had no faith for finances much less for world missions.

Offending my Offense

During that time in Alaska, we decided to bring in a visiting minister to our town who was widely known for operating in unusual miracles (keep in mind I loved the supernatural, I just had no faith for cash). I was excited. Ready to see signs and wonders. Well the first night he

42

took to the stage, I became a bit disturbed. From start to finish, the minister's the entire message was one long offertory. Since I was critical of that sort of thing, I just bit my tongue and waited for the next day's session. After all, we had him in town for a week. By the time the next day rolled around, it was more of the same. *Money, money, money.* All the guy ever talked about was money. I just held in my offense, and kept coming back to the meetings every day. And every day for the entire week, he just kept rattling off hour-long offerings.

By the last day of the meetings, I was sitting on the pew, fuming inside as he continued with his money talk. Finally, as I was sitting there, I felt as if the Lord Himself came along and spoke to me.

"Son."
Yes Lord?
"You know you do live in a trailer. *Maybe you should listen to this guy.*"

Suddenly, as I sat burning with criticism, I began coming to a realization. I remembered something that charismatic writer Rick Joyner always used to say: *criticism is the number one thing that holds people into poverty.* Then instantly, I remembered the words of the Lord, "Blessed are those who are not offended because of Me" (Matt. 11:6). Suddenly this verse appeared to me as a sort of dividing line, as if I were on one side of it or the other: *am I experiencing blessing or am I feeling offense in my pew right now?*

It was precisely at this moment that something shifted. I decided that I was going to spite my own criticism. I was going to sow against my own offense. I was going to write this guy the biggest, fattest check I had ever written. It is not that I liked the guy (still do not care much for him today), but I decided that I was going to refute my own offense and defy my own cynicism. I pulled out the checkbook, wrote down a number and followed it by a long string of zeros. I threw it into the offering.

Instantly, before I realized anything, someone came up and put a check into my pocket. Nothing like that had ever happened to me before. I had some friends in that very meeting who threw their diamond engagement ring into the offering. Later that very same week, in their remote cabin in Alaska, they randomly found another diamond ring … *double* the size of the one they had given. *Probably a coincidence?*

Something crazy and supernatural had just taken place, because in the blink of an eye – within two weeks of the offering – I received three telephone calls to my trailer in Alaska with people giving me a book contract and tens of thousands of dollars to start traveling around the world doing missions and evangelism campaigns.

Cha-ching!

Suddenly, I was a man with a revelation! I had always been a faithful tither, but I had never authentically grasped the reality that giving is an intoxicating principle designed by God attached to a solid expectancy of reaping. It was a joyous "get to," not a legalistic "have to." Suddenly on a deeply personal level, I realized, "This stuff really works!"

How many have heard the old adage: *never give to get; only give out the goodness of your heart?* While I appreciate the sentiment and agree we should give out of genuine love, this is really a misguided statement. Imagine a farmer sowing his seed. What farmer in his right mind plants seed just *out of the goodness of his heart*, not expecting a return? Some dumb farmer! "I'll throw some seed in the toilet. Toss some on the pavement. Doesn't matter. I am not expecting a return. Just giving out of the goodness of my heart." No! Old and New Testaments both appeal to expectancy in giving. *Expectancy* not greed.

Supernatural Increase

Immediately I tossed the Benny Hinn video into the garbage. No more criticism. I began chucking money at any ministry that had a drop of oil on it. If I saw someone moving in the glory, I invested into it. It was like I had an addiction – a gambling problem. I just got hammered drunk on giving. I had never experienced anything like this before.

In one year's time, I was able to give away more money than I made the year before. Imagine what your gross income was last year – would you love to be able to give that much away? I realized there was nothing stopping me except a substandard belief system. In one year's time, our income more than doubled. The year after that, it doubled again. The year after that it doubled again. On the fourth year, it went up. On the fifth year it doubled again. Somewhere in that timeframe America experienced the *economic downturn* of the mid 2000s. It was our best year to date. We were living by a different economy.

44

On our seventh year in ministry I took a modified sabbatical, cutting back my ministry engagements to only once a month. It was the first time our income slumped. By how much? *Only 10 percent.* Imagine taking a whole year off and still bringing in 90 percent of what you normally would! This was crazy! In the Old Covenant, God told His people to take a whole Sabbath vacation year off, and He supernaturally doubled their income the year before so they could coast.

Return the voice of the critic: *Well, no wonder you were bringing in all that money. All you do is go around and take up offerings all the time!*

It is quite comical how people think itinerate ministers just roll around in offering money on their hotel room beds every night while single mothers go without milk and bread. Let me clearly tell you that what was happening was utterly *supernatural.* It did not make sense. It was *stupid.* I once walked into an office supply store, and someone who did not know me from Kanye West came up with a check and said, "I haven't paid my tithes in months. Can I just give you this?" Another day I was lying on the floor during worship and received a vision of a diamond ring. I knew the Lord was telling me to invest in a certain jewelry store stock. I knew *nothing* about investing. I had no broker at all. So I just jumped online and in a few minutes figured out how to buy stock. I purchased the stock. The thing instantly jumped up over 100 percent, and I doubled my money. Now that is *insider trading!*

It was offensive how easy this all was. Just shun greed, be generous and watch it rain. I was afraid to talk about it, because I did not want people to get jealous. I knew too well how that critical, religious spirit worked. Let me say clearly that the spirit of religion and the spirit of poverty are the *same spirit.* It is that same critical mindset that "God wouldn't heal little ol' me. God wouldn't use little ol' me. God wouldn't financially bless little ol' me." Is it not ironic that the Bible Belt of America (where I am from) is also the most poverty stricken area of America? There are plenty of people who would intellectually agree that sowing and reaping is a valid principle, but somehow they do not think it would actually work for "little ol' me" so they never step out.

Addicted to Generosity

In those beginning days, set before me was now the faith to move into full-time ministry. Around that period the Lord was really teaching me about faith. At one point, I had no money to pay my bills for the month. Most pastors would strongly caution against what I did to remedy the situation, but I was unstoppable because I was a man who had caught a revelation. I figured, "Well, I obviously need a miracle since I cannot pay the bills," so I emptied out my entire bank account online and gave every last penny to a humanitarian ministry.

The next day I got a telephone call. A massive megachurch had just discovered my fledgling new book and wanted to buy every copy that I could muster up. Thousands of dollars came pouring in. Understand that I had no sugar-daddy partner list. No Plan B or alternative financial support to depend on. My vision was just being flooded by the glory of generosity. Sowing was not drudgery. *Sowing is fun!* I have four kids. My wife and I enjoyed sowing them! If you don't have that much fun sowing, chances are you have only known religious, duty-driven giving.

I began to challenge myself. Forget sheepishly splitting restaurant bills – I would dive for them and cover the whole group. As a teenager $500 was a huge amount to give, but as I became a grown-up, I needed to start thinking in grown-up amounts. I would recommend if you have never dropped $2,000 or $5,000 or $10,000 – keep pushing and offending yourself beyond the breaking point. Sometimes it feels like bungee jumping, "Am I really giving away $30,000?" Then you take the plunge and your income doubles! Someone will say, "Well, I gave $1,000 once and nothing happened." Well I am sure you have consumed more than $1,000 worth of housing, food and clothing since then. Yes this is a principle – but do not think of it strictly in observable, mechanical, transactional terms. On top of that, remember that giving is a lifestyle. Not something you try once just to test the water. It is the rhythm of the Christian life. I made love to my wife once. It was so great, I decided to make it part of my lifestyle.

The very thing that was integral to it all was that we became addicted to giving it away. We were not hoarding all this newfound income. I am even hesitant to talk about it – it is no boast. I know there are vast realms of faith I have not begun to tap. These testimonies are liberating and it would almost be selfish not to share them. Religionists say *give until it hurts*. But there is a place beyond that in which giving *feels really good*.

As I discovered that this principle really works, I started exploring it. At the time we had a minivan that smelled like toddler urine. We still owed thousands of dollars on it, but I thought, "Hey, why not believe for an upgrade?" So I started asking the Lord if I could give my van away. Pretty insane right? Who asks the Lord if they can give away their own car? I did not get a thunderous answer from the sky. My answer was already plainly declared in scripture. So we gave away the van to a struggling missionary couple. Within mere weeks the entire debt on the van was miraculously paid off and we got a massive, leather interior SUV fully loaded with a carbon footprint the size of Texas.

Bowing to the Tithers

If you think the money was just rolling in because of honorariums, think again. It was around 2008 and 2009 that we were immediately deluged with cancellations, disinvites and rebukes from massive churches and ministries which had embraced us only months before. My embrace of supernatural Christianity, effortless grace (and the fact that I liked to joke around and have fun) got me scapegoated and blacklisted from the prophetic conference circuit. Many big ministers would secretly tell me they agreed with my stances, but it did not matter. The bottom dollar for many ministries is summed up in the fear of losing tithers. The green room rumor mill began to swirl that John Crowder is too edgy or controversial to have into your meetings!

I could care less about doing a dog-and-pony show for potential bene-factors. I knew that was utterly backward and idolatrous. Let the partners go. Stick to the truth, and the Lord will send more along. Well that is exactly what happened. We had more money rolling in than ever before, even while getting kicked out of enormous churches! I cannot remember how many 1,000-person-plus conference invitations we lost in a matter of weeks. It was financially irrelevant. It was still our best year ever in terms of cash. It did not make sense!

We were having fun in the freedom of enjoying God and preaching the scandal of Christ's finished work. We relished not being controlled. At the same time charismatic churches were slamming their doors in our faces, bigger doors of opportunity were opening into secular media. Al Gore's television channel Current TV (now owned by Al Jazeera!) did a 30-minute documentary on us. *The Sun* newspaper – largest daily in the UK – did a full two-page spread on us. We even had pornographic magazines coming to our meetings because experiencing the ecstasy on God sounded fun! That's right – I was interviewed and got to preach the gospel right in the middle of a porn mag! Imagine some bloke flipping his pages: Dirty picture ... Dirty picture ... *John Crowder preaching the gospel* ... Dirty picture ... I am probably the first porn star preacher you have ever encountered (I never undressed for money). Funny thing is that the porn article was more positive than most of the stuff the church had written about us (albeit the language was much more colorful).

Needless to say, doors of favor opened up. I have turned down multiple opportunities for reality television shows – including National Geographic, Big Brother and others! I was free from making decisions based on money or increasing my platform.

Buying Favor?

The favor of God is not something we buy. This is a huge straw man misconception about the so-called *prosperity gospel* (by the way, I would much prefer a prosperity gospel to a *poverty gospel*). We are not talking about a transactional exchange like Simon the Sorcerer attempting to *buy the Holy Spirit* (Acts 8:8-25). But favor is something we can flow with or against. Wherever we invest, we are aligning and contributing and joining ourselves together with that cause. If we put time and money into the glory, we are associating ourselves with the glory. As mystical as it sounds, the oil rubs onto us – there is no way around it. While we do not "buy favor," we also cannot deny the biblical principle of sowing and reaping. These are two truths we hold in tension.

So what about the poor and persecuted? Are they unfavored?

Let me return to this common, mocking argument against prosperity. I do not suggest that people who are suffering, in chains or persecuted for Christ's sake are somehow outside of God's will (but let us stop blaming God for the horror they are facing). For goodness sake, you should see the persecution we faced during these times! The countless dozens of nasty blogs written about me, protestor lines at my meetings, thousands of condemning emails and untold hundreds of bullies I had to block on social media probably qualify me for some hazard pay (Just for fun we eventually bought our haters their own domain at www.johncrowderblockedme.com)! No wonder at any given time 75 percent of American pastors want to quit.[4] Resistance and hardship happens. That does not indicate a lack of favor. Even in the midst of resistance, this uncanny thing happens where the temporary trials *work for us*, working up a weight of glory!

We think of the book of Job as a story primarily of human suffering. Job experienced a very intense, but short period of suffering for sure. But Job was blessed beforehand, and double blessed afterward. The story is really one of God's favor and faithfulness even when we are going through hard times that we may even blame Him for. When Job was thinking back to the days of his prime – when the favor of God was on him – he said:

Oh, that I were as in months past,
As in the days when God watched over me;
When His lamp shone upon my head,
And when by His light I walked through darkness;
Just as I was in the days of my prime,
When the friendly counsel of God was over my tent;
When the Almighty was yet with me,
When my children were around me;
When my steps were bathed with cream,
And the rock poured out rivers of oil for me! (Job 29:1-6, NKJV[5])

For Job, all his children were around him. There were no dry places for Job – even the rocks poured out oil. There was no friction or difficulty for Job – no resistance! His paths were greasy, drenched with cream and butter. He slid right into the best parking spots. He had all the right connections. Things just came together easily for him. When he went into the city gates, the young men hid; the old men stood up and the princes covered their mouths. He had favor in high places.

For whatever reasons that suffering may happen (God's "answer" is rather ambiguous to Job), there is still tangible favor for us in this world – our blessings are not just *spiritual.* They exude into the natural world around us, though they are firmly established in God and from Him.

---

[4] "Top Two Causes for Pastors Leaving Ministry and More Statistics," *Standing Stone* (May 10, 2014) http://www.standingstoneministry.org/top-2-causes-for-pastors-leaving-ministry-and-more-statistics (accessed Feb. 25, 2016).

[5] *New King James Version* (Thomas Nelson Publishers, 1982).

Rather than have a causal, problem-focused approach, "Well why doesn't everyone prosper?" Instead let us have an answer-driven approach, "Hey, this is for me thanks to Jesus! Even if suffering or trouble comes my way, I am a child of favor and can expect to see more in this life!" So many impoverished areas of the world are plagued by hopelessness. We need *metanoia*. It starts not with whining about the successful, but with *me* making a difference.

Money Miracles

We must anticipate the favor that is already ours thanks to Jesus (that is faith)! Since the scriptures also appeal to our expectancy in giving, I always encourage a supernatural anticipation to be attached to our generosity. I could tell countless stories of money miracles we have seen in our ministry that are beyond human ability to generate. Gnostic tightwad religious folks should be awfully upset that Jesus pulled a gold coin from a fish's mouth, multiplied food or supernaturally filled the disciples' nets with fish. Besides my earlier example, I have received *other* God-given stock investment tips. Once I was given the name of a Chinese stock in my dream. Again, I had no investment broker, so I looked online the next morning and saw it really was the name of an actual Dow Jones commodity! I bought into the stock. I sat on it for a year, but it dipped in value. Finally, I sold the stock, thinking perhaps it was just a "pizza dream" not really inspired by God. When I sold it, the stock jumped up 400 percent! I said, "Sorry Lord," bought back into it, and it continued to climb until I doubled my money! Another example of *insider trading*. Living by revelation is much easier than toil.

In our meetings we have had numerous examples of money spontaneously appearing. Once in Georgia, our friend Kathy Drown reached into her purse during our meeting and found $1,500 in crisp, brand new consecutively numbered $100 bills. You would know if you were packing that much heat in your purse. But she had not put it there.

Once a lady in our meeting opened up her Altoids breath mint can, and money had appeared in the container! We have had numerous testimonies of people with thousands of dollars in debt (one in particular was $5,000) who experienced the glory of the gospel in the meeting. When they went home and checked their account, the negative balance had turned into a *positive* balance of $5,000! This stuff makes people either really excited or really mad!

MONEY. SEX. BEER. GOD.

Once in Fort Wayne, Indiana we were talking about *drunk money*: how God wants to get your finances so drunk that the decimal point will start bouncing around, and you do not know where the money is coming from. During the break, a lady visited the ATM, inserted her card, and the machine started spitting money out at her. Then it gave back her card and said, "Sorry, we cannot process this transaction." The ATM got drunk in the Holy Ghost! I do not know the ethics on that one, but thank you Jesus and thank you FDIC.

We once received a spontaneous offering for a widow in a meeting. When she went to the bank to deposit it, the amount had multiplied since she first counted it. So right in front of the teller, she counted it over and over multiple times. Every single time, the total continued to supernaturally grow larger and larger.

I was traveling with a friend on a weeklong ministry tour. Following a meeting one night, he counted the offering. In order to get the accurate total, I had him calculate it once more. The second time he counted, the total jumped up another $4,000. I said, "How could you miss $4,000? Count it again!" He counted it a third time, and it jumped up an additional $6,000 on top of the other four grand. I said, "Count it again!"

Honestly we have seen supernatural phenomena that would cause any academic reading this book to label me a fraud or a loon if I mentioned them. I have never been ashamed of this supernatural gospel. We have seen gemstones fall out of thin air in meetings. I was recently in Mexico and only learned afterward that 30 gemstones were found in the meeting! People with costume jewelry have seen their fake gems turn color and become authentic gemstones during meetings. We have had meetings where eight or nine people spontaneously saw the prongs of their diamond rings begin to break because the diamonds grew or doubled in size. Once on speaking about the "mustard seed" of faith, a lady reached into her purse and a handful of mustard seeds appeared! That is even strange in my book. There have been repeated testimonies of people getting new contracts or jobs as they experienced the glory of God in certain ways in meetings. I do not give personal prophetic words in a programmatic way to people in sessions the way I once did when I was associated with the *prophetic camp*. But if I randomly feel led to do so, I will. I once told a guy he was going to be given real estate. The next time I saw him, he had two house keys – both properties had been *given* to him.

MONEY. SEX. BEER. GOD.

When my youngest daughter was 11, she asked me to explain how offerings worked. I was driving at the time and made a few offhand remarks. Apparently, I must have exerted some sort of *offering magic!* Little did I know that my statements made an impact on her. From that point forward she inwardly determined that the next conference event she attended, she was going to donate *all* of her money (which was approximately $11). She is an artist. She is also a budding entrepreneur. Ever since she was a small girl, she would paint or draw pictures and set up tables to sell them in random places – on the beach, at the park ... *and obviously at dad's meetings!*

I brought her with me on a trip after my forgotten conversation about sowing and reaping. While I was preaching that weekend, I noticed she had taken initiative to set up her paintings at the back of the room. At every session, she would ask, "Dad is there going to be an offering?" I do not have routine, obligatory collections at every session. Finally, on the last day, we did an offering. I saw her run forward and throw in her crumpled $11. Immediately we broke for lunch. Less than five minutes after parting with all her money, my daughter ran up to me, "Dad, someone just gave me $900 for my painting!"

Years ago, I felt a crisis of conscience to receive an offering. I knew there were many folks giving in the plate who were so broke they could not even pay attention, much less pay bills. But the Lord strongly corrected me. *If this principle is true, it is true for everybody.* It was not about me. Let the people participate. Jesus could have told the poor widow with two mites not to bother, because He did not need the cash. He does not need *anybody's* cash. This is a participatory act in which we learn to trust and exercise faith.

Generosity Negates Idolatry

Many people in the church who criticize money talk are usually hung up on this stuff because they are internally conflicted. Some of my favorite theologians, as much revelation as they may have on certain aspects of grace, are still unwittingly Gnostic when it comes to money and prosperity. Our dualisms have blinded us. The popular evangelical teacher John Piper, whose work *Desiring God* will remain a classic, is a great example. In that book, he argues for a hedonistic delight in God, yet simultaneously Piper argues that the joy of the Lord is not a tangible *happiness*. Joy is once again relegated to a dualistic spiritual realm that does not intersect our "fallen" earthly life. Piper regularly attacks his caricatured version of the "prosperity gospel" equating all Word of Faith preachers to idolaters. My aim is not to strike out at Piper (as much as we would disagree on many points, I actually respect him and was once close friend to his son). My point is that the broad brush of *idolatry* is a categorical typecast that is good for stirring up ire in a fiery sermon, but not for dialogue between streams and building bridges over disagreement in focus.

If one argues charismatics appeal to greed in their offerings, you could also argue that the mainline evangelicals appeal to *guilt.* While we do not base theology over consensus, it is worth pointing out that charismatics and Pentecostals (the bulk of prosperity adherents) now make up 26.7 percent of the church.[6] Not saying by any means that majority rules when it comes to doctrine. And there is surely greed and idolatry in the church. But evangelicals need to watch where they wave the guns of accusation.

The problem of idolatry does not consist in the accumulation of wealth. It is ultimately the inability to be generous with it. Placing our trust in it. No doubt materialism is a massive problem in the Western world. Our longing for satisfaction is radically misplaced. We rightly recognize that money can bring *some* comfort and protection. Ecclesiastes 7:12 notes that "wisdom is a shelter as money is a shelter." But the question is, do we place our ultimate trust in the false comfort of material gain or in the infinite wisdom of God from whom all blessings flow? That verse continues, "but the advantage of (godly) knowledge is this: that wisdom preserves the life of its possessor." We know money cannot buy love, life, health or eternal security.

The ditch on either side of the road is to either vilify money or else worship it. These are Gnostic extremes. There is a fine line we must walk. But that walk is found in ultimately relaxing over the whole thing and not constantly worrying about the bottom dollar. We are in the world, but not of the world. There is a holistic way of recognizing the God-given role of money in our lives without feeling spiritually conflicted with a false sense of guilt. *Gratitude is key.* Remembering the Source. Not running off with the cash like the prodigal, but enjoying the

---

[6] Pew Research Center's Forum on Religion & Global Life, *Global Christianity*, (December 2011) http://www.pewforum.org

inheritance *with* the Father in the Father's house. Whether in plenty or in lack we are remaining faithful – not tossed to and fro by the winds of Wall Street, thinking our current financial state is an indicator whether or not God likes us. You may be so broke when you go to Kentucky Fried Chicken you have to lick *other* people's fingers. Not a big deal! God is for you, whether you are loaded or living in the garbage dumps of the Third World. I have been to those dumps ... *Jesus lives there!*

If we must drive everything to the dualistic extreme and enforce a division between our spiritual and natural lives, then Jesus assures us we surely cannot serve two masters, both God and money. He also tells us to hate our father and mother if we are to follow Him. But we rightly recognize He loaded certain statements for comparative legal value – He is not literally endorsing *hatred*. Every dualism is radically corrected in the incarnation.

The kingdom of the world has become the kingdom of our Lord and of His Christ ... (Rev. 11:15, ESV[7]).

G. K. Chesterton said, "Somehow one must love the world without being worldly."[8] Balance is not rejecting the world itself, but the undue attachments and misplaced confidence we see in the lustful modus operandi around us. Balance is not settling for less, while subjectively criticizing what we consider *excess* in the lives of others. There is true balance in these two extremes: taking the limit off how much money you can make and taking the limit off how much money you can give. Only there do our dualisms not blind us to blessing, nor our hearts become full of avarice. Balance is also found in being content all along the way – whatever economic status – yet never using *contentment* as a misplaced excuse for apathy or low expectancy.

Simply said: *gratitude, generosity and love guard us against idolatry.* These virtues keep us mindful of the Lord, our source.

Hatred of Megachurches

One pastor who has criticized my views on money (though ironically

---

[7] *The English Standard Version Bible: Containing the Old and New Testaments with Apocrypha* (Oxford: Oxford University Press, 2009).

[8] G.K. Chesterton, *Orthodoxy* (Snowball Classics Publishing, 2015 ed.), 49.

never attended one of my meetings to actually hear them) happens to struggle financially himself. Go figure. He paradoxically bashes ministries which are fiscally successful, yet every few months puts out a desperate Facebook plea for alms, saying his own ministry is bankrupting him to the point he literally can not afford to feed his own kids. Everyone but himself can see the jealous inconsistencies.

He recently made a statement on social media that highlights common faulty logic, saying, "The combined cost of just the megachurches within the U.S. is enough to wipe out childhood hunger. Think about that. I am not saying they shouldn't exist. Just pointing out a financial fact." Believe it or not, this person actually has an education. But he is clearly not an economics major nor a sociologist. Just another voice beating the pandering drum of false social justice outrage. If by the "cost of megachurches" he suggests selling off all the assets, buildings, putting clergy out of a job and sending tens of thousands of believers to start home groups, well what does he think is the derived benefit? Surely millions of dollars – lets even say a few billion – would feed the world's 3 billion people living on less than $2.50 a day for how long? I figure it would feed everyone about one warm Happy Meal.

Even the most philanthropic sociologists will tell you that the answer to world hunger is not throwing money at the problem. There is an endemic poverty mindset that must be internally addressed in most world cultures that only the gospel will solve. This goes beyond the adage of "Give a man a fish and he'll eat for a day. Teach him to fish and he'll eat for a lifetime." In many cultures there is a pervasive hopelessness and lack of expectancy for financial success. It is a core identity issue – a survival mentality that is hard to break. Surely the poor are often not equipped with financial tools regarding saving, investment or higher education. These things seem superfluous when you are living hand to mouth. And while it is surely not an issue of laziness, many who struggle in developing nations simply lose the hope to rise above the overwhelming tide of inopportunity. Often our Western mentality to throw money at the problem only further enables and cripples societies by fostering a dependence on charity, rather than building initiative within the poor to discover sustainable economic freedom.

I will admit in my younger days, I too shared a cursory disgust over the big megachurches. But our stereotypes of them are usually unfounded and lack originality. Ever since the 80s televangelism scandals, the media has ritualized a format of exposing these so-called untouchable institutions. Their fund-raising is considered suspect not because they are disingenuous, but simply because the churches are ... *big*.

The aforementioned pastor – for all his talk of helping the poor – is doing little to that end if he cannot buy groceries for his own children. Just like the media, many in the church fuel this misplaced outrage by feeding into the jealousy and mistrust of the masses. They endorse the dualistic notion that to be a Christian ministry means you must be dirt poor. Of course, you cannot help the hungry if you are dirt poor – but that is just pointing out a *financial fact*. It is a catch 22.

They're all After Money?

I am not classified as a "Word of Faith" *money preacher* nor do I have a particular affinity toward televangelists or megachurches – but I am going to throw the underdog a bone for a moment. I have defended Catholics, Reformed, charismatics and Orthodox for various reasons – which does not make me popular when one camp pigeonholes another. And every stream has its strengths and weaknesses.

I readily admit I too am wary of the propensity of large churches to compromise for the sake of money, numbers and man pleasing. Many would consider my own ministry to be a *large machine.* I do not feel I have ever turned tricks for dollars or followers, but I have definitely irritated many. We must differentiate personal preferences from prejudices. While larger ministries do merit critique, our individual distaste for the style or size of these organizations can taint our view. A ministry's size or bankroll says nothing about its character, fruitfulness, depth of teaching or effective outreach. They still fill a vital role, reaching many sectors of society that other churches do not.

Big is not bad. Our problem with big ministries goes back to our subjective concept of *how much is too much*. The danger with big churches is when the structure stops serving the people and the people start serving the structure. But this can also happen with small churches (which conversely to have a greater propensity to turn stagnant, inbred and irrelevant).

If McDonalds sold organic kale salad, certain people would still hate them because they are *big*.

To highlight the bias against large ministries, I will point out a recent report from an ABC news affiliate in Australia that ran an *exposé* on the massively successful megachurch Hillsong. The tone of the article implied that Hillsong is a "money making machine" that squeezes exorbitant amounts of cash from its followers. The news agency, operating off the assumed idea that all big churches are shady, *did not even contact Hillsong before running the piece*. Knowing it would feed viewers' bias, the station skipped journalistic ethic and just threw together a stereotypical, quickly generated sound bite. As a former newspaper editor, I can attest that newsies are always in a rush to fill as much airtime with as little legitimate research as possible.

Rather than send a reporter or a camera crew, they just recycled stock footage from a massive Hillsong conference to convey imagery of a huge Christian empire. The only other bit of investigation was a quick Google search into Hillsong's financial reports (which the church transparently publishes online). The report centered on the massive bottom line revenues: $85 million a year in 2013. That is a lot of money. They must be evil, serving the almighty dollar!

But others broke it down the report with more objectivity. Extracting the Bible College and conference revenue puts the church's annual income at only $16 million. That is with an average weekly attendance of 31,400. Do the math and this means that the average Hillsong attendee gives just over $2,000 a year. That is far less than a "tithe" of each person's income. "Rather than being a money making machine, Hillsong is almost as poor at gaining offerings as the rest of Christianity," writes John Sandeman with Mediawatch.[9]

Wasted on Jesus

Yes Hillsong is successful. Their songs are sung by 30 million people, hitting top charts; and they have millions of online viewers. But as it turns out, Hillsong is nowhere nearly as monetized or shady as the hypocritical team at ABC news. On top of it all, they contribute countless dollars to social justice causes and ministry to the poor in developing regions. Big ministries make big targets. They feed the same sus-

---

[9] John Sandeman, "Hillsong get Sledged by Channel Nine," *Mediawatch* (April 23, 2015) http://www.biblesociety.org.au/news/hillsong-get-sledged-by-channel-nine (accessed Aug. 15, 2015).

picions we have against big corporations, government and media. I do not listen to Hillsong, but size alone does not indicate they are sellouts.

Although they have their limitations and are not for everybody, why is it my prerogative to criticize someone who wants to worship in a stadium instead of a small chapel? Do congregants necessarily lack meaningful relationships just because there are lots of people? Big just means big. They can make a massive beneficial impact, or a hugely compromised one. But size does not matter (despite what you read the *Sex* chapter).

The only reason I am hammering the point, is because many of our biases directly equate success with idolatry. If we pull out our calculator and figure cost per congregant per square foot of building space, I doubt there is much difference between a storefront church at a strip mall and Joel Osteen's Astrodome. People are still in an uproar over building the Crystal Cathedral in Orange County in 1980 (worth about $60 million today) ... "You could give that money to the poor!" Sounds eerily familiar. Remember this story, when Mary emptied out a year's worth of wages in extravagant *wasteful* worship on Jesus:

> But one of his disciples, Judas Iscariot, who was later to betray Him, objected, "Why wasn't this perfume sold and the money given to the poor? It was worth a year's wages." He did not say this because he cared about the poor but because he was a thief; as keeper of the money bag, he used to help himself to what was put into it.
>
> "Leave her alone," Jesus replied. "It was intended that she should save this perfume for the day of my burial. You will always have the poor among you, but you will not always have me" (John 12:4-8, NIV)

Who was it that said to never give extravagant gifts to preachers? Oh right ... now it is coming back to me. That was *Judas Iscariot*. Never criticize someone else's act of worship, no matter how over-the-top or non-utilitarian it may seem to you. Jesus is basically drawing a line here: *Even if you have to choose between helping the poor and worshipping me ... worship Me.* Obviously our gifts to the poor *are* an act of worship. But beyond social justice alone lies the one true thing that ever matters – the love of God. Paul writes, "If I give all I possess to the poor ... but do not have love, I gain nothing" (1 Cor. 13:3, NIV). The gospel is no mere ethical message of good works. It is first and foremost about an intimate union with God. This is not an indictment against charity! The fact is if we are not giving to the poor, then the love of God is probably not in us. Nevertheless, as the great commandment goes, we love God first and then our neighbor. Sometimes that means spending ourselves in ways that look foolish or impractical.

Can the Rich Enter Heaven?

Generally, the more money one has, the more we distrust their character and feel liberty to judge them – this goes true for our entire society. For the rich, we have all but lost hope for their very salvation. I am well aware of our Lord's statement that it is easier for a camel to go through the eye of a needle than for a rich man to enter heaven (Matt. 19:24). Consider in context that the Jewish society of the day thought their Messiah would come in regal pomp. They were not expecting Him to come as a lowly day laborer. In the same way, that society considered economic clout and power a divine seal of approval. But Jesus was clarifying that not even the elite can buy their way into His kingdom. Let me add that the *poor* cannot enter the kingdom of God any easier! Back then, society already figured the poor were hopeless (cursed by God) – but Jesus leveled the playing field putting the trust fund babies on the same plane with ghetto kids. *No one* can merit his own entry to heaven. *No one can come to me unless the Father who sent me draws them, and I will raise them up at the last day* (John 6:44, NIV).

The Lord's deconstruction of a tiered, monetary spiritual hierarchy was soon hijacked by Gnostics. Inverting His words, they made it a *virtue* to be poor – something the Lord never intended. Believe me, you should get the romantic idea out of your head that all poor or homeless people are cuddly little Oliver Twists skipping through the lollipop forests to paradise ... they too can be absolutely nasty! Go sleep under a bridge with a few meth heads and tell me every single poor person is a saint.

Rich or poor is irrelevant. Money is not a seal of divine approval, but it *can* be a fruit of us trusting in the approval we already have thanks to the finished work of Jesus. Consider the patriarchs Abraham, Isaac and Jacob. Somehow we have a Sunday school felt board mindset of Abraham as a dirty, hippie shepherd smelling like goats living in a tent in the wilderness. *Abraham trusted God and was filthy stinking rich.*

Abraham and Lot were so prosperous; they had to take two separate countries (I'll take China, you take America). Abraham defeated five kings and owned the wealth of more than five nations (imagine modern terms of owning five European countries), plus he was so generous he gave all the money back to them. He was overrunning with servants, flocks – people and families – and enormous amounts of gold. But his economic earthly authority was seamlessly integrated with his spiritual heavenly authority. Abraham ate with angels, was a friend of God, and he prayed one prayer over King Abimelech causing the entire nation to be instantly healed of barrenness (Gen. 20).

Solomon's Gold

Having a successful job is one thing, but the church gets frightfully scared to talk about our role in macroeconomics. *Really* big money – the world financial sector – must be the prerogative of the antichrist and the mark of the beast! Clearly we do not usher in the kingdom with money and power. The kingdom is already at hand thanks to Christ. We are ushering in an awareness of it by the Spirit and the Word. So does that mean the world itself is *not the Lord's* and that Christians have no role in world economic affairs? I honestly do not care what the *beast* is doing – I will be living by a different economy!

Thank God we do not have religious zealots sitting on the Federal Reserve Board – but imagine if we had some genuine, humble believers whose hearts were full of charity allocating trillions of dollars and creating new economies in developing nations? The church has abused its secular power in centuries past. But I believe the Lord wants to entrust us and restore a level of participation with world economics in the coming days that is healthy and fundamentally sound. I am not arguing for a theocracy, nor can I even conceive the ideal balance between church and state. But one thing is certain – we must think bigger.

Let us think for a moment of the richest man there ever was or will be ... *Solomon.*

Most billionaires in the world today own between $1 to $3 billion dollars. The richest of them on the planet own $80 to $100 billion. But by today's standards, Solomon would have owned *$1.3 trillion.* That is more than the current annual GDP of Australia.

MONEY. SEX. BEER. GOD.

There was so much gold in Solomon's day that silver became as worthless as the stones on the ground (1 Kings 10:21-22). Imagine throwing away all the silver in your house! In today's equivalent, you would think, "*Why on earth decorate my house with aluminum cans?*"

Every year, the scripture tells us that Solomon brought 666 talents of gold into his coffers. That is metric ton after metric ton of gold! Now it does not take a theologian to tell us the number 666 is not normally considered a *good* number. The mark of the beast! Here is the thing: *either you are going to serve money or money is going to serve you.* Just like your physical body, money is just matter – material substance – that can be used for good or evil. When the slave master of sin owned you, your body was used for wickedness. But possessed by the Spirit of God, your body is a holy vessel used for righteousness. Money is a tool that enables the inward compulsion of the heart. It can fuel you to save lives like an Oskar Schindler, or it can drive you on a self-destructive crack bender like Charlie Sheen.

Maybe you are not called to be Solomon, but there are applicable principles here for all of us. Let us look at the beginning of his story when Solomon first dedicated the Temple (2 Chron. 7; 1 Kings 8). As an extravagant sacrifice, Solomon killed a thousand bulls. The smoke of God's glory rolled through the place so thick the priests were all pinned to the floor, twitching under the weight of it. That night, the Lord asked Solomon, "What would you like buddy?" (Crowder paraphrase) "Here's the menu. We can cook up anything you want in the kitchen."

Did Solomon ask for cash? *No.* Did he ask for his enemies to be killed? *No.* What did he ask for? *Wisdom.*

Who is Wisdom? *Christ is the Wisdom from above* (1 Cor. 1:30). Solomon had his priorities in order. He put God first, and gold began sticking to him like static cling. He put first the kingdom, and *everything else was added to him*. Scripture says lovers of wisdom "inherit wealth, that I may fill their treasuries" (Prov. 8:21). But this verse only speaks of *spiritual* wealth since *Solomon* wrote it? Prioritize God; get wisdom for "long life is in her right hand; in her left hand are riches and honor" (Prov. 3:16, NIV). That sounds like a health and wealth gospel. Solomon was the richest man on the planet; he was also the most famous. Not only did every king want to sit under his wisdom; men from every nation wanted to sit under him. He was more famous than Michael Jackson. The rumors were surely flying concerning Solomon's wealth. There was no snopes.com to verify all the facts.

"I hear Solomon has a golden toilet! I hear he wipes with silk!"

Tales of Solomon's wisdom and fortunes traveled all the way to Ethiopia. The Queen of Sheba heard of this and trekked all the way from Africa to visit Solomon to check it out for herself. What motivates world rulers? *Cash.* Solomon's depth of insight floored her. The riches were so extravagant; she was overwhelmed by the minute details of the cutlery (boggled by spoons). She was blown away at the ornate detail of the servants' clothing (golden clad fast food cooks). Finally she saw the extravagant offerings of God's people and she *fainted.* Passed right out on the floor. *They're just giving money away??* She said that *not even half* of his riches had been told to her (1 King 10; 2 Chron. 9).

"Solomon's toilet wasn't golden boys. It was platinum. And he doesn't use silk – he uses $100 bills!"

I believe Solomon gained his perspective from his father David who got hammered drunk on generosity. It was Solomon who said, "He that gives to the poor lends to the Lord, and He will give him his reward" (Prov. 19:17). Solomon understood extravagant giving from David.

David's Drunken Offering

Do you remember the story where David moved the Ark of the Covenant from Obed-Edom's house to Jerusalem? They had previously tried to move the Ark by their own manmade devices in a cart, until Uzzah got zapped. So they parked the Ark on Obed-Edom's front lawn. Would you like to have the Ark in your back yard? Parked on your bank account? Everything Obed-Edom touched prospered. His carrots grew bigger; his radishes grew bigger; his wine vats overflowed. Finally David said *that's enough! We need to get the Ark into Jerusalem.*

This time, David realized they needed to move the Ark the proper way. So every six steps they took, they stopped and killed a bull. Sacrificing a bull in those days was like killing a Volvo. A bull was like a Chevy or a Toyota. So here was this long massive trail of bloody sacrifice for nine-and-a-half miles! Do not miss the point. Yes it was an extravagant, expensive offering. But this was not a quiet, seeker-sensitive type of offering. The kind where the pastor says, "If you feel led, you can slip an envelope in the offering box on the way out the door. Do not let your left hand see what your right hand is doing. Please don't feel any pressure." There is surely a place for not letting the left hand see what the right hand is doing. But there is another zone in which you are so love-crazed-drunk that you do not know what *either* hand is doing! The scripture tells us in 2 Samuel 6 that David literally danced his clothes off! Imagine how wild and celebratory and out-of-the-box this was ... Here was David dancing and killing bulls in his bloody underwear!

All around him was a chorus of instruments in wild, unfettered worship with shouting and rejoicing. And David *umesachaq* before the Ark (1 Chron. 15:29).[10] This single-occurring word in scripture means "to frolic," and is connected to the root word *Isaac* which means "to laugh." David is frolicking in the offering, dancing himself half-naked, thoroughly intoxicated with a frenzy of generosity. Not exactly what you see when you pass the plate most Sundays. The absolute key to generosity is to get drunk on giving. You become unstoppable. This is the heart of a true hilarious (*hilaros)* giver that God loves (2 Cor. 9:7).[11]

The whole city of Jerusalem erupted in celebration with eating and drinking as David fed everyone bread and meat and wine. But glaring down from her window was David's old stagnant wife Michal. She was seething with hatred. She must have thought, "I could have shopped at Gucci with all that bull!"

Michal was critical of David's lavish offering and she was barren for the rest of her life. David returned home that evening, cow blood still dripping from his nose, knife in hand, "Long day at the office dear. What's for dinner?" She turned on him (paraphrase), "Look at you O King of Israel making a fool of yourself, dancing half naked with the slave girls" (2 Sam. 6:20). David responded, *"Honey ... It's going to get way more undignified than this."*

Jesus Christ, the Son of David, danced through those very same streets. Not in the blood of bulls or goats, but a body was prepared for Him. Not just down to the underwear, but even that was stripped away

---

[10] James Strong, *Exhaustive Concordance of the Bible* (Nashville: Abingdon, 1890), See entry H7832.

[11] Ibid., See entry G2431.

and gambled off. And with a sacrifice of everything He had, He destroyed not only the curse of poverty itself, but the entire fall of mankind and brought to an end the old man in Adam.

God rescued the earth with a physical offering. Did you know the scriptures speak exponentially more about offerings than they do about *love?* Understand me clearly – love is the underlying current, goal and objective of it all. And the Beatles were right; money can't buy me love. It is just that so many Christians give lip service to a fuzzy, ethereal concept of love but never express it materially in tangible, real world gifts or acts of service. They don't *do* love. I have met countless Christians who never contribute a dime to gospel endeavors, because they have some metaphorical excuse, "My entire life is an offering." They think they are giving everything but really giving nothing at all. Paul said in one of his offering spiels to "show the proof of your love" (2 Cor. 8:24). Proof is in the pudding.

It is in our DNA to be philanthropic. When manipulation and spiritual abuse are leveled to wring the flock of their earthly fortunes, it works the opposite. Pastors and leaders understand that money is necessary for ministry, and they know that the fallen Adamic mind is chintzy. But employing law, pressure and fear of lack is not the gospel way. When people get a revelation that *God is for them*, they catch the inherent delight in grace giving, motivated by the kiss and not the baton.

Tithes, Offerings & Sacrifice

A tremendous amount of rewiring needs to occur in our thinking. I hope this book is the tip of the iceberg for you. Whenever I begin to approach the topic of giving from a perspective of grace, people immediately think, "Hooray! So you're telling me I don't need to pay my tithes anymore?" I am a preacher by trade ... *I would never tell you that.*

If God commanded 10 percent under the law, is He going to bring us from generosity to stinginess in the New Covenant? What if we started giving 80 percent of our income and watched it double every year?

See the question about tithing is a loaded one. Countless times I have heard people say they do not want the pressure of giving 10 percent, because they want to give *more* than 10 percent. But the underlying objective is usually a desire to get out of any obligation to ante up. As for legal obligation, we are not *bound* to anything. We are no longer under the law of sin and death. However, we are under the *law of the Spirit of Life in Christ Jesus* (Rom. 8:2). If the Spirit encourages us to stockpile and end up on the next episode of Lifetime TV's *Hoarders* then so be it. But God's very essence is *Giver* not hoarder.

Tithing is not a *have to* law (I am aware of the New Testament reference to Abraham and Melchizedek in Hebrews 7). But in a shadowy way, tithing can indicate a bare-minimum issue of our heart … if we are not giving to that least degree it can be a good reality check for us. As a people of grace, we do not want to settle for "legal minimum" and live below our design. Who wants to be a stagnant, Dead Sea end-recipient? We are springs and fountains and sources of blessing.

As for technical terminology, an "offering" is sometimes defined as a gift above and beyond the tithe. In scripture, this is the *above and beyond* realm of generosity that is often accompanied by crazy miracles and blessings in scripture. Not because you are buying them, but because you are walking in alignment as the radical grace giver that you really are. Ironically the expression of faith exerted in giving is so synonymous with faith for healing that we often see healings *during* offerings. One has to be careful in explaining this, however, else the occultic religious mindset thinks you are "purchasing a healing."

Even beyond *offering*, there is an extreme place of sacrificial giving in scripture. You see this in Acts 4, where people are laying houses and lands at the apostles' feet. In the same breath, Luke tells us a heavy weight of glory is manifesting on the church – signs and wonders start popping like popcorn. Prosperity was flowing through *everybody* in the seed church of Jerusalem. Heaven was manifesting everywhere. Barnabas, who is a priest, gives his land up. Priests were not even supposed to own land (Deut. 18:1). A few chapters later, we see that Barnabas is ranked among the apostles. Again, be careful not to think Barnabas "bought" his apostolic mantle. Nevertheless there is a mystical connection here between the state of the giving heart in submissive charity and, "If you are faithful in little things, you will be faithful in large ones" (Luke 16:10).

We know that by one sacrifice, we have forever been made perfect (Heb. 10:14), and yet His love is what inspires our own responsive sacrificial love – pouring ourselves out like Mary in abandonment.

MONEY. SEX. BEER. GOD.

A Source of Blessing

I could rattle off chapters of biblical principles on money, but until we see the heart of the Father – until you know His love and providing care for you – it may never break through to our hearts that He has abundance for us. We must change our minds. Jesus came to demolish the throne of poverty in our hearts. In trusting His loving provision for us, we open our hands to be His provision for others.

God has made you a resource provider to the nations. You do not need a blessing; you are a *source of blessing*. God hates poverty, and we get to do something about it. The same guys who harp against materialism at Christmas (a celebration of the material world's redemption through the incarnation) are often the real idolatrous, cheeseparing misers – not the generous souls shopping at Nordstrom for their loved ones. You do not have to be a Wall Street tycoon to idolize cash. The religionist tirade, "Why are you buying that latte? Don't you know you could have fed an orphan with that latte?" Newsflash! Did you know God is big enough to give you an orphan *and* a latte? Maybe you can set up a Starbucks in the Third World garbage dumps! Why do we embrace the very spirit of poverty we are aiming to break, in order to break it? Heaven is a different economy. Let us stop shuffling around our few clams down here, and look up to the source of all abundance.

Do not let religionists put their trip on you that the God-given desire to succeed is to be confused with the evil of greed. God does not want to make you stand in line at the soup kitchen; He does not want to stamp out your desire to thrive and achieve the best.

Being broke may be a temporary disposition, but poverty is a mindset. Prosperity is not just about accumulating *stuff*: the rice cooker and treadmill you never use; the boat; the George Foreman grill. When you know that dollars will not scratch your infinite itch – when you know that He Himself is the ultimate source of your pleasure and fulfillment – when mammon is cast down from its unrightful position of worship, paradoxically that is when the shekels roll in to bow their knee and serve you. Do not settle for squeaking by in life. Expect to operate in overflow so you can radically bless the less fortunate. So you can usher in kingdom dynamics that impact multitudes. These are holy desires. Money is neither the answer, nor is it inherently corrupting.

66

If you have no desire for financial gain, that is completely fine. There is no condemnation. Maybe you feel a particular call that is different – if you are a monastic for instance, that is an honorable calling. But remember that is a *preference*, so do not think it is more spiritual to reject the natural world. Money is a tool. Sometimes having the tool means the difference of reaching four people or 400,000. Maybe you are not shooting for the stars (you live in Newfoundland content with pastoring four), but if this book encourages you to at least loosen up the purse strings and buy your family a vacation … well I have done my job. God is extravagant toward us. Let us at least stop giving Him a bad rap. Our Father provides for us and wants us to enjoy it. God said of Abraham:

> *I will make a great nation of you and bless you and make you famous for your bliss; those who bless you, I will bless, and anyone who curses you I will curse, till all nations of the world seek bliss such as yours* (Gen. 12:2-3, MOF[12])

God wants to make you famous for your bliss. Imagine the thing all your neighbors chase and worship – money – is the very thing you are always giving away like Abraham? And somehow you still have more of it than they do! Whether you are broke or not is irrelevant. But if you are poor, you do not have to settle there and build a monument to lack in your life because religion tells you to hail your poverty as a virtue. You can dream and do something spectacular if you so desire.

Final Thought

Let us just change our thinking. If you are at the bottom, the only direction left is up. Do not feel paralyzed by your current economic condition. If God is calling you to something, take one baby step at a time toward that goal. We currently operate two children's homes for orphans in India and depend by faith for our 50 some children to be fed every month. However, when we began building our first home we had no clue where to begin. With no money for the project, we took a baby step and used what little we had to buy the land. Then more money came for the foundation, then the walls, the water well, etc. until the dream was realized. Do not get stuck when you are at point A because you feel so far from point Z. Just one faithful step at a time along the

---

[12] James Moffatt, *The Bible: James Moffatt Translation* (San Francisco: Harper Collins, 1922/1994).

way. So many young people feel ill equipped to make a difference in the world, because they have no money or no degree. Do not let your vision be limited by your bank statement. Start taking some steps. Go to school. Do not let religion diminish your dreams.

I did not have to write this book. It can only stigmatize me as a *prosperity preacher*, a *pervert*, a *homophobe* or a *wino*. I am already misbranded by numerous incorrect epithets: *antinomian, universalist, irreverent, charismatic loon*. But this particular topic triggers me. As a preacher I constantly deal with an unspoken standard that all ministers of the gospel should be beggarly paupers. Preachers' kids should only eat generic brand cereals − not Applejacks or (God forbid) something organic from the health store. I have found in certain regions church folk are more sticky on this than others. A minister friend recently traveled to Europe to speak. His hosts were utterly insulted that he would receive a love offering. "But we flew you in," they said − shocked that he thought to be paid for the time he traveled around the world to feed his family. After all, they bought his ticket to come work for free! If any other occupation on the planet expected people to work for nothing and starve their own kids, it would be a joke. Apparently ministers should only live on oxygen and the love of God. It is disgraceful. I have a thousand such stories I could tell. Certainly men of the cloth should serve me for nothing … they just talk once a week while *other people* throw money at them? I am not closing with an offering. Just an exhortation to remember the poor as well as those who labor among you.

I was delivered from generations of poverty and the Lord has given me faith in this area. I am unapologetic. I will attack that asinine, critical, religious spirit of selfish idolatry any day of the week. I am grateful to be one of the few preachers who do not need to *preach for money*.

My prayer for you is to experience wholeness in life. That the Spirit would energize your trust in God. May you engage creative ideas with the faith He supplies. May you be met by multiple streams of income. Residuals. Royalties. Unexpected sources of funding and favor beyond what you could generate in your own strength and talent. All for the glory of God.

SEX.

The Doctor is in

If you skipped the other sections and jumped here first, I totally understand. My wife graciously (hesitantly) entrusted me to enlighten you on the forbidden subject. If candid terminology and snarky innuendos are problematic for you, this may be the wrong book. Sex was designed by God to be both fun and funny. Know for starters this is not a Christian *Kama Sutra*. I am not drawing obscene diagrams of what transpires beneath your Sunday dress, but there is some semi-tactful graphic explanation sprinkled with a dab of ridiculous lingo. We do need clarity in what is possibly the most confusing area of many people's lives.

Joking about sex is a great way to keep it from becoming an idol. The sobriety that the subject demands in hushed tones – in whispers unutterable from the pews of Christendom – proves we view sex as a dark goddess only deserving of somber reverence. We pay homage to our fears she will enslave us. Our views of sex may be too low or too high. Cheapened to a quick animalistic fling in a truck stop bathroom. Or conversely, over-idealized with soft-focused lens and violins playing, we fashion it a sort of X-rated Disney rhapsody of enchantment complete with rose petals, fireworks and a six-packed prince giving his damsel a bareback ride on a sweaty white stallion.

In reality, sex is usually more of a clumsy, lumbering roll in the sheets with a lot of buildup and fanfare; then it is over. Loads of fun and plenty of returning customers – but more a quick, bumbling caper than anything else. I never finished my psychology degree, so I cannot give you free therapy here if you are looking for directions to the truck stop or Disney. Yes sex is both primal and romantic. But we project a lot of mental and emotional baggage onto this area of life, replete with all manner of odd sexpectations and unrealism. I cannot address the thousand-some-odd hang-ups that may seek release through your genitals.

Also keep in mind this is not a *marriage* book per se. Sex is just one piece of that complex jigsaw puzzle. We do address marriage and dating (primarily as it relates to our subject matter), but most of our discussion is limited to biblical protocol for the party in your pants. Biblical, not *religious* (those are not synonyms). Mostly I hope to liberate you from religion's disparaging, Gnostic view of the body and get you comfortable in your skin; but I cannot completely rescue you from *awkward*.

I will note that if your husband gave you this book, it was a setup. Do not demoralize him for it. Just humor him and read on. Think of him as a starving puppy who may just need to get his little tail wagged more often. He has been barking and whining for a treat, but did not know how to tell you. Like Lassie he finally pointed his snout toward this book expecting me to do all the talking for him. Typical. *But humor him.*

In full disclosure, I am a preacher, not a sex therapy doc. That should not lower your expectations per se. Whatever your reason for reading, I am sure you will find a few nuggets of wisdom nestled among the frat boy humor. You will read church history, some exegesis and even some strange testimonies. My prayer is that God brings you some clarity. But getting all wound up over this topic never helped anybody.

Laughing at Venus

C.S. Lewis alerts us to the laughter and banter that must be present when dealing with the topic of lovemaking. "But sensible lovers laugh. It is all part of the game; a game of catch-as-catch-can, and the escapes and tumbles and head-on collisions are to be treated as a romp," he said.[1] We are most in danger when we view Venus, the goddess of love, with too much solemnity. He notes:

> *We must not be totally serious about Venus. Indeed we can't be totally serious without doing violence to our humanity. It is not for nothing that every language and literature in the world is full of jokes about sex. Many of them may be dull or disgusting and nearly all of them are old. But we must insist that they embody an attitude to Venus which in the long run endangers the Christian life far less than a reverential gravity. We must not attempt to find an absolute in the flesh. Banish play and laughter from the bed of love and you may let in a false goddess. She will be even falser than the Aphrodite of the Greeks; for they, even while they worshipped her, knew that she was*

---

[1] C. S. Lewis, *The Four Loves.* Kindle Edition (Houghton Mifflin: 1971), 100.

"laughter-loving." The mass of the people are perfectly right in their conviction that Venus is a partly comic spirit. We are under no obligation at all to sing all our love-duets in the throbbing, world-without-end, heart-breaking manner of Tristan and Isolde; let us often sing like Papageno and Papagena instead.[2]

Extracting the frolic and fun and play of this pleasure has only served to contort its God-given role in our lives. But the Gnostic dualisms adopted by the early church onward cast a dark cloud over the providential joys of sex. Professor John Noonan notes that, "if one asks ... where the Christian Fathers derived their notions on marital intercourse – notions which have no express biblical basis – the answer must be, chiefly from the Stoics."[3] Stoic Greek pagan philosophy modeled subdued, dispassionate intercourse that was justified only by its procreative element in the church for centuries. *Eros* (romantic love) was always considered a vulgar competitor to *agape* (divine love). Eros can truly be an idol if it is an end in itself. But eros and agape were never meant to be competitors. Eros was always meant to be baptized in the sacrament of marriage. It is a love wholly given to the other. "Sexual desire, without Eros, wants it, the thing in itself; Eros wants the Beloved," writes Lewis.[4]

The Church's Coital Confusion

The church has been confused about sex for 2,000 years. It is no wonder half the church thinks their body is nasty and the other half uses it for some deviant sexual addiction: from the foundation even the church fathers were clueless and sexually stifled. Understand there is tremendous benefit in reading the church fathers. They were enormously strong in Christology, the Trinity, etc. – but in other areas many were completely blinded by the dualisms of their day.

Origen (184-253 A.D.) took Jesus' words about removing the offending member quite literally and nipped his own chicken nuggets right off.

---

[2] Ibid., 99.

[3] John Thomas Noonan, *Contraception: a History of its Treatment by the Catholic Theologians And Canonists* (Cambridge, MA: Belknap Press, 1965), 68.

[4] Lewis, *The Four Loves*, 94.

MONEY. SEX. BEER. GOD.

Ambrose (337-397 A.D.) equated absolute celibacy with holiness – he expected Christians to stop having sex even if they were married! Sex itself was sin, married or not. Augustine (354-430 A.D.) once caught the glance of a young hottie, got a pup tent under his tunic, then jumped in a cold lake to cool off. He immediately renounced his secular life and resigned himself to become a monk (overreaction perhaps?). Jerome (347-420) attacked marriage vehemently as inferior to celibacy. If he ever felt a bit randy, Jerome threw himself into a thorn bush.

In the fourth century, a fellow named Jovinian came along who is by far one of my favorite heretics. I would recommend a book about him by David G. Hunter called *Marriage, Celibacy, and Heresy in Ancient Christianity: The Jovinian Controversy.* It is a great academic overview on some of the bizarre sexual beliefs taught by the early church fathers in the West. It highlights one solitary voice of sanity in the midst of it all. In this section I will borrow from his research. This fellow Jovinian was eventually ousted as a heretic because of one scandalous idea: *that virgins held no greater merit in the eyes of God than married people.*

Why is this such a big deal? Because we are talking about a time when ascetic renunciation of all earthly pleasures was equated with absolute holiness – and the physical body was deemed very suspect. Jovinian also daringly taught there is no difference in fasting from food or receiving it with thanksgiving. Needless to say, many early church leaders tore him to shreds. Sex itself was taboo, married or not (an idea our Jewish forefathers would never have conceived, noted Jovinian).

Celibate or Celebrate?

Our poor Catholic brothers still struggle with these ideas today. Celibacy was enshrined as a virtue by the fourth century when Jovinian was speaking out. Sex was a necessary evil to continue the proliferation of the human race, but it was not *good.* Priests have been forced to remain celibate, not taking wives since the fifth century. In all due respect to our priestly friends, is it any wonder they slip into perversion and widespread pedophilia on such an enormous statistical scale? The Western church rejected married priests because of our dualistic disgust over the body. But our Eastern Orthodox brothers have always allowed married priests. Martin Luther said such laws against a married priesthood were not of God but the devil, and I could not agree more. These satanic parameters only encourage deep perversion.

Jovinian likely had no direct personal motives for suggesting married people are just as holy as virgins (he himself was a celibate monk). Nor was he calling for licentious sexual indulgence as his detractors claimed. He simply argued that promoting celibacy as a virtue wrongly divided Christians into two classes of merit. He accused leaders of promoting Manichaeism (a term that basically meant Gnosticism: it also rejects the natural world) for their forbidding of marriage and promotion of fasting and asceticism. A massive scandal unfolded.

Jerome composed the *Adversus Jovinian*, a long scathing attack, full of venomous character bashing as was common in early heresy hunter writings, throwing the kitchen sink of heretic labels at Jovinian. He presented a problem for men like Jerome. Known for translating the Bible into Latin (the Vulgate), Jerome was a very learned man and a prolific writer. But a huge part of his shtick was to rub shoulders with the high class Roman elite of Christianity, playing the role of the "humble ascetic" who would live off the patronage of rich widows, encouraging them to divest their resources to the church and give all their daughters to absolute celibacy. Asceticism was Jerome's *niche market*.

Since marriage was a culturally acceptable and respected institution among Roman aristocrats, Jerome's ministry was challenged. For Jovinian to advocate a biblical *acceptance* of marriage (something Romans already thought was good) this could put Jerome's ascetic religious ideas out of business. Jerome was in the virgin market.

Jovinian accused men like Jerome of being the *actual* heretics because of their heavy-handed promotion of asceticism. Jovinian did not espouse their work-oriented view of salvation, but regarded all who were baptized into Christ as saved.[5] Jovinian did not oppose celibacy; he just did not think it should be elevated above marriage. While Jovinian's writings have been destroyed, we can learn much of what he said through his opponents who quoted him. He had concern with the "pride" that was often displayed by virgin ascetics who assumed themselves to be spiritually superior to others.[6] "No act of ascetic renunciation, Jovinian insisted, could achieve what had been bestowed through the death and resurrection of Jesus Christ," says Hunter.

---

[5] David Hunter, *Marriage, Celibacy, and Heresy in Ancient Christianity: The Jovinian Controversy* (Oxford: Oxford University Press, 2007), 31.

[6] Ibid., 32.

Jerome's Virgin Co., Inc.

Jerome wrote extended treatises praising the virtue of certain female ascetics, often elevating them as examples of supreme piety to shame other priests. The early church's roll of confirmed saints are overwhelmingly lists of virgins. We know little in comparison about normal, conventional Christians from those days because of the lack of attention given them in writings of men like Jerome. There were often political reasons for Roman families to consecrate one or more of their daughters as a vestal virgin. As Christianity came into political favor over paganism, sacrificing one of your kids on the altar of sexual repression was viewed as a pledge of dedication to the emperor. In addition, a number of women would have actually been drawn to the ascetic lifestyle because of the relative freedom and autonomy it would have allowed in a predominantly patristic society. If she had enough financial resources, a female ascetic virgin would have had more opportunity for an education, travel and freedom to build non-marital, near-equal friendships with other male ascetics.[7] She would not be encumbered to the duties of a repressive husband. Celibacy served as a prototype of women's liberation.

By leveling the playing field between virgins and married people, Jovinian's views threatened to topple the notion of clerical, celibate hierarchy that had emerged in Roman society. With the political adoption of Christianity, these tiered systems had been strongly integrated into the church. Virgins were at the top.

Prior to this fourth century controversy over Jovinian, early Christian leaders varied on the degree to which they accepted asceticism. Ignatius of Antioch in the second century wrote about the disruption caused by the asceticism of celibate Christians. Together with Clement of Alexandria (150-215 A.D.), the two suggest that a troubling elite class of ascetics was emerging that posed danger to the community in which celibates were claiming higher spiritual authority or gifts.

Sex Before the Fourth Century

Iranaeus is a church father who, in the second century, opposed the *Encratites* – a sect of Christians who forbade marriage and required

---

[7] Ibid., 79.

fasting. Encratite means "self-control." Iranaeus was strong in his condemnation. Iranaeus (the disciple of Polycarp, a direct disciple of the apostle John) was focused on the concept of union – union between the Father and Son, and our union with God thanks to Jesus. He was instrumental in articulating this union in the Nicene Creed. His theology was much more incarnational than the dualisms of later leaders.

Between Iranaeus and Clement, a tenuous line had been drawn by the third century – the outright rejection of marriage was viewed as unorthodox (as was radical encratism). But rolling into the third century, men like Origen, Cyprian and Tertullian would again echo the Gnostic disdain for marriage. While the silent majority of Christians were married, there was still an underlying motif that celibacy was the *higher way*. You would surely not become clergy unless you were single. The voices of moderation and short-lived victory for Christian marriage would soon be overrun again by extremism.

Just because he allowed marriage, do not think Clement of Alexandria viewed sex favorably. Clement was a deeply conflicted man. His dualisms blinded him. While he allowed for married couples to have sex, they should surely not *enjoy* it! "Pleasure sought for its own sake, even within the marriage bonds, is a sin and contrary both to law and reason," said Clement.[8] "Intercourse performed licitly is an occasion of sin, unless done purely to beget children."[9]

Clement wholeheartedly adopted many of the Greek dualisms of Plato, baptizing them in the name of Jesus. While vocally battling Gnosticism on the one hand, his theology was still chock full of it. He held a cautious view about sex common to the second century. Nevertheless, even Clement said Plato's view of the body was excessively negative, and he defended marriage on the grounds of a doctrine of the goodness of creation. "The basic error of all the heretics, Clement argued, was 'hatred of what God has created.' To reject marriage and procreation is simply to 'blaspheme under a pious cloak both the creation and the holy Creator, the almighty only God.'"[10]

---

[8] Clement of Alexandria, *Christ the Educator* (From *The Fathers of the Church*, Vol. 23 [CUA Press: 2010]), 170.

[9] Ibid., 175.

[10] Hunter, *Marriage, Celibacy, and Heresy in Ancient Christianity*, 107.

MONEY. SEX. BEER. GOD.

Unholy Matrimony?

In 208 A.D. Tertullian's *Exhortation to Chastity* was a treatise declaring God's "preference" for celibacy – and thus to not follow what was essentially *God's will* was a sin. His earlier writings said marriage was a mere *allowance* as it was better than fornication. But his later writings argued that marriage itself is a sin. This would be later adopted and exponentially hammered out by Jerome and Ambrose, who believed marriage and sex itself were both evil. "Tertullian and Ambrose preferred the extinction of the human race to its propagation through sin, that is, through sexual intercourse," notes church historian Leland Ryken. He adds that for Tertullian, "Marriage and adultery ... are not intrinsically different, but only in the degree of their illegitimacy."[11]

And let us not bypass Origen here. "On the whole, Origen tended to view the physical world, the body and sexuality as profoundly ambiguous, even dangerous," writes Hunter.[12] "For Origen, the body could be little more than the locus of perpetual temptation. Like the rest of the material world, the body was meant to be transcended." Origen castrated himself before entering the ministry at 18. While he affirmed that procreation in marriage has been ordained by Providence, he too was a conflicted man. Origen saw a fundamental incompatibility between sexual activity and a person's union with God. Like a good dualist, Origen allegorized nearly *everything* in scripture, but interestingly he held to a very literal interpretation of anything to do with sex. He even appealed to Old Covenant ritualistic purification ceremonies, preaching sexual abstinence before prayer and communion (don't say your prayers tonight if you've had any nookie).

For Origen there was a "disjunction between the sensible world and the intelligible world. The implication of that dualist way of thinking was very far-reaching: 'the invisible and incorporeal things on earth are copies of true things, not true themselves,'" remarks theologian Thomas F. Torrance.[13] Origen held a near carbon-copy worldview of Plato – that the material world was not "real" but the spirit realm was. He was profoundly versed in scripture but nearly everything he read there was

---

[11] Leland Ryken, *Worldly Saints: The Puritans As They Really Were* (Grand Rapids: Zondervan, 1990), 40.

[12] Hunter, *Marriage, Celibacy, and Heresy in Ancient Christianity*, 124.

[13] Thomas F. Torrance, *The Trinitarian Faith* (London: T & T Clark, 1991), 35.

76

a metaphor of some higher spiritual reality. The concrete world around him was *false* if not dangerous. Origen said that "every marriage takes place in darkness" while our consummation in Christ is in the light. He even drew from Paul's discussion of fornication with prostitutes to characterize the nature of marital union.[14] Origen and Tertullian allowed Christians to marry, but they were clearly considered *lower class* Christians at the bottom of the spiritual totem pole.

By the fourth century, any *serious* Christian would never marry. One teacher Priscillian absolutely loved the apocryphal and Gnostic books, for they seemed to declare that Jesus' resounding theme in the gospels was to give up sex. Pope Siricius stated a common emerging idea that, "Surely we do not treat the vows of marriage with contempt ... but we bestow a greater degree of honor on virgins who are consecrated to God. ..."[15] To deflect accusations of Gnosticism/Manichaeism, writers like Jerome would stress a difference between "orthodox" and "unorthodox" versions of asceticism – justifying his own harsh views that were extreme even among his sexually frigid peers. At the heart of Jerome's doctrine was the same heresy held by the encratites: that sex is a symptom of original sin. Other leaders like Ambrosiaster, Epiphanius and Filastrius would stress the original created goodness of sex. As stated, most Christians still married. Ambrosiaster implies that Jerome's extreme anti-sex, anti-marriage views were not the norm in Roman society, which again is why Jerome felt challenged by Jovinian's claim that virgins were no more spiritual than married folks.

Protestant reformers would later critique Jerome for his attack on Jovinian. Luther in 1522 writes of Jerome, "He treats virginity as a thing existing in its own right. He neither relates it to faith nor uses it to build up faith. If this kind of teaching goes on – it is only human teaching – no good work or virtue can be taught without disaster and danger."[16]

Philip Melanchthon says of Jerome, "He disparages marriage and rails at it with abusive language, which is by no means worthy of a Christian. He collects badly distorted passages of Scripture as if they disparage marriage, such as: 'If you live according to the flesh, you shall die', and similar passages. He expressly states that there is no differ-

---

[14] Hunter, *Marriage, Celibacy, and Heresy in Ancient Christianity*, 127.

[15] Ibid., 17

[16] Martin Luther, *The Judgment of Martin Luther on Monastic Vows*, 1521.

ence between one who marries a second time and a prostitute. Likewise, he says that we must observe not what God allows, but what he wills, as though God does not will marriage."[17]

Low views of sex and dualist thinking further compelled Jerome to cement an already formulated doctrine that was enshrined in the fourth century known as the *perpetual virginity of Mary*. It attests that Mary remained a virgin her entire life. Furthermore, that Mary supernaturally gave birth to Christ without breaking her hymen. Despite later Protestant objections that Jesus clearly had other brothers in scripture, the doctrine remains a cornerstone of Mariology in the Catholic church. Some rightly charged that this could amount to *Docetism* (that Jesus was just a *spiritual being*, not a flesh and bone baby who stretched the living daylight out of His mother's womb like any other little newborn crumb snatcher). Let me assure you on that first Christmas Eve, there was blood, sweat, screaming and placenta all over the barn, with poor Joseph standing in the corner wringing his hands in need of a drink.

St. Augustine's Penis

Augustine, who would emerge as the chief theologian for Western Christianity, thought that original sin was transmitted through sex. Augustine had converted to Christianity from Manichaeism. And while he taught against its doctrines, he still retained a sharp worldview of dualism. Augustine tried to find a middle ground between Jovinian and Jerome. He said that celibacy was God's preferred choice, but that marriage was not itself sinful. Writers like Jerome suggested sex only occurred *after the fall* of Adam and Eve as a symptom of sin. Augustine held this same view in his earlier years, but later softened his stance, remaining ambiguous as to whether any bushwhacking could have occurred prior to the fall.

John Chrysostom had earlier argued sex came after the fall. Gregory of Nyssa thought Adam and Eve had no original sex drive – had they not fallen, they would have magically produced babies in some other way, "that mode by which the angels were increased and multiplied..."[18]

Despite his relatively moderate position between Jovinian and Jerome,

---

[17] Hunter, *Marriage, Celibacy, and Heresy in Ancient Christianity*, 7.

[18] Gregory of Nyssa, *On the Making of Man*, Ch. 27:4

Augustine was still influenced by the Stoics and worked hard to have complete control over his body. He still could not quite control those erections under the tunic. He viewed his involuntary movements as disobedience. In his book *On Marriage and Concupiscence* he attributed all sexual urges to man's lower nature. Today, the Catholic church still bases its concept that sex is for *procreation only* on Augustine's prescription we should not just hump for *fun*. "This lust, then, is not in itself the good of the nuptial institution; but it is obscenity in sinful men, a necessity in procreant parents, the fire of lascivious indulgences, the shame of nuptial pleasures," he writes, equating even marital bonking to *lust*.[19] This is also where Catholics base their rejection of all birth control. "It is impermissible and shameful to have intercourse with one's wife while preventing the conception of children," he writes.[20] This strictly functional approach to log jamming is still the bedrock of the evangelical Protestant world as well, which views Augustine as the proto-Protestant. Augustine was by no means alone in statements like this. Clement said, "To indulge in intercourse without intending children is to outrage nature, whom we should take as our instructor."[21]

In Genesis 2, Adam sang over Eve, "This is now bone of my bones and flesh of my flesh." The two became one. Sex not only happened before the fall; it was an integral part of creation – which God called *good*. Adam did not grow a penis after he ate from the Tree of Knowledge. Sex enables us to *know* our spouse and foster oneness and unity. It is not good for the man to be alone. Sex is a gift; it is not gross.

Cults Love Perversion

In the early centuries, all manner of strange ascetic heresies popped up with weird sexual dynamics. It seems to be a hallmark of any cult to have a proclivity toward aberrant sexual views. The *Adamians* gathered to worship naked like Adam and Eve. The *Valesians* imposed compelled celibacy with forced castration. The *Cathari* did not allow second marriages. The *Origenists* were a sect that cohabitated and masturbated to appear celibate to outsiders.[22]

---

[19] Augustine, *On Marriage and Concupiscence,* Ch. 13

[20] Augustine, *On Adulterous Marriages* (*De adulterinis coniugiis ad Pollentium* 1b.II c.12 (PL 40 [1887] 479B).

[21] Clement of Alexandria, *Paidagogos*, II, 9-10.

[22] Hunter, *Marriage, Celibacy, and Heresy in Ancient Christianity*, 150.

The religious rejection or twisting of sex has produced some incredibly perverted practices up until this very day. If the privates are not given their proper course, they will always cut a perverted path. The Oneida Community founded by John Humphrey Noyes in 1848 in New York practiced something called *complex marriage*, in which everyone was "married to one another." They also practiced *male continence*, wherein men were not allowed to ejaculate. So anyone could have sex with one another upon board approval; they were just not allowed to orgasm. They gave detailed lessons on how to pull the hot rod out of the garage at just the right time.

Joseph Smith, founder of the Mormon church, upon being busted for his multiple affairs, said an *angel told him* to embrace polygamy and have numerous wives. Quick thinking Joe! Dutiful servant of the Lord that he was, he wed as many as 40 women, some as young as 14. Even Mormon church officials acknowledge that his first wife, Emma Smith, likely had no clue of the extent of his plural marriages.[23] It was not until threat of losing their tax exemption status and assets in 1890 that the Latter Day Saints reversed their stance on polygamy (another divine directive of course, that did not apply to the old geysers on the board who had already collected their harems).

No wonder the world is confused over this stuff. Despite the oddball sexual deviancy of cults, even *mainstream* Christianity had odd pagan views on sex from the very beginning! We have understood sex no better than the sects. By the Middle Ages, the church was obsessed with regulatory enforcement curtailing how often spousal sex was allowed and what positions were permitted. You could not just throw her over the barrel any day of the week and show her the 50 states:

Intercourse was banned on all Sundays and all the many feast days, as well as the 20 days before Christmas, the 40 days before Easter, and often the 20 days before Pentecost, as well as three or more days before receiving Communion (which at that time was offered only a few times a year). These forbidden days altogether totaled about 40% of each year. Penalties of 20 to 40 days of strict fasting on bread and water were im-

---

[23] Daniel Burke, "Mormon Founder Joseph Smith Wed 40 Wives," CNN (Nov. 11, 2014) http://www.cnn.com/2014/11/11/living/Mormon-founder-polygamy (Accessed Aug. 21, 2015).

posed on transgressors. Clergy routinely warned believers that children conceived on holy days would be born leprous, epileptic, diabolically possessed, blind, or crippled. Intercourse was also forbidden during the menstrual period and pregnancy, partly out of concern for protecting the fetus. Pope Gregory I decreed abstinence should continue until a baby was weaned. Because intercourse was only allowed for procreative reasons, various penitentials (rule books) also forbade intercourse between sterile or older partners, although never assigning a penalty. Oral and anal intercourse were often punished by more years of penance than for premeditated murder, as they prevented conception from occurring. Although practice varied, menstruating women were often forbidden to attend Mass or receive Communion, and women who died in childbirth could not be buried until they had undergone a purifying ritual to forgive their sexual activity. Canon law until 1917 labeled contraception as murder.[24]

The Gnostic disgust with sex from the early church to the Middle Ages continued to flourish in subsequent eras. One might expect me to discuss the Puritans here as well (after all, their very name is synonymous with repressed sexual piety). But in fact the Puritans were far less *puritan* than the modern term entails. They were actually more balanced with food and song and sex and booze than history gives them credit. In fact, Puritan men were sometimes publicly charged for *not* fulfilling sexual duties to their wives! No limits were set on enjoying the gift of whoopie in the confines of marriage.[25] So let us cut Puritans some slack and instead fast-forward a bit to the nineteenth century.

Victorian Secrets

The Victorian era of the nineteenth century is known as one of the most prudish times for despising any and all sexual activity. Sex was for procreation only. Only lower classes and prostitutes were thought to *enjoy* it. Women were thought to know little about sex, to have no desire for it nor derive any pleasure from the act. It is highly unlikely that

[24] "Catholic Teachings on Sexual Morality," *Wikipedia, The Free Encyclopedia,* https://en.wikipedia.org/wiki/Catholic_teachings_on_sexual_morality (accessed Aug. 26, 2015).

[25] See Leland Ryken's *Worldly Saints* for a better description of Puritan life.

most men were well versed in how to please a woman. If a woman did express sexual desire, it was viewed as an illness that required extreme measures that may even entail removing the sex organs. Only men were thought to possess any sexual appetite.

The very discussion of the boom boom was taboo in this period, and many lacked a basic mechanical understanding of how the operation worked. Sex was repressed and considered dirty even within marriage (undoubtedly contributing to the thriving prostitution industry and hypocritical hook ups that occurred out of wedlock, though none of that was culturally acceptable). Most people were confused on basic sex education. The only published material was a rudimentary midwifery book titled *Aristotle's Masterpiece* (which was not a masterpiece, nor was it written by Aristotle). It gave anatomical instruction, along with pointers such as: "If she is ugly, the advice is: do it in the dark."

Is it not ironic how religious constriction is the very thing that promotes immorality? Piano legs would be covered up, because they looked suggestive. But by the late 1700s, more than 10,000 prostitutes worked the streets of London! Many men gained illicit sexual knowhow from hookers before marriage. Women were to remain virgins until their wedding night, but were never even *told* about sex. Most had no clue how their own anatomy worked. Many did not even know where babies came from prior to having their bottle corked on their nuptials.

A likely parodied account of the Victorian period in 1894, supposedly authored by an old dry prune named Ruth Smythers sums up the evolution of society's "Christian" views on sex. The book is titled: *Instructions and Advice for the Young Bride on the Conduct and Procedure of the Intimate and Personal Relationships of the Marriage State for the Greater Spiritual Sanctity of this Blessed Sacrament and the Glory of God.*[26] The main concept? Avoid sex with your husband at all cost.

"Give little, give seldom, and above all, give grudgingly. Otherwise what could have been a proper marriage could become an orgy of sexual lust. ... Most men, if not denied, would demand sex almost every day," writes Smythers. "Feigned illness, sleepiness, and head-

---

[26] Ruth Smythers' *Instruction and Advice for the Young Bride* is considered a parodied commentary of Victorian sexual views purportedly written in 1894 due to the unverifiable nature of its historicity.

aches are among the wife's best friends in this matter." She also recommends that "arguments, nagging, scolding, and bickering also prove very effective, if used in the late evening about an hour before the husband would normally commence his seduction."

We see that her husband Reverend Smythers was not allowed much creative liberty in the bedroom as, "Most men are by nature rather perverted, and if given half a chance, would engage in quite a variety of the most revolting practices. These practices include, among others: performing the normal act in abnormal positions; mouthing the female body; and offering their own vile bodies to be mouthed in turn." She adds, "Sex, when it cannot be prevented, should be practiced only in total darkness. She should let him grope in the dark. There is always the hope that he will stumble and incur some slight injury which she can use as an excuse to deny him sexual access."

For your entertainment, here are a few of her pointers that I would not recommend trying at home:

- "The wise bride will permit a maximum of two brief sexual experiences weekly — and as time goes by she should make every effort to reduce this frequency"

- "A wise wife will make it her goal never to allow her husband to see her unclothed body, and never allow him to display his unclothed body to her."

- "Many women have found it useful to have thick cotton nightgowns for themselves and pajamas for their husbands — they need not be removed during the sex act. Thus, a minimum of flesh is exposed."

- "When he finds her, she should lie as still as possible. Bodily motion could be interpreted as sexual excitement by the optimistic husband."

- "If he attempts to kiss her on the lips she should turn her head slightly so that the kiss falls harmlessly on her cheek instead. If he lifts her gown and attempts to kiss her any place else she should quickly pull the gown back in place, spring from the bed, and announce that nature calls her to the toilet."

Unsexed Wives

While wives kept the sheets unsullied for the Lord, their husbands were often sowing their diverted oats elsewhere contracting syphilis in the brothels. Despite the religious austerity, undersexed wives had needs too. It was not on the Victorian menu for a women to even desire sex, much less would husbands consider the courtesy of giving their wives an orgasm. No one even knew female orgasms scientifically existed until the late 1950s with the research of Masters and Johnson. No doubt a few explorers of the nether regions had pioneered these delights over the past few millennia outside the laboratory, but what God-fearing soul would dare mention it? Nevertheless, ladies in the nineteenth century were not getting their switch flicked by husbands who did not even know what a clitoris was. And where there is an unrequited need, there is always an odd perverted way to fulfill it – even amongst Victorians.

We will soon meet Plato in the *God* section of this book – the founding father of this confusing mess (the term "platonic love" is named after him for a bond that transcends the *lower* state of gross sexuality and achieves something more akin to the divine). Plato's negative views on the body included the odd belief that a woman's uterus wanders around on the inside of her, strangulating other organs and causing shortness of breath. Five hundred years later, the physician Galen would define Plato's strange concept as an illness called "hysteria" (meaning *from the uterus*), labeling it as a uterine disease caused by sexual deprivation. Passionate or emotional women were considered susceptible to it. What today we call "hysterics" was formerly an official medically diagnosed condition until 1952.

Hysteria became a blanket condition given to at least a quarter of all women in the Victorian era. Any symptoms ranging from faintness, insomnia, nervousness, shortness of breath, loss of appetite or irritability fell under the umbrella of "hysteria." *Feeling any emotion whatsoever in our stoic society? Ah ... you must have hysteria.* Medical books from that era loved this catch-all term. Today, any kid that merely acts like a kid is diagnosed with ADD and put on drugs. And back then, any woman who merely acted like a woman was diagnosed with hysteria. The term was even used on women who experienced divine ecstasies in worship or revivals (the term was also used condescendingly on emotional men as if they had a uterus).

All of these female hysterics (um … *emotions?)* needed a release. And during the nineteenth century, the odd practice of doctors lubing up their fingers and offering "pelvic massages" became a common solution. Virgins, widows, unhappy married women and even nuns would be rubbed below at the clinic for minutes or hours until they experienced a "hysterical paroxysm." This bizarre cultural acceptance of physicians manually stimulating women to orgasm eventually led to the invention of the vibrator, and was the subject of a 2011 historical film *Hysteria.* The practice also highlights society's utter ignorance and comical yet sad confusion about the biblical joys and proper outlet for sex. After all, the mind-over-matter dualism is more accommodated in a clinical setting with a doctor's hand under the sheet than a wild, passionate romp with the spouse. The church said, "Don't enjoy it at home," so you stealthily bought it at the red light district or the medical exam office.

More Doctrines of Demons

I believe the divorce rate and level of marital infidelity in the church today is unacceptable. We should be salt of the earth. But it is the fault of religion that it continues. Let me tell you that there is a move of grace coming that will not be marked by moral failures – it will be marked by husbands and wives spooning in the back of church!

This twisted concept that married couples having sex are "less holy" than unmarried priests who turn by droves toward child molestation must finally end. If natural desires are forfeited their proper outlet, they run a perverted course. Religion will never diminish a desire; it only warps them. This Gnostic renunciation of real-world pleasures is clearly denounced by the apostle Paul in his first letter to Timothy:

> *The Spirit clearly says that in later times some will abandon the faith and follow deceiving spirits and doctrines of demons. Such teachings come through hypocritical liars, whose consciences have been seared as with a hot iron. They forbid people to marry and order them to abstain from certain foods, which God created to be received with thanksgiving by those who believe and who know the truth* (1 Tim. 4:1-3).

My embrace of mystical Christianity and preaching of radical grace offend people: I am often accused of teaching "doctrines of demons."

That is just ignorant tripe from vacuous critics who idolize their religious traditions but have never flipped their flipping Bible open. Because what does Paul define as a *doctrine of demons? Commands to fast. Commands to abstain from marriage.*

We have all seen the charismatic fasting cults. But a perfect example of demonic doctrine was the *I Kissed Dating Goodbye* craze that blew through in the 1990s. Thank God I kissed dating hello and met my wife! *I Kissed Dating Goodbye* is one of only two books I ever threw across the room. Marriage is a glorious thing to be pursued. Date responsibly, but date for crying out loud. I absolutely despised that book as a single man for its implied elevation of celibacy over marriage as a superior spiritual state. It is time we throw this gospel train out of reverse and start preaching the truth again. Married couples need fun, spontaneity, freedom and play in their sex life. Not guilt, shame and religious restriction. If you devalue the sex life, you are diminishing a cornerstone the whole house and family is built upon. Unless we are preaching an incarnational gospel, then distortion, destruction and separation will continue to pervade society.

Clearly from a historical perspective, we have shown the biblical gift of sex has been exponentially skewed and devalued from the church's start. The physical body and its pleasures have been vilified as evil. In a moment, we will transition into the nuts and bolts of God's perfect recipe for good hot monogamous sex. But before we get XXX-rated, covering the steamy details of allowable positions, masturbation or the ethics of wearing a two-piece bikini, we need to back things up a bit.

Fun with Morality

We need to look further back than the early church fathers to the scriptures themselves. We need to ask ourselves, what does the New Testament *really* have to say about sex and marriage and celibacy? What if the scriptures offer a Wet 'n Wild water park of sexual fulfillment and we did not even know it?

Our theme is as follows: *God gives us natural pleasures as a gift. And these pleasures should be filtered through the word since He has our ultimate satisfaction in mind.*

Remember that He gives us parameters because God loves us and wants to bless us. It is important to heed instruction and not go our own way. Only in directing our passions according to their design do we ever see them fully flourish as intended, rather than destroying us.

Sex is designed for one man and one woman in the sacramental bond of marriage. In today's culture, that means *with a marriage certificate.* I do not mean, "We decided to get *'spiritually married'* in the back seat at 2 a.m. after a make-out session." You do not make lifelong commitments in a late-night moment of frenzied passion. Those are pheromones. So cool off big boy and take a cold shower. But before we can talk about dating, the marriage bed, singleness and the whole lot, we must acknowledge that scripture has a place in this discussion.

In my introduction, I made the case that New Testament moral guidelines are veritably *recipes for satisfaction.* Not prohibitions to quench your party. They are parameters to aim you toward the fullness of life in this world according to God's design. We are not bound by old Jewish ceremonial or civil laws about tattoos or how to plant your garden. But sexuality is an issue of morality – an issue of the heart and how love is expressed toward others. The New Testament does not write off morality; it has written morality into you – so deep down that you *know the truth.* It resonates when you hear it. It frees us to live holy lives from the inside out. Morality does not equate legalism. Eating pork will not hurt you, but porking your neighbor's wife will.

Sexuality is an issue on which the apostles were extremely clear. It is something to be celebrated. It is also one of the chief areas in which we can be selfish and self-destructive if not enjoyed in God's format.

I know we have prejudices regarding morality. The church is quick to jump into the morals business. But the gospel is highly scandalous. On the one hand, forgiveness is radically *immoral* – it gives us what we do not deserve. We are in the forgiveness business. And living a moral life is not a way to pay off God so that He loves us. That said, the gospel does grab us by the scruff of the neck and propel us with an inward desire to live like the good boys and girls that He says we really are thanks to Jesus. Grace compels us to live right.

Today, *grace teachers* are so afraid to talk about morality. Because a law message has been shoved down our throats by religionists our whole lives, there is a guttural reaction against moralizing. No one wants to be caught *mixing* law and grace. Trust me, grace has to be drunk straight – no law added. Yet Paul, the grace apostle, talked about morality *all the time!* Not in a fix-me-up program sort of way. We live pure *because* we are holy, not because we are *trying* to become holy. Knowing the truth of who we are enables us to live in liberty.

We live holy lives not out of fear of punishment, but out of the bliss that is inherent in righteousness. Sin has its own negative consequences. It is self-destructive. Stick your arm in a meat grinder; it will hurt. Touch the stove; you get burned. Walk across the street to the porn shop, and you are stepping out into open traffic. If you cheat on your wife, you are going to experience torment: emotionally, financially, and your kids and friendships will suffer. If you sleep with someone's future wife, while you are both still single, there will be regret over those stolen waters. You are never *missing out* on pleasure by being a moral person. Fornication and perverted sexuality is never going to make you a happy person. Nothing outside of an ethical biblical sex life will ever really bring you the deepest fulfillment you are created for. Despite what Hollywood tells you, the best sex on the planet is found in a monogamous, heterosexual union. It has been very under sold. Monogamy is God's perfect and only recipe for wild, salacious, romper room enjoyment free from dishonor, betrayal, shame and noncommittal shallowness. Monogamy was instituted *for your fun*, not to kill the party.

With all that settled, now let us get down to the bits and bobs of sex.

Sex is Yummy

Countless married couples who grew up in the church are extremely frigid and locked up in this area. Religious worldviews have absolutely paralyzed people psychologically and emotionally regarding sex. They have been brainwashed into believing their body is bad. Their marriages grow cold and standoffish.

I once knew a couple in Australia; the husband was a worship leader. They were serving under a rather co-dependent sort of inner-healing focused church that promulgated the "we're always going to be broken, sinful people" mentality in their flock. The wife in the relationship had experienced an extremely religious childhood. One day in desperation, the husband admitted to me that his wife had a strong phobia of sex. She would physically seize up if he ever tried to sexually insert himself.

"How long has this been going on?" I asked.

"Since we've been married," he said.

"You mean you've never had sex *once* since you've been married?"

No, they had not. How long had they been married? *Five years.* That's right. The poor guy had been married half a decade and had never once crashed the custard truck thanks to religion.

I cannot imagine the horror. My Australian friend had been on a long dry walkabout, without ever actually going down under. While I admire the man's patience, I can assure you his wife was not going to get fixed at the self-help church. We must recognize the gospel reality that we are both *whole and holy* – body, soul and spirit. Many people have hurts not just from spiritual abuse but sexual abuse as well. I want to assure you that Christ entered into your brokenness to make you whole. Years of therapy only keep you thinking you still need a fix. The gospel says, "You're okay champ. Give that pink pony a ride." There must be a fundamental shift in the religious mind that sex is yummy and our bodies are pure. Sex is healthy and recommended in copious amounts in the marriage bed. So many have been conditioned, "Sex is filthy. Sex is filthy. Sex is filthy." And since it is so filthy, that is why we *save it for our spouse?*

No Religion in the Bedroom

I once knew a professor who had spent years in study in a theological institution. His wife also had an extremely religious upbringing. The man was quite frank with me about his sex life. I started to realize that, although they were young – they literally went months at a time without making love. Now they did have children – so they had clearly figured out how to work the pipes. But you do not spend months apart unless you are so old your heart cannot handle Cialis anymore. So I began to prod. Turns out the problem was chiefly from her side. She was just not fond of the ol' *bow-chick-a-wow-wow.*

I figured I would play Dr. Ruth and help him out a bit. *Was he encouraging her by bringing her to orgasm?* If a woman is getting nothing out of it, this is probably because you are not fully meeting her needs, I told him. You have to unleash the inner tigress. I could tell the conversation was going nowhere unless we spoke in specifics.

"Do you give her oral sex?" I asked.
No she doesn't like that.

I am thinking that he surely must not have done it correctly to get that result. You've got to shuck the oyster. Take a stroll down and have lunch at the Y. But nevertheless, if he cannot bring her to orgasm, his sex life could forever be a pitiful existence. Do not buy the excuse that it is physiologically impossible for some ladies. Keep giving it the college try. If it takes an hour, well it may take only forty-five minutes the next time. I had to make sure he was still trying ... so I gave it one more shot.

"Look," I said, "You've at least used your hands? You've got to flick her switch. Do you know where that is?"

"I know where it is, but *she doesn't like that*," he said.
Doesn't like that? You've got to show her what she likes!

I am a man of joy. But that day I almost gave up on life. I came to an overwhelming realization that a vast majority of Christians are absolutely stuck. Forget oral sex, upside down sex, stuck in an elevator sex ... no ... there are people so religiously damaged that they *don't even want their privates touched with their spouse's hand.* Just hop on top and get the functional marital duties over and see you in a few months.

Let me tell you married folks – you do not want any religion in your bedroom. I pray for roller coasters, hot air balloons, cotton candy machines and dancing mechanical bears ... glory in the bedroom, glory in the hallway, glory in the kitchen and glory in the garage. *The whole house is full of His glory.* There is a cornucopia of delights for you.

Maybe you are old and think your glory days are behind you. "Well, my prime is over; the South will ever rise again." I pray Holy Ghost Viagra to overtake you. Just like father Abraham, that tent will start shaking again at 100 years old! And for heaven sake, if my prayer does not work, go buy a little blue pill and thank God for modern medicine.

If there is an underlying subconscious belief that batter-dipping the old corn dog is an unspiritual, necessary evil, you are trying to strip yourself of the very humanity God gave you, and it will tear you apart. Folks with stories like these may intellectually *know* this is a wrong way to perceive sex, but deep-seated religion can cause us to schizophreni-cally partition off that part of our lives. As frustrating as it seems to the casual reader – who wants to just shake them out of it – trust and openness in this area comes by over time from God. But there also comes a point you have to stick it in there and just churn the butter.

Single is Better?

As I said, we must skip past the Platonic leanings of the church fathers and return to Holy Scripture on this matter. I believe Gnosticism was artificially wedged between just a few verses in Paul's letter to the Cor-inthians, and it has had our collective sacred panties in a wad for 2,000 years. I want to walk us through the passage in 1 Corinthians 7 where Paul seems to indicate it is *better* for a person not to marry.

Firstly, I must put this epistle into context. Paul is dealing with *two* Gnostic extremes in Corinth. As discussed in the introduction, there are two main brands of Gnosticism: *Greek and Roman*. Both of them believe the material world is intrinsically evil. But how they approached the physical world was different. The Greek Gnostic leans toward ex-treme asceticism – fasting, abstinence, avoiding earthly pleasure. But the Roman Gnostic figures, "The world's all screwed up anyway so who's counting right and wrong? Let's have group sex!" The Greek turned to legalisms and the Roman turned to worldly licentiousness.

The Greek Gnostic said *no* to *all* sex – even in marriage. There were cohabitating married men and women who were not even buttering the biscuits with their own spouses after the kids went to bed. On the other hand, the Roman Gnostic said *yes* to *all* sex – he would tap anything that moved. Understand that Corinth was sin city. There was a temple to Aphrodite that likely employed upward of 1,000 male and female temple prostitutes. The place was a slimy den of dirty friction.

And so the passage of 1 Corinthians 7 begins:

> *Now concerning the things about which you wrote, "it is good for a man not to touch a woman"* (verse 1).

For starters, let me confess I used a bad translation here. Why? Be-cause that is how I first read this as a new believer. I thought, "Don't even touch a woman? Is that literal?" I was not even sure if I could give an elderly sister a side-hug on Sunday morning. Even worse translations say it is not good for a man to "marry" a woman. *That is not correct at all.* Just throw that particular Bible translation away.

Paul does not mean *touch.* He is talking about *touching that stuff.* The question being, "Is horizontal refreshment good or bad?" It is a general question: *is sex right or wrong?*

Plus, catch an important newsflash: *This is not even Paul's statement!*

Paul never said, "It's good for a man not to paddle the pink canoe." No, he is quoting a question that the *Corinthians* themselves had written him to ask, "Paul, tell us if sex is good or bad?"

The very nature of their question underlies how ignorantly confused they were. They were trying to figure out if *all sex itself* was right or wrong. Dumb Gnostic question. In this chapter, Paul will essentially tell them, "There is nothing wrong with feeding the kitty. But make sure it is your own cat! Don't feed the neighbor's kitty, because that thing should not be coming around the house." (Crowder paraphrase).

Hit it or Quit it?

See some Greek Gnostics in the church were not even having "business time" with their own spouses every Wednesday night. In order to be more *spiritual* they were refraining from the hokey pokey altogether even though they were married. On the other hand, the Roman Gnostics in the church were on constant booty patrol. In Corinth there was cross-dressing, homosexuality, adultery. One guy was shagging his own stepmom and everyone seemed to be okay with it. The Roman Gnostics would ride the bologna pony with anyone.

So their utterly misguided question, "Is sex okay?" Was answered by Paul's resounding, "Absolutely – but only with your spouse."

> But because there is so much sexual immorality, each man **should have** his own wife, and each woman **should have** her own husband (verse 2).

If I could have the brief courtesy of proof texting for a moment – let us just look at this as a standalone verse. Paul is not saying you *should* be single. Never once in scripture does he say you *should* be single. God bless you if you are single. That is a special gift. But why on earth do we think being single is a higher spiritual stratosphere? We are all on the same level of holiness my friends. If you think you will forfeit marriage just to get special heavenly space cadet points for celibacy, you are deluded. If you are called to celibacy, you will *want* to be single. But if you *want to have sex* – let me assure you, that is proof positive that you are called to marriage at some point (like most of humanity). Singleness and marriage are both gifts but not a hierarchy. Just different. For instance, if you are single you can binge watch Netflix nonstop for six months and never once shower. No one will nag you for smelling like rear end. Put a pool table in your living room. Drink milk straight from the jug. Not an ounce of negative feedback. Brilliant.

It's Business Time

Wanting sexual intimacy is a telltale sign that marriage is on the horizon for you. And Paul says here that marriage is good – even if for the sole reason of protecting us from temptation. This is a reason why married people should lovingly serve one another *always* if requested – whether you are sexually in the mood for your spouse or not. At a very minimal level, marriage safeguards us from temptation – so do not leave your spouse hanging out to dry if he or she is feeling hot to trot and you are not. There is mutual submission here.

The husband should fulfill his wife's sexual needs ...
(verse 3a).

Dear God is that a Bible verse? (Single people close your ears now).

This is simple: fellows ... take care of business! There are no excuses. Take it from Snoop Dogg, *"You've gotta take it slow ... she gonna get hers before I get mine."* If I could give one *practical* piece of advice for any man's love life it is that. As they say: happy wife, happy life. When young Christian men get married they are never schooled in this art by their local elder board. On the honeymoon night it is all fists and fur and frenzy. You do not know how to handle all those woman parts, and it is all over faster than the Flash on coke. Take your time. Learn to bring your wife to complete satisfaction. Discover what she likes. If you are both new at this, maybe she does not know what she likes. There is joy in the discovery, but take your time. Be a Victorian doctor and learn how to bring her to *hysterical paroxysm*; but whatever you do – do not just move on while she has unfinished business.

Get in a habit of playing three-minute wonder boy – giving her nothing in return before it is over – and it takes no rocket scientist to figure out why she does not want to romp around as much anymore. This is key to loosing her inner Kraken. Slow and steady wins the race. You will know when she is done. You will soon realize that key to your own pleasure is submitting and giving her pleasure first. That is what love-making is all about. It is also why a habit of watching porn and rubbing one off in the shower is the most horrible psychological thing you can do in preparation for a real woman in your life. It is not that every single playtime you have together needs to be an hour-long siesta under the stars with candles and Enya music. Sometimes in the middle of the day you may have five minutes before an appointment and decide to knock out a quickie in the kitchen. That is great! But do not get in the habit of satisfying your own urges without first assisting her.

Finally, if you married men have not realized it yet, women have a bizarre definition of foreplay. It involves *talking*. This chapter is on the rumpy pumpy – it is not an all-inclusive marriage guide. Sometimes the bedroom suffers if there is no communication or acts of kindness in other areas of your life. Sometimes you need to sing to her heart before you go yodeling in the valley.

Hear ye the Word of the Lord

Now, back to the Bible … *Oh dearest Lord!* This verse is still going:

> … *and the wife should fulfill her husband's needs* (verse 3b)

There is a God. (Yes, Virginia, there is a Santa Claus) … *wives fulfill your husband's needs.* Surely the Big Guy had me in mind when He wrote this. I am not a woman, so ladies I cannot address this from your perspective (I have never had that bent). After 15 years of marriage, one thing I know for certain is that I certainly know nothing about how a woman thinks. But I can tell you exactly how your husband thinks because all men are wired exactly the same on this point. He wants you to be bold. He wants you to initiate. If you are ever wondering, "Is this too far?" I can assure you it is not far enough. Whatever you think may be too *dirty*, I promise you *he will be absolutely comfortable with it.*

Your husband loves it when you switch things up and surprise him. Serve him. Sex should be frequent and enjoyable. In serving your spouse, you are actually being obedient to the Lord! Give no room for temptation outside the marriage bed. Sex should never be used as a tool for negotiation or a bargaining chip. It should be free and often. Surprise him. In Song of Solomon, it is actually the *woman* who initiates the playful banter and love. Do not make excuses. Ladies, herein lies is a wonderful remedy for headaches.

It is never acceptable for one spouse to simply say *I don't like sex*. It is a huge biblical part of marriage. Let us not be hearers of the word only, but doers of it. And do not be passive. So often, a person is waiting to be *pursued* by their spouse. But the more you take initiative in the sexual pursuit, the more your spouse may begin to do the same. Do not go to bed angry (Eph. 4:26). Often couples withdraw sexually after an argument, when in reality that is the very opposite thing you should do if you are looking for reconciliation! If you have to fight, try fighting naked. You may end up in gland-to-gland combat. To the best of your ability, be willing to experiment and explore in freedom and fun.

> The wife's body does not belong to her alone but also to her husband. In the same way, the husband's body does not belong to him alone but also to his wife (verse 4).

You are not your own. Be responsive to one another's needs. Often when there is timidity, or someone comes from a frigid, religious background it may be awkward to start exploring your freedoms. But out of love and service of your spouse, decide to communicate about your desires. Especially if it comes to trying something new or controversial, you need to talk about these things. "Well talking about it is awkward." Newsflash: *Sex is awkward!* Most often it is the man who wants to try new things or positions. While wives have a responsibility, men are likewise not to be demanding. Never make demands in the heat of the moment if your spouse is uncomfortable with something. Peter tells husbands to be considerate with your wives and treat them with respect (1 Peter 3:7). This means being patient and encouraging your wife, not just using her. Often if there is hesitation involved, there are reasons behind it. Fears. Previous abuse or past relationships. These can be opportunities to work through things and overcome some issues. Communication is needed, so be clear about any hang-ups, hurts or previous sexual sins from your past. You do not need to go into sordid detail, but you need to talk. If you are a man who has been addicted to pornography and have some strange obsessive fantasies that your wife is not comfortable with, you may need to lay those things down. Esteem her higher than your fetishes and do not press the issue. As she becomes the sole object of your affection, you will find her much more satisfying that the weird trappings you were demanding.

If You're Married it's Allowed

Scripture is quite specific on things not to do outside of wedlock, but the freedom within the sanctity of the marriage bed is pretty open ended. As long as the motives are loving and respecting of one another – not addictive preoccupations – go for it. No one is going to write you a citation. Scripture does not address specifics here – and since this stuff is rarely ever discussed in church – people tend to get their information from secular media or deviant sources like pornography. But whatever you choose to do, just let your conscience be your guide without placing control on your spouse. Oral sex, mutual masturbation – nothing is off-limits, and in fact we encourage *a lot of it!* But do things that promote oneness – not going off into another room to pull your own pickle. That is unhealthy. Anything done together (and exclusively together) endorses unity and is glorious. There is no place whatsoever for pornography in the marriage bed, because that involves other people – nor should you fantasize about someone else. Let your spouse be your standard of beauty, and guard your heart. Do not compare them to others, which will only breed discontentment. If you want to lock the door, set up a tripod and make your own smut movie for private viewing (and your spouse is okay with it), well have at it Steven Spielberg. Just make sure it does not end up on Facebook. I am not suggesting any particular fetishes; just saying when things are kept exclusive between the two of you, the sky is the limit. It is all about freedom, not requirements. If something is painful and your spouse is not ready for it, let it go for now. Do not force things.

If you have some certain things you are into (toys, anal sex, duct tape, hand puppets), just be sure these things do not become obsessions that master you. If you cannot just be with your spouse in an ordinary way without always *having* to do this stuff, it may be enslaving you. But just because something is out of the box, or because it has been done illicitly in a non-marital context does not make the action itself bad. Pastor Mark Driscoll, whom I esteem as refreshingly honest, clear and

96

balanced on sexual ethics, puts it this way, "I have been working in missiology for a long time, and at our church we use the language of 'receive, reject, redeem.' In the world there are things we can just receive. I don't know if a pagan invented the telephone or not, but we can receive it and use it. There are things we have to reject. We have to reject pornography. There's no such thing as Christian pornography. Then there are things that God created good that are defiled through sin but can be redeemed. So there may be certain sexual practices or positions that were introduced to someone in a sinful context, but they're not sinful in and of themselves. They may be able to be redeemed within marriage, if both parties have a clear conscience and are willing."[27]

Tighten Those Abs

Returning to our verse in this chapter: *your body does not belong to you alone*. This is broader than requests for oral sex. Do you shower? Use personal hygiene? Own a toothbrush? There is something to a bit of upkeep for your mate. You cannot walk around smelling like a decayed squirrel in the basement and expect to get cuddled. When I became a grown man of my 30s and my metabolism finally hit a wall, I realized as a traveling preacher eating late night pizza was not doing my midsection any favors. No woman wants to be married to a manatee. As a southern boy I grew up eating anything healthy (salad, broccoli) *as long as it was deep-fried*. My gracious wife never complained that I was a blimp, going through pant sizes like daily Starbucks cups.

I decided to take initiative to start eating better and hitting the weights at the gym, not just for her but also for myself. Did our love life improve? How could it not? Please understand I am not talking about embracing unhealthy eating habits or obsession with your appearance. The last thing you want is an eating disorder or some legalistic pressure driven by insecurity. Granted our society is shallow and image oriented. But there is a reasonable contribution we can make toward serving one another's preferences. My wife hates seeing me in out-of-style cargo shorts, so I have reluctantly stopped wearing them. One

---

[27] Interview by Katelyn Beaty and Marlena Graves, "Q & A: Mark and Grace Driscoll on Sex for the 21st-Century Christian," *Christianity Today* (Jan. 2, 2012) http://www.ctlibrary.com/ct/2012/januaryweb-only/mark-driscoll-sex-marriage.html (accessed Aug. 27, 2015).

day I woke up, realized I am old and the 90s are over. There are things you can do within reason to serve your spouse in terms of maintenance. I knew of a guy who would literally go months at a time without showering, slovenly obese, who stopped working and would spend hours a day playing video games. Surprise, surprise his wife cheated on him and left. I am not threatening fear of divorce. I am not fat-shaming or condemning anyone (you cannot always fix ugly anyway). It is just common sense that your body is not your own and there are basic self-maintenance things to be done in a relationship. You can go too far by worrying or not go far enough by not caring. Do not beat yourself up with insecurity, but use some common sense. Do not wake up to fistfuls of red velvet cupcakes every day (just some days).

Married couples learn pretty quickly that it is unhealthy to put demands on their spouse's appearance. I have never done that – and honestly I am overwhelmingly satisfied with my wife; I married up. But when you become aware of your spouse's preferences, try your best to accommodate them. My wife hates the smell of cigars (which I happen to enjoy). I may not forfeit them altogether. But when bedtime boogie is on the horizon, I give a valiant effort to scrub away the stench.

Fasting or Fondling?

Now to the next verse that preachers and prudes have long used to *mentula statur* (ahem … Google that in Latin).

> *Do not deprive each other except by mutual consent and for a time, so that you may devote yourselves to prayer. Then come together again so that Satan will not tempt you because of your lack of self-control* (verse 5).

Paul is not telling you to keep the banana out of the fruit salad for a while to be spiritual. Yes, it is fine to skip a day or two from the love couch if you are preoccupied with some other spiritual stuff. Sometimes I get lost in writing or study and forget to go to bed until 4 a.m. But this verse is so often wrongly interpreted to mean that people *should* pull away from the bonestorming in order to pray. Paul is *not at all* encouraging you to fast the four-legged foxtrot.

No, Paul's whole point is to *come back together!* How could such a pro-sex verse be interpreted in an anti-sex manner? Remember the context here. You had Greek Gnostics who were not even testing the suspension with their own mate, because they thought the bedroom rodeo was sinful. Paul is making a concession, not a command!

What I have just said is not meant as a command but as a suggestion (verse 6).

Paul is not playing referee. You want a few days off? *Fine*. But come back together. Pray with your knees upward. He is not commanding you to refrain from hiding the canoli. He is not even suggesting it!

I wish that all men were as I am. But each man has his own gift from God; one has this gift, another has that (verse 7).

How is Paul that we should be like him? Primarily he is *content*. He is not saying everyone should be single as the verse has routinely been suggested. Is Paul now contradicting himself, after telling folks they *should* have a spouse, reversing the directive and saying they *should* be single? Let us read on ...

I say to those who are unmarried, especially to widows: It is good for them to remain like me (verse 8).

Some translations say unmarried "*and* widows," but the phrase is akin to "namely widows." It is more accurate to say Paul is speaking *specifically* to unmarried widows. While scripture is unclear on this, a number of scholars believe Paul is addressing widows "like himself" as *Paul may have been a widower.* This is highly likely, because for Paul to be a member of the Sanhedrin, marriage was a requirement. In other words, many scholars believe Paul is essentially saying this: *Maybe you're an old cow that has already gone to pasture. You have had your fun in the sun – your romp in the park. If you are not interested in stirring up that old love machine again – if the thrill is gone – then just be content like me and stay the way you are. That's fine.* Widows should not feel some sort of financial or societal pressure to get married again if they do not want to. But even this is not a command! You want to go driving Miss Daisy? That's fine. Take Grandma to Applebee's. Widows and widowers are still completely free to remarry if they would like:

But if they cannot control themselves, they should marry, for it is better to marry than to burn with passion (verse 9).

Paul's whole point of this entire passage is to encourage a good, healthy married sex life. He is not trying to elevate singleness and celibacy to a standalone virtue. Do not religiously diminish the sex life in marriage, neglecting this cornerstone of the home and family. If you have been frigid, not putting out for your spouse, repent. If you have some psychological hang ups, then talk about it and *get over it*, but do not keep carrying on under the delusion that your marriage will be fine without copious amounts of copulation. A ravenous sexual appetite is wholesome and strongly encouraged in the marriage bed. Get this disgusting mistake out of your head that God is competing with your spouse for affection. God is the *source* of all love and affection for your spouse, and you literally worship God through the service of your mate.

Joy for Eunuchs

It is true that in some cases, people do *prefer* celibacy or they will not experience marriage for various physical reasons.

> *Jesus replied, "Not everyone can accept this word, but only those to whom it has been given. For there are eunuchs who were born that way, and there are eunuchs who have been made eunuchs by others—and there are those who choose to live like eunuchs for the sake of the kingdom of heaven. The one who can accept this should accept it"* (Matt. 19:11-12)

In modern terminology, a eunuch is someone born with genitalia that do not allow sexual relations (physical deformities, impotency, etc.); your body has been physically altered intentionally or accidentally (castration, mutilation, etc.); or you just have no appetite for sexual relations and want to live like a eunuch by choice. That choice may entail a desire to focus on solitude, prayer, study, ministry, missions etc. (for the sake of the kingdom).

In saying that "not everyone can accept this" does not mean the Lord is implying that some are not spiritually advanced enough to handle celibacy. It essentially means, "this word is not for everyone." It is not because some are called to "higher positions," but that some are called to "different roles." I would encourage anyone who is physically incapable of sex to know this does not define you. Perhaps you have had a surgery or medical condition that makes it impossible. Sexuality is an im-

100

portant part of life. But our identity is not rooted in the exchange of bodily fluids – what an empty existence that alone would be! The Lord has made other plans to fulfill you, and depression is not your portion.

If physical reasons prevent you from intercourse, that is out of your hands apart from the Lord growing you a pair of testicles (something I have prayed for pastors for years). You can have a wonderful, non-sexual life. Do not be embittered or despise yourself. Although it is not an elevated "forsaking" of the lesser in lieu of the greater, the Lord says eunuchs are not missing out. Do not think you are a *dry tree*. He says not to complain in Isaiah 56. You cannot have physical sons and daughters; the Lord says He has something *better tailored* for you – a spiritual lineage, a *memorial in His temple and an everlasting name*.

Single and Desperate?

As for those single people reading this, know that there is grace for you right where you are. Those pheromones do not have to be agitated until the proper time. Jesus lived life a virgin. Paul was single. A perfect life lived does not have to include sex. If you have already been sexually active, do not believe the lie that once your appetite has been whetted, it is impossible to go cold turkey. Living a holy life is your first and primary nature. You are a new creation. Holy Spirit sustains you. Sexual temptation does not have to be a constant struggle. It is religion that says you are a sinner and that you must constantly battle lust.

Neither single nor married folks are second-class citizens. There are different gifts in life and different seasons. No need to compare ourselves with one another like apples and oranges. Every married person was once a single person that can fully empathize with the struggle of wanting to be married. I get it.

If you are currently single, you may be wondering, "Will I be single forever?" Again, the fact that you want marriage means you are not called to be a monk. If you *do not want marriage* – perfectly content with absolutely no desire for sex and matrimony – go for it! You can stop shaving, trek across Greenland and carry your entire groceries home on a bicycle. The possibilities are endless. Stop obsessing over what you do not have, and focus on the opportunities that you do.

There are two extremes to which we must never fall prey:

1) That sexuality is wrong.
2) That sex is okay outside of marriage.

Let us be crystal clear on this point that inside marriage, all sex is good. And outside marriage, all sex is off limits. Period. Noticing that someone is attractive is normal and healthy. That is not the same as lusting and obsessing. God made us with a sex drive. It would be odd not to recognize beauty in the opposite sex. These are not bad feelings; yet those feelings need not control us in an improper way. Self-control is really God-control – allowing ourselves to be overmastered by His love so our lives blossom in the direction of His Spirit's guidance. Sex is such a holy and pure thing inside of matrimony that we would never want to spoil the intended oneness it entails – we should realize it belongs to the right person. There is grace for mistakes. But grace is also the antidote to temptation. As I drink daily from His presence, there is an overmastering satisfaction that outweighs all else.

Your desire for sex is a good indication that you should start *preparing* for marriage, not just continually thinking about sex itself. Marriage is so much bigger than the physicality aspect. In the meantime, in the grace to wait, you are learning the disciplines of faithfulness and drinking from the well of satisfaction that is Christ inside of you – something a spouse can never replace. In your preparation for a lasting relationship, you are ensuring that you do not enter marriage in a broken, co-dependent state expecting your mate to solve your problems. You are learning to live out of the new heart He has given you. And that lesson will continue after marriage. Studying, working hard, learn to love and serve others, and growing in maturity. Rather than obsessing over what you *do not yet have*, focus on what is currently at your disposal to achieve in life. One day you'll be jerking it where she's twerking it … but that is not the primary objective. Rest assured big boy, one day you will have a mortgage, a car and a king-size bed.

Maximize Your Singleness

Singleness is a gift that should be fully lived to the hilt. You have boatloads of time on your hands to do things in life a person married with kids never can. Work an 80-hour week and you still have time galore! You are tired of hearing that from married folks, but it is true! Singleness is not a curse. It is a blessing, so receive it as a gift. It will not be this way for you forever. Do not wish your life away in the meantime. In hindsight I wasted loads of time as a single guy. I could have learned eight languages, how to play the cello, opened a bourbon distillery, earned a doctorate and become a black belt in three martial arts.

Maximize your singleness for God. Missions. Ministry. Service. Not everyone is called to preach or become a full-time missionary to Ghana. Whether you are called to business, medicine, the arts or whatever – just do not waste your time away idly spinning your wheels, only wishing you were married. Occupy your time with study, work and being a source of assistance to others. Fight injustice. Create. Be a big brother or big sister to someone who needs a mentor. Very soon you will be working a full time job, juggling several kids and a spouse. Above all, grow up! Yes we should play hard and learn to rest. But do not spend all day on Xbox or taking a hundred selfies on Snapchat. Live life and accomplish something. The benefit of marriage and having children is we learn to think outside ourselves and realize our lives are truly fulfilled in loving and serving others. In raising family, wasted time is not an option. How amazing to learn these lessons while single, some day looking back over your shoulder with no regrets.

Do not despise your singleness. If you do look forward to marriage, do not try to "kill" your desire for it or ignore your emotions. Do not succumb to a resigned fatalism because you have hit your late 30s and are still going stag. It is perfectly healthy to want to have sex and want to have a spouse. It is just an issue of self-control and patience in the meantime. There is a content balance in which we recognize natural longings, yet do not try to stir them up. There is God-given patience to direct them toward our future mate without succumbing to temptation. This is an area where you may learn to daily depend on grace. We channel our desires, not vilify them. Otherwise, the legalistic attempt to exterminate our emotions will only cause them to find a twisted outlet. Yes there is tension in the journey, but do not close down the fact that we are sexual creatures to the point that (when you do get married) you have become a religious frigid creature that is averse to stuffing the turkey when you finally tie the knot.

Ready to Date?

It is only common sense not to pursue a serious romantic relationship if you are not in a season of life in which you are ready to marry. If you are in school and do not intend to walk down the aisle anytime soon, why pursue a relationship? Why put yourself in an emotionally and physically compromised situation? If you are not in the position to glaze the donut, why go sniffing around Krispy Kreme?

Our society today is far removed from the venerable safety of the courtship traditions that marked almost every culture until the mid 1900s. While there were healthy aspects of courtship, it is delusional to expect our society to hop in a time machine back to the 1950s. The fact is that family and faith do not influence the institution of dating the way they once did, and we live in a sexually charged culture that sets up many young people with recipes for failure. Countless morally compromised parents actually *encourage* promiscuity in their teens today!

Many religionists would seek to prohibit dating altogether. But unless you are Amish and sew your own flour sack dresses, chances are you must navigate the world from within the parameters of your own conscience without the benefit of the external societal norms. So what does this look like? If you are 16, odds are you are not ready to get married. I am not saying all dating is off the table. But you must determine to keep things light and relatively unattached. Consider yourselves friends, not lovers. Otherwise you are only tooling around with one another's emotions. In your longing to transition into adulthood, playing "pretend marriage" is not a sign of maturity. It is actually immaturity. Also do not resign yourself to "messing up" just because you have been told this is a "tough age." You have God Himself within you. Take advantage of this time. Get off the PlayStation and dive into the things of God. Work wonders. Explore the beauty of the path He has chosen for you, without getting overly serious with a premature relationship. Keep your focus on the greater destiny that lies before you without caving to unnecessary distractions. God will sustain your emotional needs beyond your greatest comprehension.

If you are young, it is healthy to keep your relationships in the context of groups. Spending inordinate amounts of time alone together is not going to be beneficial. Even here, do not be legalistic about dating. We allowed our daughter to date in high school. Rather than enforce a "no dating" policy, we preferred that she learn to do it in a healthy way with boundaries and parental input before leaving the house to blindly navigate relationships on her own in college. If you are a parent, be sure to engage in open and honest communication with your teen about these things. Take the time. Do not be lazy or timid to address these issues.

Do not expect YouTube to parent your child. Deep down they appreciate the love and boundaries you give them. They crave it. If you are raising teenage daughters, be sure the young buck who comes rutting around your house does not just pull up and honk for her to come out. He should walk through the front door, look you in the eyes and ask your permission to see her. Take him for a drive, scare the living hell out of him and make sure he is crystal clear in understanding he will be keeping his hands and mouth to himself. Be clear about these things; anything left uncommunicated is a loophole that will be exploited. Be a parent, not a buddy. Your child will eventually thank you.

Kiss Dating Hello

If you are a legal adult and the time is ripe for a serious relationship, recognize that it is better to marry than to burn. Do not let the pressures of societal expectations delay you until you have accumulated all your degrees and obtained your dream job. Be open to marriage, even at a young age. So many leave behind the carnage of emotional scars from aborted relationships that were shelved by the idol of career.

For a Christian, dating is not about playing around, but should be done with the prospect of finding a spouse. Keeping to a group dynamic is healthy for a teenager. However, when a young man grows up, he needs to man up. In order to get a date, you have to ask a girl out. It takes something called courage. Do not pass her friend a note like a second grader to see if she likes you. Put on some nice clothes, stand upright, walk up and take the initiative to ask her out. If you are a single lady being asked out, you have the freedom to say "no" if you are not interested. And you have freedom to say "yes" if you are interested.

In church circles, so often we see young men who are paralyzed with fear that they are moving outside the will of God by asking out a lady they like. So many 20-somethings are "just friends" within a social circle, but they think it is wrong to date. They are expecting a lightning bolt visitation from the Son of Man on a pegasus to reveal the hour in which they might ask a chick to a movie. Many of them feel awkward to just ask out a girl. If you never go on dates, it is not because you are unattractive or inept at relationships. It may just be that you are a chicken. You can live a life of eternal bromance with your buddies, or you can grow a set of cajones and overcome your fear to ask her out. People who over think this step become the 40-year-old virgin. Ever notice a very attractive woman with an ugly little pug of a spouse? Often times she just fell for the first guy who was brave enough to take her out for a coffee!

Manhood seems to have long disappeared from our culture. The exfoliating, moisturizing, metrosexual 2000s gave way to the skinny-jeaned, effeminate hipster 2010s. Now masculinity is embodied as a sentimental artifact with recent trends like the "lumbersexual" (post-metrosexuals who now wear exquisitely well oiled and groomed beards, flannel T-shirts and decorate with cute retro mannish things like taxidermy deer heads and vintage toolboxes in remembrance of that museum relic once called testosterone). To even mock the castration of American pop-culture can get me labeled a heterosexist-caveman misogynist, but I am really okay with that and beyond catering to anyone's opinion. I appreciate the finer things in life and am in no way a primitive, non-cultured redneck. One can be a Renaissance man yet still be a real man. Women are attracted to real men. So if you are a young fellow interested in women, you should make that clear and occasionally act straight.

Laundry List of Perversion

Once a dating relationship kicks off, even in the church today hardly anybody blinks an eye at fornication. Desensitized by modern culture, a large percentage of new believers do not even know what that word means *(fornication is any sex outside of marriage)*. As Driscoll has often pointed out, "Today, we have a bunch of teenagers who don't even think oral sex counts as sex."[28]

The choir boys, in their Greek Gnosticism, are too skiddish to do a Starbucks date – while Roman Gnosticism flourishes in the "friends with benefits" mentality of other "Christians" having casual sex without a hint of a moral compass. The apostle Paul clarifies this topic in which the New Testament scriptures are resounding clear:

> But among you there must not be even a hint of sexual immorality (Eph. 5:3, NIV[29]).

---

[28] Ibid.

[29] *The Holy Bible, New International Version* (Grand Rapids: The Zondervan Corporation, 1973, 1978, 1984). International Bible Society.

106

People do shifty things in their minds to justify sexual activity before marriage. They figure any sort of work-around outside of direct penis-to-vagina interaction is somehow fine with the Boss. Just for your personal enlightenment, allow me to clarify exactly what constitutes sexual immorality. The goal here is not to have a "sin consciousness," but you better believe this list is to pull you out of the delusion and moral ambiguity that this stuff is somehow okay.

With anyone who is not your spouse, there should be absolutely no sexual interaction – this would include dry humping, mutual masturbation, hand jobs, oral sex, anal sex (Some would literally ask, "Aren't I still a virgin if it's anal?"). Oral sex is sex (who could blame you for not knowing that? ... Even President Clinton was confused). Mutual masturbation is sex. If you are not married, do not do it. If you are married, do a lot of it. Think of it this way: you should not do anything physically with your date that you would not do with your grandmother. This person is not your wife or husband. Until you put a ring on it, you are defiling someone else's future spouse as far as you are concerned. The shame and guilt – the cheapening of a spiritual and emotional connection that is reserved for the lifelong mate alone – is beneath you as one who is a carrier of the image of God in Jesus Christ.

It is a complete delusion to think anything outside of direct vaginal intercourse does not count as "sex" and therefore not sinning. You should not be sexting, sharing nude images, sharing explicit video through technology or having erotic conversations with anyone that is not your spouse. And we can broaden the definition of sexual sin to things that no one should be doing, married or not: swinging with multiple partners, rape, pedophilia, polyandry (one woman multiple husbands), bestiality, polygamy or homosexuality. Furthermore it is wrong to engage in incest, adultery, prostitution or orgies.

That is not an exhaustive list of perversions – I am sure you could think of more. Jesus used word "porneia" to lump together all manner of sexual sin. The Lord knew if He merely gave you a list of naughty stuff like the one above, you would still find some other twisted way to get your rocks off that was not on the list. So the word porneia essentially means everything that is sexually immoral: any other sick way you plan to engage in sexual behavior outside of marriage.

The issue is not "How far can I go?" The issue is not to get going until you are married. A focus on what one can or cannot do is indicative of a low level of morality. No better than a base legalism that shows our heart is in the wrong place. The more advanced question is "How can I show honor to this person? How can we best demonstrate the light and life and gospel of Jesus Christ in our relationship? How can I exhibit faithfulness and enjoy the glory of God in the happiness of holiness?"

Spiritually Married?

If one is always pushing the technicalities of what is or is not sin, they are playing foolish definition games. And so often people are enslaved by sexual addictions, using coping mechanisms and self-deception to justify unbiblical lifestyles. They build structures and thought patterns in their minds to excuse their behavior as if they are an exception to the rule of biblical morality. "We are 'spiritually married.' We are 'married in the eyes of God.'" I can promise you His eyes are furious toward the sin and compromise you are corrupting yourselves with. If you are "spiritually married" without the rock solid commitment before God and society in a legal bond with a certificate, you are not fooling anyone but yourself and the person you are defiling. If you are not willing to make the lifelong legal commitment to bind yourself together – including your possessions, your name, contractually and obligatory in all things certi-fied – you are merely in fornication. You do not love the person if you have not even put your wallet on the table. Go to the justice of the peace and baptize the relationship.

Granted there may be rare historical or cultural reasons where gov-ernment sanctioned marriages are not possible for Christians (i.e. Mel Gibson's *Braveheart* in a secret ceremony by night). There are rare cases of cultures that outlaw or persecute Christian marriage (think of Muslim convert to the faith in some nations). If you are a fugitive or face some bureaucratic loophole, etc. that prevents you from making it legal, there would clearly be exceptions. Marriage is indeed and fore-most a spiritual bond that could be witnessed by the church with holy vows, even if the government disallowed it. But overwhelmingly in 99 percent of "shacking up" today, legal avoidance is merely an excuse to play Animal Planet without the real life commitment that true marriage entails. If for some obscure reason the government will not endorse it, you should at least make your vows before witnessing believers before you start taking the skin bus to tuna town. I have personally known of only one such case. A woman's husband ran off and disappeared altogether – he virtually fell off the planet for years. In the UK she was not allowed to remarry until he signed off on a divorce. Her life was thrown into limbo because of this deadbeat absconder. Years later, she wanted to remarry, but was not allowed. So she and her new mate got married in a service before God and the church, even though they were not allowed to get official marriage papers.

Depleted finances are no excuse to shack up. If you avoid a legal contract for the sole reason that you are personally unwilling (yet you are willing to play hide the porpoise with your girlfriend) then you are in sin. You may think you are too spiritually advanced for a government certificate, but you are just a coward afraid to commit. There are "one flesh" unions or "soul ties" that are deep spiritual bonds designed for lifelong commitment. Not shallow, ambivalent game playing with no ramifications. To think cohabitation does not constitute "sin" because you are "under grace" means you are deluded by Roman Gnosticism.

Today there is a plethora of bizarre theological reasoning to justify sexual immorality. Whole denominations today do back flips arguing that every passage on homosexuality does not mean what it clearly says. "That's not what the Greek meant." Or they endorse an evolving hermeneutic, "Yes the Bible says it's wrong, but we've transitioned beyond that. Revelation is progressing." Some things in the New Testament were cultural (women speaking in church, dudes having long hair). But scriptural admonitions against sexual immorality were not just culturally contextual and open to change over time.

Freedom From Sin

Whatever the sexual sin may be, countless Christians develop systems of self-justification. Often they just schizophrenically decide their sexual deviancy is only "one part" of their life. "I don't have it all together in that area, but everything else is okay in my spiritual life, so I'll just live with it." They have learned to identify with and excuse self-destructive behavior. This is further enforced by the double-minded, non-gospel message of indwelling sin preached from most pulpits today. Folks are not clearly told they have been liberated from their old nature. Therefore, excuses for sin are commonplace in the resounding idea that "nobody's perfect," "you're only human," or the nauseating unbiblical notion that you must always battle your old sinful fleshly self.

109

We do not condemn ourselves if we have struggled sexually. Guilt and shame are not going to help us. We must know we are forgiven, but we must also know we *really can rest* as new creations who do not have to engage with this stuff another day. We also do not judge others who are in sexual sin. But we must be honest in love. Obviously we should deal with Christians differently than nonbelievers. Why should we even expect a nonbeliever to have a Biblical compass? Pointing out their sins is not going to help. However, if we are in relationship with other believers, there are times when we must be honest. If a brother is in fornication, adultery or some lustful addiction, let us gently seek to restore him. Scripture is clear that we should approach him, and if necessary, bring someone else into the conversation as well. If they refuse counsel, we may have to put distance in the relationship. The apostles knew this was a big deal for the health of the community. The biblical mandate to "expel the immoral brother" sounds harsh to our tolerant modern ears, but we must know the heart of the apostles was not one of anger, bitterness or condemnation. Love protects wholesome body life and makes no room for predators. Our communion of believers is a place of safety and soundness. Not an open door for corrupting influence on the innocent. This does not mean we disfellowship and shun every Tom, Dick and Harry who struggles with internet porn. But there must be a humility, teachability and willingness to grow in these areas without blatant, willful intent to sin against others in the name of Christ.

At the end of the day, we are not referees blowing the whistle calling fouls on one another. And ultimately we cannot fix people anyway – it is Holy Spirit's job to reveal their true identity and holiness. But our fear of being legalists does not excuse us to be cowards. If you are a leader, do not make room for sexual immorality in your congregation. Confidently and clearly communicate what the holy life looks like.

Freedom from sexual sin is found in "considering dead" your earthly members to immorality (Col. 3:5). It is vanity to try and "kill" sinful appetites that have already died with Jesus. Sexual appetites are God given, but the false identity in Adam tried to pervert them to be explored outside the sanctity of marriage. That perverse nature is a false identity. It is not you. Christian growth is about realizing we are already free from those delusions. Do not shadowbox this thing as if it is a legitimate part of who you are, which you have to combat. Sure we are waking up to the reality of who we are - but it does not have to be a difficult lifelong struggle. As we put our focus in the right place, every-thing becomes a breeze.

Everyone has struggled with sin. You are not "more depraved" than others if you have dealt with this stuff. But sexual sin does have further reaching implications on ourselves and others than many other things. It brings upon us shame, guilt and a sense of condemnation. But be-yond personal, emotional and psychological damage, it also produces the bad fruit of divorce, broken families and ultimately a fatherless, vio-lent, impoverished society whose turmoil can carry over to future gen-erations (at least those generations not aborted because of it).

So we are not *sin conscious* – constantly trying to battle and fight it and giving it a life of its own. Nor do not deny sin's negative effects. Yet our objective is a positive one – become aware of the presence of Christ and his finished work in destroying our old perverse nature, so the de-lusion of darkness flees in the light. We find our struggles dissipate like the smoke and mirrors they always were.

Again, the New Testament writers are holding this perspective of our righteousness in Christ while still spending a lot of time clarifying mo-rality issues. Often, we can talk about grace and freedom without ever dropping the delusions about the lifestyle we are living. We are free *from evil*, but that does not mean we are free to *act evil* by redefining a moral standard of "anything goes" now that we are under grace.

> But strong meat is for the mature, even those who by reason of use have their senses exercised to discern both good and evil (Heb. 5:14).

Let us be mature. Not viewing sexual guidelines as stark legalisms. God is adamant about you having a wonderful healthy sex life, and that is the very reason why He gives us parameters. God's "No" to sexual immorality is a resounding "Yes" to the glorious bliss of marital un-ion. The No is always a Yes in disguise.

Pressure to Accommodate

So often in a dating relationship, women feel a pressure to accommo-date a man's desires. Even if she would not ordinarily be prone toward immorality, she feels an obligation to please him. Understand clearly that if he is willing to disrespect you by not waiting for marriage, tell him to go to hell. You do not want that kind of scumbag. If he is not willing to wait for marriage, then he is not marriage material. Men can be masters at manipulation, lying and flattery to get what they want. Some women are so lonely and needy for affection they essentially prostitute themselves for the first guy willing to buy them dinner and a movie. Do not compromise your integrity on a person of compromise. His long-term odds of being faithful are not going to be good anyway. Value yourself. Do not lower your standards for a sleazebag. The same is true for men in a similar scenario. In today's culture, women can be sexually aggressive as well – the same temptation applies. There are truly moments when you must decide who you are going to worship when illicit opportunity comes knocking on your door. Flee temptation. If it gets thrown in your face, run. Take your cue from Joseph. When Potiphar's wife enticed him to spelunk her bat cave in Genesis 39 he ran away faster than Usain Bolt. Do not flirt with temptation. Escape it.

If as a single woman your boyfriend is trying to get into your pants – not respecting the sanctity of marriage as the ordained place for sex – why on earth do you think he will respect the boundaries of marriage after you tie the knot? Is he suddenly going to become sexually moral after you say vows? There will always be times when you are apart when you are married, so you need a foundation of trust. While the physical aspect of your relationship is vitally important, love transcends physicality. If he cannot respect your physical boundaries, his love for you is either shallow or non-existent. He is selfish and using you. Do not expect him to magically demonstrate self-control after you are married, if he lacks it while you are dating. Self-control is a fruit of the Spirit anyway – it is not human generated. It may be good to reevaluate priorities and see where God's role is in the relationship. It is imperative to be clear on your shared goals of purity before you go deep with any dating relationship.

It is idolatry to offer your body to a created being outside of marriage. But it is worship to your Creator to offer your body to your spouse within the sacrament of marriage.

Don't you realize that your bodies are actually parts of Christ? Should a man take his body, which is part of Christ, and join it to a prostitute? Never! Do you not know that he who unites himself with a prostitute is one with her in body? For it is said,

"The two will become one flesh." But the person who is joined to the Lord is one spirit with Him. Run from sexual sin! No other sin so clearly affects the body as this one does. For sexual immorality is a sin against your own body. Do you not know that your body is a temple of the Holy Spirit, who is in you, whom you have received from God? You are not your own; you were bought at a price. Therefore honor God with your body (1 Cor. 6:15-20).

God does not put limits on sex because the act is gross. Rather, it is such a strong, mystical bonding mechanism that its power must be contained to the two souls it is meant to tether and join. Like a nuclear reactor, it must be sealed in such a way that it does not melt down and destroy the lives it is meant to bless. Sex is for a husband and wife in marriage without anyone else being involved in any other way – this is not a restriction or limitation, but a protection for our ultimate satisfaction, joy and emotional prosperity. Only a moron would think the dangers of non-marital sex are just external (i.e. worries about venereal disease or pregnancy). No the issue goes much deeper to the eternal regions of the heart, for the effects are spiritual and psychological.

You are in union with Christ. Your body is His body. This is a mystery. But He will not be part of your fornication. Do not put yourself in such a dangerous situation attempting to act "apart from Him." Sexual sin is the only sin the scripture says is done "in the body." Do nothing you would not want your own spouse doing with someone else. This is not legalism. It is the law of love. This is honor. This is respect and living in godliness. Your freedom is not freedom to molest someone else's current or future soul mate for your own temporary gratification.

Expect to Succeed

For young adults with the prospect of marriage, dating is a great way to meet and bond with a potential spouse. Although we should guard our hearts to have healthy boundaries – the dangers of sexual sin should by no means instill fear and trepidation in this area. You are not *running from danger* as much as you are protecting something valuable. Set your expectations to succeed in this area and know that failure is not an option for you. But avoiding dating due to religious fears is tantamount to those doctrines of demons forbidding people to marry. Keeping it pure, healthy and innocent should be a shared goal.

Dating is much more than finding a potential lifelong boot knocker. The only objective is not to harness that mule. Find someone with whom you have shared goals regarding career, family and theological beliefs. Date someone you are attracted to – do not date out of pity or some twisted religious obligation to punish yourself by going out with an ugly person (yes some people do that). Find someone with whom you share a spiritual and emotional connection. Do not date a non-Christian. What is the point? So often people become "unequally yoked" with a nonbeliever and foolishly wonder why they end up not sharing the same moral values or ultimate vision for life. Maybe you feel a strong passion for a non-Christian, but "missionary dating" is always a bad idea. This may sound like a legalism, because you feel this person is "the one," and you are just positive you will lead them to the Lord. But have some wisdom here. You are not their savior. If you do not share the most fundamental priority in life from the beginning, you are setting yourself up for a long-term nightmare.

Some set the bar of expectation too low. Ladies you do not need to date the hunchback of Notre Dame just because he is the first guy to ask you out. If your only qualification for a date is that he has a pulse and most of his teeth, I would encourage you to lift your standard. Conversely, other folks are *way too picky*. Their expectations are through the roof. When you are 20, you can hold out for that perfectly symmetrical Adonis. But some end up single until they are 45 because they are so indecisive. You could find a supermodel Harvard graduate with Mother Theresa compassion with a stand-up comedian's sense of humor, but you would still anal retentively pick her apart because her hair is an inch shorter than you prefer. Do not be that guy. The one who frustrates all your married friends because you cannot see the forest for the trees. They could parade a harem of beautiful godly ladies before you; but you have this idolatrous, imaginative caricatured woman in your head that is nonexistent, whilst being totally oblivious to the hot mess that is standing right in front of you in the real world.

Guard your heart in dating. Do not give it away too early if the other person is not there yet. Also be open to love if the Lord brings someone across your path who may not meet your preconceived criteria list. Of course use wisdom, but sometimes love may override your checklist of expectancies in a future spouse. You might overlook a good person for various reasons: they are not affluent, there is an age difference, they are divorced, they have a kid, etc.

When I met my wife, she was single mom. This was not something I was expecting in a potential wife, but I loved her and knew the relationship was from the Lord. I also immediately loved my daughter whom I adopted as soon as her mother and I became married. On the same token, I probably did not fit all of her criteria list for a potential husband. I was literally a lawnmower man living in a one-room cabin with an outhouse in Alaska. Not exactly a billionaire swooping her off her feet in my private helicopter. I was not even a full-time grass cutter; *I was a temp!* I was driving no Mercedes. I had a minivan (not usually what a player drives, but to her it screamed *commitment)!*

So Holy Spirit may guide us into situations we were not looking for. Conversely, sometimes we may be in an unwise relationship that we are justifying. Our judgment can become cloudy if we like someone and think, "We can work through this." Look at character. Is this person kind, patient, serving ... do they love God? Is the man a leader? Is the woman willing to follow her husband's leadership? Are they abusive? Are they flirtatious with others? Are they addicted to pornography? A potential spouse should also want children.

Making Babies

As a side note, opinions on birth control vary in the church. I see nothing at all wrong with using it in marriage (unless it is an abortive type, like the "morning after pill"); but if a couple is adamant about *never* wanting a kid, that is a massive indicator of selfishness. Viewing children as a hindrance to career or inconvenience to one's lifestyle is a new phenomena of modern society; historically they were always seen as a blessing from God. Procreation is not the *only* reason for sex, but it is a *massive* God-given part of it. When Paul says *women will be saved through childbearing,* this is has nothing to do with one's eternal fate resting on her nether regions. It is about the constant recognition of our dependence on God through raising kids – as well as a constant reminder to think outside ourselves (1 Tim. 2:15). How many children have been sacrificed to the altar of human selfishness in the abortion industry? Be clear that abortion is *never* an acceptable means of birth control. Life begins at conception, and abortion is *always* murder.

Some men do not want kids because they do not want to grow up and work and take responsibility. Some young women have a hyper-feminist orientation, or people just delay childbearing for financial reasons that are selfish or greedy. Children are a blessing, but you are not commanded to have them (being fruitful and multiplying is not just a dictum on having rug rats). Jesus did not have kids. You might use birth control because you want to wait; or you are done having them; or you cannot have them for medical reasons. If you physically cannot have kids but want them, consider adoption. There is freedom here. The sin of Onan spilling his seed is not applicable to all uses of birth control. People can be legalistically for or against birth control. Some deadbeat religious zealots will heap 20 kids on their tired, ragged, homeschooling wife, unable to support them financially – all because of some self-righteous, anti-contraception dogma they try to push on everyone else. There is freedom here: but do not be selfish.

The anti-contraception crowds are often the same groups who think sex is *only* for procreation. Sex makes kids. But sex also makes us happy. A woman's body comes factory-direct from God with certain parts that bring her pleasure, yet those parts have *no creative purpose* whatsoever for childbearing. This tells us sex is not strictly a utilitarian tool for reproduction. We can take the bald-headed gnome for a stroll in the misty forest for no other reason than the fun of it.

Finding "The One"

Besides building a family, there are some common sense things to consider in a potential spouse that Christians may overlook if they think "this is the one." Ladies, if your guy is not willing to get his act together, get a job, move out of his parents' house, finish school or stop playing computer games all day long, how committed and responsible do you think he will be toward you? Will this person lay down his life for you? Again, do not be too picky, but also do not think you must settle for the first douche bag who asks you out. Do not settle for a little immature boy who wants to dip his carrot but does not want to grow up. If your boyfriend does not have eyes for you alone, that's a big red flag. If you feel a pressure to be more sexually alluring to capture him, that is not a good sign. If he is into you, he will be all about *you.* If his eyes are elsewhere, the problem is not with you. Do not think you need to *do something* to make him committed. And do not think you can correct a character flaw in him like that.

Overall, I am a huge fan of short engagements. If you are trying to fix up your character before you get married, realize that Jesus is the one who perfected you. Yes we mature, but part of marriage is growing together. Stretching out engagements brings unnecessary temptation. Some break up after two years only to have an emotional divorce. So you had an argument? Well decide who you *do* want to argue with the rest of your life and marry that one. If you feel this is "the one" and want to get married, then just get hitched. And how do you determine if this is "the one"? Do you love them? Do you want to spend your life with them? Are they godly? Sometimes the pros and cons list is a good indication of the divine call. You do not need a visitation from Enoch and Elijah. Rest assured that once you get married, *this is the one!* There is no point wondering if you made a mistake. Do not go looking for a better spouse. *Become a better spouse.* Stretching engagements out excruciatingly long (meanwhile telling your hormones "no, no, no") can not only produce temptation, but also cause frigidity problems in marriage after years of stifling desires that were created to be expressed in matrimony. You are unnecessarily battling against the sex that you should already be having as a married couple, growing resentful toward your "gross" desires. Some people date for two years, then mess up sexually – and suddenly think, "This isn't the one because we botched it!" Maybe you should just stop botching and marry!

Waiting, Boundaries & Guiltless Sex

Do not buy into the ridiculous idea that you should try multiple sex partners to make sure your potential spouse is "good." Wait until marriage and you will not know any difference – *it will all be good!* This is an area you are going to grow together in anyway. I have heard of people being bitter at their conservative Christian upbringing. They held onto their virginity until their wedding night and their first experience with sex was clumsy and painful and awkward. Newsflash: *everyone's first time having sex is clumsy, painful and awkward!* It only gets better over time. Give it few more tries. Soon you will be skinning the dingo upside down.

If for whatever reason, your fiancé is unwilling for a short engagement, then you must gauge your love for him or her and determine if you are willing to do what it takes. *Jacob served seven years to get Rachel, but they seemed like only a few days to him because of his love for her* (Gen. 29:20). Consequently, if your fiancé is unwilling to shorten that time and commit because of parental pressure or misplaced obligation, there are two things to remember. One, you should honor their par-

MONEY. SEX. BEER. GOD.

ents. Two, unless they learn to make a clean break from their parents' wishes at some point and emotionally leave and cleave to you, there are going to be lots of issues and baggage coming into the marriage. And chances are, that long, religious engagement can mess you up.

Finally, with dating, have some common sense boundaries. Do not sleep over at one another's house or spend all night spooning on the couch alone. There are a thousand reasons (financial or otherwise) that lead people to shack up before they are in a committed marriage. Proverbs 6:27 says, "Can a man scoop fire (*khathah* "take burning coals") into his lap without being burned?" The answer is obvious: *No.* Even if you are not "doing anything," why bring reproach on your girlfriend and dishonor her by putting her in such a position?

Maybe you think you are mature enough to live together without burping the worm in the mole hole. Get real. You owe it to yourself and your fiancé to elevate your moral standard. Every line you cross will be like a domino effect into wanting more physical intimacy. Your objective is not to figure out how much tongue is okay. The objective of true love is to set the course for a solid, honoring relationship and ultimately a thriving sexual relationship in marriage, built on trust. Let your question be "What can we do to honor God and ourselves in this relationship?" Err on the side of purity. I speak as a man who made many mistakes in this area. If I could do it all over, I would not have kissed anyone until I was married. Before marriage you are still building intimacy, even with the physical boundaries you set to honor your lover.

Pornography Hurts

God wants us to have an exhilaratingly spicy sex life, and I have made the case that marriage is the divine recipe. But we need a tremendous amount of clarity on this, as today's porn-driven media bombards us. It has cheapened the glory of human sexuality and desensitized us to the bliss designed for the marriage bed.

Consider the following statistics: American children begin consuming hardcore porn at age 11 (I was first exposed at age 5 or 6). Thirty percent of the Internet industry is porn; it is a $97 billion industry worldwide. Child pornography is a $3 billion industry. Porn sites attract more visits than Netflix, Amazon and Twitter combined. Nine out of 10 boys and one out of three girls report using porn; and seven of 10 youth have accidentally come across porn online.[30]

If you are a porn user, you are actually contributing to child abuse, the sex slave trade and the horrors of sexual immorality. Even if you are looking at some free site that puts viruses on your computer, you are still contributing to the culture of death, psychological depravity and family destruction that this industry promotes with every single click. Whether you are paying for it or not, porn corporations are driven by advertisements you are watching.

Let me say that if you are using pornography, the first practical step is to stop. It is dishonoring to God and ourselves. Confess it; do not justify it. Set boundaries for yourself. Do not give room for it anymore. Depending how deep you are into it, it may be good to get accountability with others who have shared this same struggle.

Most of us born after the so-called sexual revolution of the 1960s were born into a climate where sexual deviancy is considered normative. Let me be clear that porn is a deviant *perversion* – it is an aberration. And people who get locked into it constantly become desensitized and crave more and more depraved types of pornography. Whatever kind you may be trying to justify to yourself — whether it is romance novels that primarily female readers use to create fantasies in their minds, to role playing sexual video games or technology — it is all destructive and desensitizing. Just because it is a busty, anime, cartoon squirrel lady you are lusting after does not make it okay since it is not human.

Your Brain on Porn

God created our bodies to enjoy sexual pleasure to bind us together in marriage. This even happens on a physiological level. During sex, nerve endings release neurochemicals in the brain that give a euphoric feeling which neuroscientists say affect the brain similar to heroine or opiates.[31] If we are visually associating this euphoric sexual release

---

[30] "Pornography Statistics," *Enough-is-Enough* (accessed Aug. 25, 2015) http://www.internetsafety101.org/pornographystatistics

[31] Gert Holstege, Janniko R. Georgiadis, Anne M. J. Paans, Linda C. Meiners, Ferdinand H. C. E. van der Graaf & A.A.T. Simone Reinders, "Brain Activation

with pornographic images, proven psychological damage takes place. Even secular science confirms this. Just on a physical level, numerous studies have shown that pornography consumption is directly connected to erectile dysfunction. It is a brain issue, not a penis issue. Your neurological pathways get conditioned to finding a release from this stuff to the degree that your brain does not even allow you to enjoy a real human spouse.

Doctor and researcher David B. Samadi of New York City's Lenox Hill Hospital says, "Due to the pornography available on the Internet, we are finding out that this type of sex dysfunction is a real entity. ... You need more and more stimulation as you build up this tolerance, and then comes your reality with a wife or partner, and you may not be able to perform."[32]

"Too much porn can desensitize a man to sex, and, eventually, he can be unable to get excited by ordinary sexual encounters," says Samadi. It is a physical reality that you are harming your own body (besides the spiritual defilement of breaking faithfulness and trust). Even if you are unmarried, honor your future spouse by not giving yourself over to it.

I am not heaping shame on addicts, but you should know what you are doing to yourself. With pornography, your God-given appetite for sex gets misdirected to this outlet, and your brain chemically associates the imagery with a release of this pleasure. Social worker Nicole Sachs writes "Sex is half in your head and half in your body, and it takes work to treat the psychological component. ...There is no pill to treat these issues."[33]

Divine Ecstasy

Ironically, the same neurotransmitters that cross and block passages in the brain with sex do the same thing in ecstatic spiritual states. This is

During Human Male Ejaculation," *The Journal of Neuroscience* (Oct. 8, 2003) http://www.jneurosci.org/content/23/27/9185.full (accessed Aug. 26, 2015).

[32] Denise Mann, reviewed by Pat F. Bass II, MD, MPH, "Erection Problems? This Habit May Be Why," *Everyday Health* (Feb. 4, 2014) http://www.everydayhealth.com/news/erection-problems-this-habit-may-why/ (accessed Aug. 25, 2015).

[33] Ibid.

a proven neurological fact. The practice of the presence of God is a very outlet of divine pleasure, ignored by vast swarths of the church. We are hardwired for ecstatic fulfillment in Him in such a tangible, physiological way that there is an intrinsic satisfaction available to everyone. I am not saying that divine ecstasy is better or superior to sex — comparison is apples and oranges. God designed us to attack the pink fortress in the marriage bed and that is a glorious thing. But if you are not married yet, there is grace to satisfy and thoroughly fulfill you until you have tied the knot and start rummaging in the root cellar.

Colleen Shantz, author of *Paul in Ecstasy: The Neurobiology of the Apostle's Life and Thought*, further clarifies that divine ecstasy, like sex, has neurochemical effects on the brain similar to opiates.

"Another phenomenon of intense ecstatic experience is the release of a number of body chemicals that have analgesic and euphoric effects. Together they leave the mystic with a profound sense of wellness and pleasure lasting for as long as days or even weeks. In this way, the cognitive experience is amplified by somatic, chemical phenomena," writes Shantz.[34]

It is imperative that we guard our eyes in what we choose to gaze on. The body becomes habituated by seeking pleasure down these same neuro pathways. In a rudimentary way, it is not dissimilar to Pavlov's dog. Once the dog associates an action with a treat, it will automatically and habitually go that direction.

Now my wife is an amazing treat. If I associate her alone with the release of my sexual pleasure, I become obsessed with her. My mind is not comparing her with a thousand other bodies of all types in the fantasy world of porn. So I am not craving something deviant yet never satisfied. No I actually *possess my obsession*. I have my cake and I eat it too.

Our minds and hearts can get conditioned in a dark way; we can quickly gravitate toward becoming powerless addicts. Our choices even get bolstered and enslaved by physical endorphins, oxytocin and dopamine in the brain. You are a holistic person; your spirit, emotions

---

[34] Colleen Shantz, *Paul in Ecstasy: The Neurobiology of the Apostle's Life and Thought* (Cambridge University Press, 2009), 98-99.

and body do not operate independently from one another. Do not partition off this part of your life thinking, "Well I'm a good Christian in other areas, so porn is just this one little side thing I'm going to allow myself to struggle with. I'm doing fine otherwise."

You are hardwired for the pleasure of God. And this works for marriage. Imagine sole sourcing your pleasure receptors to be conditioned habitually to find satisfaction in one person. You build deep-seated emotional, spiritual even biological connection to that one person — this is what you are designed for. Do not build deviant behaviors that cause destruction. Porn is like crack. We can lie to ourselves about it – that we can casually dabble around with it. If you think you are not addicted, try going three weeks without it.

You're Better Than That

You cannot worship God and do porn. They just do not go together. Porn does not have a place inside or outside the marriage bed. The porn industry is the fuel behind so many horrible statistics today, such as the fact that one in four women have been raped. Even one in six men have been sexually assaulted. We were not created for our sexuality to be dispersed out like waters from which anyone can drink. First Timothy 3:2 and Titus 1:6 both tell us to be faithful husbands to one wife. This is the same principle that should apply to our hearts.

Porn use involves lust or adultery of the heart. Lust is different from simply recognizing beauty. Again, "feeling sexual" or noticing beauty is not wrong, bad or dirty. It is what we do with that. Do not suppress the fact that you are attracted to the opposite sex. But to feed into those feelings with no proper outlet for it in marriage only causes frustration.

You say, "All things are permissible!" Paul says, "Not all things are beneficial." If you are into grace, but are enslaved by porn and fornication in the name of "freedom" you are not free. You are a servant to those things. Compulsion to disobey God is not freedom, it is sin and it is destructive. Roman Gnostics justified their sexual immorality by saying "Hey this whole planet is messed up anyway. God will destroy it all. What does it matter what we do with our bodies?" Paul clarifies:

> You say, "Food for the stomach and the stomach for food, and God will destroy them both." The body, however, is not meant

for sexual immorality but for the Lord, and the Lord for the body (1 Cor. 6:13, NIV).

Jesus came in the body to liberate your body from brokenness. He was tempted in every way so that you can be free. He bore your temptation.

You are not your own, you were bought with a price — therefore honor God with your body. This stuff affects your relationship with God. He has not gone anywhere — He is not pulling back from relationship — but sin separates *you* from God: you slink back into shame, guilt and insecurity ... pulling away from Him like Adam hiding in the bushes.

Let us steward our bodies He gave us to honor Him, and in doing so we truly honor ourselves and others ... and our spouse.

Cultivate a hatred for sin. This stuff causes catastrophic damage to kids and relationships when it fully blooms into a spouse running off with someone. As a child product of numerous divorces, I have had eight or nine parents. I should be a statistic, except for the grace of God. But I can tell you that there is no ultimate joy in sexual immorality.

Sex only works in marriage.

So if you are single and not preparing for marriage, not conditioning yourself to be with a real woman — if you are just sitting around doodling the noodle: grow up. Be mature. A real man is one who walks in fidelity and integrity. He is not a guy who just knows how to shave and wants to be sexually active without the commitment of marriage.

Restoration is Yours

Clearly know if you have struggled with porn or any sexual sin, you are forgiven. God loves you tremendously. There is no reason for you to be slinking around in guilt and shame. That only compounds addiction anyway. In drawing a clear moral line, the aim is not to heap guilt on you if you have messed up. It is just to show a better way of living.

Yes I have used lots of sharp language toward the sexually immoral in this section (pervert, predator, coward, loser, deadbeat, scumbag, douche bag, etc.). Scripture uses even more lucid language! But that is not the *Real You* – it is the role you were handed. You are better than that. You do not *deserve* a healthy spouse – *no one does*. It is a gift and a privilege, which is why we grow up and begin walking into the role of responsible, faithful representative of Christ.

Sexual sin in your past does *not* mean you are prevented from having a good sexual relationship in marriage. Do not buy into the accusation or condemnation that you are impure, or damaged goods. Where sin abounds, grace abounds all the more. Forgiving yourself is huge. And do not let performance orientation push you over the edge. Once we have messed up, we can sometimes let ourselves go completely, after failing to live up to a certain standard we were upholding.

I failed miserably in the area of sexual sin before marriage. And like most men, had a strong addiction to pornography. These things do take a toll on your soul. But my life is an example of the power of restoration. I have an amazing, healthy marriage. I am living proof that in marriage you grow in love, can find satisfaction, and the sex always ... *gets better*. It is a lie that monogamy is dull or that sex gets boring by staying with the same partner. Stay vulnerable to the Lord and you will always be growing to a deeper level of intimacy. Know that past hurts and abuse do not own you. There is grace to liberate you right now.

The Bible is far more concerned with who you are than what you are doing. To experience freedom in this area, we must have revelation of identity. That your old wounded, addicted self has been swallowed up in Christ. You do not need a self-help manual. Just realize your worth.

Homosexuality

We cannot close this section without touching on the trending topic of homosexuality and gender confusion. It is like we woke up, and overnight everyone is a gay hipster. Jumping into an admittedly hot social issue as volatile as this one can discredit you in a way that people cannot hear the gospel from you. At the same time, the gospel is the very key to inform social issues.

Cultural trends cannot dictate our theology. Christian conservatism and Christian liberalism are two bandwagon ideologies with extremes on both ends. I am admittedly liberal in some areas and staunchly conservative in others. I want the Spirit and the Word guide me, rather than *consensus* orthodoxy. The liberal, diehard, religiously pro-gay

124

agendists may be angry that I adhere to the biblical model that marriage is between a man and a woman. Holy Scripture is the guiding truth for moral standards. I will not waste time exegeting the crystal clear New Testament passages stating homosexual behavior is wrong.[35] There is a flood of new culture-driven, pro-gay spin on those scriptures where folks do back flips to say the Bible is okay with gay.

The Bible clear as day tells boys not to poke around with other boys' choccy starfish. And it tells girls to stay out of one another's whisker biscuit. Interpret sexuality through the lens of scriptures, but do not read scripture through the lens of a pre-existing agenda on sexuality.

So am I a hater? *I do not have an iron in the fire.* Your decisions are your decisions and I am nobody's judge. If the scripture told boys to get their Twinkie stinky, then I would say enjoy the back packing!

So if liberals think I am primitive, well the conservative camp on the other side of the religious fence dislikes me as well. Because I am not gay bashing or constantly moralizing on this issue. I preach grace and inclusion. But I also hold the scripture to be inspired. I do not think America is going to be burned to the ground like Sodom and Gomorrah because all the boys have sugar in their britches (actually Jesus said religious folks will get a harder bill than Sodom and Gomorrah [Luke 10:12, Matt. 10:15]).

How do you categorize a minister who hosts love missions to the transsexual, transgender ladyboy prostitutes of Thailand without even trying to straighten them out? We do not conveniently fit people's paradigms. While everyone is barking up the tree with his or her opinions on the whole homosexuality deal, I have actually been to the seedy underbelly of the gender-bending capital of the world. I have invested time, resources and hugs on some of God's most beautiful creations.

Are Sexual Guidelines Arbitrary?

We can love people without endorsing self-destructive behavior. We can pick our battles. I legitimately love gay people. I do not need to post rainbows all over Facebook to approve that lifestyle.

---

[35] See 1 Tim. 1:10, Jude 1:7, Rom. 1:26-28, Mark 10:6-9, 1 Cor. 6:9-11

I am not going to rehash the same old verses from Leviticus that prohibit homosexuality. Legalists think we plop our finger anywhere in the Torah and do everything we read (they have no revelation on the New Covenant). You have a vast majority of Christians who still think it is a sin to get a tattoo or cut your beard a certain way.

Others think Leviticus puts homosexuality on the *same plane* as these frivolous regulations against tattoos, beard trimming or wearing two types cloth (as if *all* of Leviticus is a haphazard list of irrelevant regulations that do not apply to us today). Sadly, much of the church lacks a basic understanding of rightly dividing the word. They do not know the difference between outdated ceremonial rituals (hand-washing, eating regulations, blah, blah, blah), versus universal moral guidelines that carry over into New Covenant life. In fact, the Levitical prohibition on homosexuality is in the same chapter prohibiting incest, child sacrifice and bestiality. Most folks still recognize those as unhealthy practices today. We cannot just write the book off. We need to read it properly. That means reading it through the lens of Christ and following the admonitions of the apostles He sent to explain the gospel to us.

The action of bum chumming in itself (not the person involved) is one of the few things listed as an actual *abomination* to God. We do not like the word "abomination," but we must understand that God hates the things that destroy us because He loves us! While we do not pick on certain sinful practices, we must recognize that certain practices have greater negative impact than others. Stealing a loaf of bread to feed your family is not the same as killing six million Jews in the Holocaust.

In that light, we can rightly argue the *degree* of detriment of sexual immorality. That gets subjective. But we must honestly admit sexuality is part of the morals package Paul carries over into the New Testament. Sexual immorality, like greed, alcoholism, etc. is a thing grace enables liberty from, not gives license to hurt ourselves with. In some ways the New Testament even raises the bar on sexual ethics against stuff that was tolerated under the Old Covenant (like polygamy, divorce). Jesus is also sharp in His decree to love, not judge, sinners in these acts.

But what if I love my girlfriend — should I not follow the law of love and love her up in the back seat? That is selfish. Scripture says true love manifests in obedience. Obedience not to satisfy an arbitrary command of a legalistic God. It is following clear guidelines established for humanity for the proper health of society, personal relationships and our own psychological development.

Gender Confusion

Scripture does not always tell us *why* to align with its guidelines. It appeals to our trust of an all-knowing, all-loving Father who has our best interest in mind before we ever get the understanding on it. There is a glory on walking in design. He designed us with one of two sets of parts. I know there is a lot of confusion about gender. It is usually the simple stuff that confuses us. God did not make three genders, eight genders or fourteen-and-a-half genders. *He made two.*

He created this fantastic formula: *put this bit into that slot ... not only is it fun, but BOOM creation happens!*

How can we argue with our created design? We did not pick our gender; we did not pick our race; we did not pick our mama. I completely understand the conservative church's frustration with the lack of common sense in this area. But humanity just gets confused because we have deep-seated *wants* — call them sexual orientations if you will, or whatever — but they are deep-seated *desires*. Realize that even *desires* are from God! This is what makes them so incredibly strong! So when you have a strong longing and you get a simple "no" to that longing from the text, it is extremely frustrating.

I know this sounds controversial, but I do not believe anyone is *gay*. I just see humanity in an identity crisis. All humanity is made in God's image, loved and included in Christ. Yet we get deeply confused about what will make us happy.

We like to dispense with sharp (yet biblical) words like "perversion" because we do not want to come across as sounding archaic or judgmental. Yet if we could return to this word for a moment and recover its definition: *It refers to a God-given desire that has been misdirected.*

We might identify with contorted longings, but that is not the *True Self*. No doubt these can be strong, seemingly unquenchable desires (orientations?) but the problem is when those God-given desires get misdirected (disoriented?) toward the wrong object by which we think they will be fulfilled. Consider the sin of covetousness. I believe God gives us a strong desire to succeed and prosper in life. That is healthy. But when that desire gets misdirected to greed or envying our neighbor, it can consume a person. There are plenty of people out there born greedy, but we do not justify that orientation. God-given appetites can be perverted toward inappropriate outlets.

What is a Pervert (and Where Can I Get One)?

C.S. Lewis brings clarity on how the wires get crossed in his discussion on the four Greek words for love. Some confuse *eros* sexual love, with *philia* brotherly love.[36] In most societies throughout history, even in the non-western world today, brotherly love is much more tactile. Men hug, kiss and show their affection in a way that is bereft of any sexual overtones. Perhaps if healthy fatherly affection were freely demonstrated in our society today, some of the confusion between eros and philia might dissipate. Lewis was not critical of homosexuals; he just felt bad for them. Not in a condescending way, he recognized their brokenness.

No doubt desires are strong as a torrent, and in the delusion of a fallen Adamic state they absolutely own and occupy us. Were you born gay? Why not? We are born into Adamic confusion where we assume twisted desires identify us. But the gospel reminds us that Christ defines us. Rather than fight against those torrents of desire, it is more

---

[36] For further reference, see C. S. Lewis' *The Four Loves*. (Houghton Mifflin: 1971).

than possible to recognize the proper God-given channels for intimacy and sexuality (call it reorientation?). The gospel recasts and directs our longings in a transcendent way; it does not endorse their confusion.

I do not mean trying to "pray the gay away." And rest assured, trying to talk a gay guy out of homosexuality is a waste of time. He already has his defenses armed and mounted for any argument. I cannot fix anyone. Transformation is God's business. At the same time we need to be clear on what is the fruit of the righteous life. It does not mean giving in to every misdirected urge we feel – no matter how strong.

If we could spend as much time loving people as moralizing on specific sins, we may see more fruit. Morality cannot be legislated. We must recognize that people are broken, hurting — so many have deep childhood wounds of abuse. Everyone has wrestled with something. As a teenager I was obsessed with sex. Given half a chance I would have tapped anything with breasts and a pulse! I needed to learn self-control and patience for the proper outlet for my urges. All manner of longings — for sex, money, substances — can run so deep that we *own them* as the fabric of who we are. All misdirected appetites are *perversions*.

Consider substance addiction. Talk about owning a false identity! The addict gives up any hope whatsoever that he can overcome this impossible ravenous urge that consumes him. He *is an addict* as far as he is concerned. Who could change this? With man this is impossible, but with God all things are possible. Christ simply says, "Stop wrestling. Wake up to the truth of who I say you are."

As mentioned earlier regarding porn, our brains simply get conditioned to associate neurochemical release with certain practices. *Metanoia,* changing the way we think, is entirely possible. At the end of the day, the only thing that keeps us in bondage is a wrong way of thinking – believing lies about what will provide ultimate satisfaction. Change seems impossible until we recognize our focus has merely been off.

There is a place for moral instruction, but it must flow out of the grace and identity of the gospel. We do need clarity in this area of sexuality. But as long as the church stops short, only barking the "no" of the law, then beauty of the "yes" will be cloaked. Instead of only bashing homosexuality, let us put more focus on the beauty and mystery of marriage.

129

A Mystical Sacrament

For all their harping about gay marriage, it might be beneficial for the *church* to actually understand what marriage is. The church calls marriage a *covenant*. A covenant is a legal agreement between two parties. If that is all marriage amounts to, it is bound to fail (at least in our hearts). No, marriage is a *sacrament*. A sacrament is a visible, tangible representation of the grace of God. A sacrament is a more than just a "symbol," there is something *mystical* about it. Not magical … *mystical.*

Consider the sacrament of the Lord's Supper. Jesus did not simply say, "This is *like* my body." He said, "This *is* my body." More than a symbol, communion is a direct expression of something sacred. In the same way, Paul did not merely say the husband and wife are *like* Christ and the church. He said, "This *is* Christ and the church."

> *This is a profound mystery — but I am talking about Christ and the church* (Eph. 5:32, NIV).

The man and the woman, like Adam and Eve, are a sacred representation of God and humanity. So what is the essence of marriage? Marriage is a union of two distinct things. It is not sameness, but two different complementaries coming together. Husband and bride. Heaven and earth. God and man. Ocean and sand married at the seashore. It is the positive and negative magnetism in nature. The yin and yang as our Buddhist brethren would say. It is written throughout creation and in the conscience of every culture. It is Christ and the church. Not Christ and Christ. And definitely not the church and the church. This is why Paul lumps homosexuality in with idolatry (Eph. 5:5, Col. 3:5, Rom. 1:18-27): attraction to your own image versus the transcendence of God's otherness mirrored in a partner altogether different from you.

It was not man, but man and woman together, who jointly were created in the image of God. God made them both: two sides of one whole to reflect His likeness. Mirror Bible translator Francois du Toit notes that when God put Adam into a deep sleep, He put him into "ecstasy" and Eve came out of his side.[37] There is a bliss in this exotic otherness. Rick Joyner used to say that homosexuality was on the rise because of

---

[37] James Strong, *Exhaustive Concordance of the Bible* (Nashville: Abingdon, 1890), Entry H8639 from *tardemah* "trance."

the church's homo-*sect*-uality: only relating with people who are the same as us. We need to connect with other voices and perspectives outside our sectarian tribes. It keeps us from becoming stagnant, cultic and homogenous. True creativity and exploration otherwise dissipates.

I would agree with the eminent theologian N.T. Wright that to redefine "marriage" undermines the intrinsic nature of what it represents — the merger of the two binary *others* — something this word has always represented in every culture from the dawn of time.[38] A union of complimentary "differents." Anything less undermines the very incarnation and the gospel — God and man seamlessly united as one in Jesus Christ. It is otherly and divine because one is plunged out of oneself and thrust completely into the other – the unknown. And it is not safe ... I have been married over 15 years and still do not understand the woman God gave me! Marriage is not familiarity. Not sameness. Not an idolatrous fashioning of an object of love into one's own image.

Sex Sings of Divine Union

For all the bad rap I gave our Catholic brothers at the start of this section, I acknowledge their forward strides in recognizing marriage as a sacrament in the early 13th century. Our Orthodox brothers believe the same and even allow married priests. Reformers like Calvin and Luther, however, while recognizing the sacredness of marriage, only accepted *baptism and communion* as sacraments. Calvin wrote, "(Marriage) is a good and holy ordinance of God. And agriculture, architecture, shoemaking, and shaving, are lawful ordinances of God; but they are not sacraments. For in a sacrament, the thing required is not only that it be a work of God, but that it be an external ceremony appointed by God to confirm a promise."[39]

In this, Calvin and the reformers were wrong. Paul has clearly stated the husband and wife are the "mystery" of Christ and the church (Eph. 5:32). This is literally where we get the term *sacrament*: a holy mystery. A husband and wife are a far clearer depiction of the gospel than shoemaking or shaving. In his *Theology of the Body*, Pope John Paul II highlights this:

---

[38] Matt Robinson. "NT Wright on Gay Marriage." YouTube video, 5:00. Posted [March 25, 2014]. https://www.youtube.com/watch?v=xKxvOMOmHeI

[39] John Calvin, *Institutes of the Christian Religion* (IV.19.34).

Throughout Sacred Scripture, the most common reference that Christ uses when speaking of heaven is that of a wedding feast. Thus, marriage is intended to be a union that draws us deeper into the mystery of our creation and provides a foretaste of the heavenly marriage between Christ and his Church, where man and woman are no longer given in marriage. In heaven, the eternal wedding feast, men and women have now arrived at their ultimate destination and no longer have need of the Sacrament (or sign) of marriage.[40]

Sex is a temporal institution. In the resurrection, we will always have bodies — there will always be an incarnational dynamic to humanity. But we will not always have sex and marriage. It is not a wrong or a forbidden pleasure. It is just not part of the age to come. That does not mean we should have a low view of it now, nor disavow the essential *goodness* of its role in creation. Marriage though a sacrament of our divine union, does not carry over into the future heavenly kingdom. Does that mean it is "less" spiritual than abstinence (since no one will be having hot pudding for supper in Beulah Land)? By no means! Just because there are other graces in our final future heavenly consummation at the feast of the Lamb by no means indicates that sex in this world is a "lesser" pleasure to be forfeited in lieu of a celibate state.

We would not strip physical bread and wine away from the communion table in lieu of "only" higher spiritual communion with Christ. We need not empty our baptismals of earthly water, just because we are "spiritually" baptized in Christ's death. These are graces for now. Tangible sacraments. Not to be strictly compared with what is to come, but surely not forfeited in a vain attempt toward a higher spiritual state.

God is better than sex. Song of Songs says it all. Sex is the best image we have for divine union here. Sex is a veritable grace given us in this world and a foretaste of something greater. So take the spouse out to dinner tonight and play a round of harpooning the salty longshoreman.

---

[40] *Theology of the Body* is the topic of a series of 129 lectures given by Pope John Paul II between 1979 and 1984. From summation at: https://en.wikipedia.org/wiki/Theology_of_the_Body (accessed Aug. 26, 2015).

BEER.

It Started with a Drink

Many preachers begin their ministry career by graduating from some Pentecostal Bible school. They shake the dean's hand, receive their certificate then sign off on a form saying they will never have another drink in their life.

How did Jesus begin His earthly ministry?

With a kegger.

By today's standard it is estimated that the six jars of water turned to wine at the wedding feast in Cana of Galilee in the second chapter of John held up to 180 gallons, or 680 liters. Quite a bit of vino. Imagine showing up to a single party with nearly 700 bottles of wine. And that is after everyone had already emptied out the coolers of the cheap stuff.

You can tell right away, "This Jesus fellow is the kind of guy I could hang around with!"

Perhaps at the aforementioned Bible school you were taught Jesus turned the water into unfermented grape juice. I will not argue scripture with you here. I will just mention this little thing called *science*. Up until the late 1800s there was *no such thing as grape juice.* Not until a dry-as-a-ship's-biscuit, sourpuss pap of a Methodist minister

133

named Dr. Thomas Welch invented a way to stop the God-given process of fermentation to prevent the evil of alcohol from touching the lips of his congregants during communion.

It is often said, Jesus turned the water into wine 2000 years ago, and the church has been trying to change it back ever since!

Said Robert Capon, "Unless I am mistaken, it was Mr. Welch himself (an adamant total abstainer) who persuaded American Protestantism to abandon what the Lord obviously thought rather kindly of."[1]

So the Good Lord kicks off His earthly ministry with free draft on the house ... and how does He wrap it all up in the end? By sitting around the table tipping another one back with the boys! Is it not a marvel what symbol Jesus chooses to represent the New Covenant in His blood? He could have used a butterscotch milkshake. He could have used a vanilla bean latte, or God forbid, a green kale smoothie. But what icon does He choose to represent your faith? *An intoxicant.* That is right; the entire Christian faith is represented by *booze* ... a cup of wine. Something that is illegal in most world religions. Oh blessed saints, how we have enshrined that cup in the stained glass windows of our cathedrals ... but have we not polished a religious veneer over the scandal of it all? God chooses a cup of hooch to represent His love and union with mankind!

In fact, the very word "grace" has direct overtones of divine drunkenness. In the very start of the introduction in his very first published work, the preeminent theologian Thomas F. Torrance writes of the pre-Christian, pagan origins of the word *grace*, stating, "in its original and fundamental sense (grace) is applied to what awakens pleasure or secures joy. It is the quality giving pleasure or thrilling the aesthetic sensibility."[2] *Grace* was a term used to cover a wide range of attributes like beauty or charm, with direct overtones of supernatural potency – a divine elixir connected with the gifts or attributes of the gods to men. Goodwill. Endowment. Bathed in royal ornament – the good regard or condescension of a god. But this element of *joy* ... of *pleasure,* this is

---

[1] Fr. Robert Capon, *Supper of the Lamb: A Culinary Reflection* (New York: Doubleday & Co., 1969),

[2] Thomas F. Torrance, *The Doctrine of Grace in the Apostolic Fathers* (Edinburgh: Oliver & Boyd, 1948).

key. Torrance says the word grace was directly associated with the Dionysian vine – with Bacchus, the god of wine. Grace literally conveyed the idea of drunkenness, party or celebration *from above.*

And thus the natural vine has always been a symbol and gift, used in moderation, as an echo or representation of a distant land, where the wine of divine love will be drunk down without limit. As the well-worn proverb often attributed to Ben Franklin states, "Beer is proof that God loves us and wants us to be happy."

God's people have historically always enjoyed alcohol. But there is also a long history of religious prudes who have balked at its consumption. Gnosticism has always thrived in attacking the natural pleasure of booze. Of course this is a Greek-influenced, Christian era problem. Our Jewish brothers never vilified drink. Biblical Hebraic culture is chock full of drinking and feasting.

The Agape

The early church carried over its Jewish roots by celebrating the *love feast* – or "agape." It was a time of meal and fellowship where the poor were invited. This was a holdover from the old sacrificial system. An animal would often be butchered – obviously no longer for sacrificial means (Christ died once and for all); but perhaps it was a prophetic *reminder* of the cross – just as the ancient sacrificial system was a prophetic *foreshadow* of the cross. And of course, there were barrels of wine … not thimbles of grape juice. Communion was community feast.

Relationship does not happen in the rows of a pew. It is in the conversations, the joys, the battles and the mix of life. It happens over tables and in the mirth of celebration. The love feast was perhaps one of the richest things we lost to Gnostic religionists. But it is restored today in the warmth of brothers enjoying life and celebration over pints together in unity. Spirituality is integrated into the festivity of living. God is reintroducing healthy, holistic celebration to the church today and setting us free from the dour pietism that robs our joy, creativity and freedom.

As dualism crept into the early church, bolstering the "kill yourself" mentality of the religious order, many over-ascetic people began to despise the love feasts, largely because of the wine that was served. Ascetic heresies flourished, as folks gravitated toward beating themselves up to curry favor with God. Religionists contended that only water should be used at the Lord's Table instead of wine. These were the same sticks-in-the-mud who argued against marriage, eating meat or anything else remotely enjoyable in their miserable existence.

These ascetics mainly argued that a few bad apples were getting as loaded as a grocery cart at the love feasts, therefore a blanket rule should be levied against the sauce. But the Council of Gangra in 355 A.D. actually anathematized these dry, religious scoundrels who despised "the agapes based on faith." The church fathers were clear that wine *must* be used in communion – not water. Otherwise it was deemed *heresy!* And why? Because they said the wine symbolized the intoxication of the Holy Ghost.

Wine's role in communion would remain. Unfortunately, the ruling in favor of the love feasts was dramatically reversed a few years later; they were forbidden from being held in churches. Is it no wonder the later decision was rendered in Laodicea? Instead of drinking a few goblets at a party, you were given one sip at the end of a sermon.

A bit of time has passed since those days. But God in his patient forbearance has not yet rid the world of party poopers. When it comes to positions on alcohol in the church today, everyone essentially adheres to one of four commonly held views:

Position 1- Sucking it back like spring break at Daytona Beach
Position 2 - Prohibition
Position 3 - Abstention
Position 4 - Moderation

Allow me to explain each one of these commonly held opinions.

Position 1 – Free for all Drunkenness

I will begin with the first school of thought (the Daytona Beach scenario), which we can easily dismiss. Nearly everyone, even a total lush, knows alcoholism is unhealthy and immoral. Unless you think it is fine to be a raging drunk since you are "under grace," then common sense should tell you to avoid getting wasted. Remember it is the delusion of Roman Gnosticism which says, "Do whatever you want; nothing counts as a sin anymore." Scripture is abundantly clear that drunkenness is a sin.[3] Other bad behavior associated with drunkenness in scripture includes violence, adultery, incest, mockery, brawling and poverty.[4] Alcoholism leads to ruin on many fronts.

There are a number of guidelines specifically regarding leaders in their alcohol consumption. In the Old Covenant, priests were not to drink while performing their ministerial duties (Lev. 10:9), but they could enjoy it while off the clock (Num. 18:12, 27, 30); and kings were not to let drink cloud their judgment while conducting the law (Prov. 31:4-5). Under the New Covenant we also see that elders/pastors cannot be drunkards (1 Tim. 3:3; Titus 1:7); and no drunkard will inherit the kingdom of God (1 Cor. 6:10; Gal. 5:21). But every apostle drank *some wine* (Luke 5:33). Being a drunkard is not the same as being a drinker.

The Bible never once says alcohol consumption is a sin. Only drunkenness – overindulgence – is the problem. Just as *Roman Gnosticism* says to guzzle the whole keg, on the opposite end, *Greek Gnosticism* commands you to never drink a drop. These are the two most extreme of the four positions listed above: *drunkenness* (party till you drop) versus *prohibition* (no brewskies at all).

We need not deal further with the view that "drunkenness is okay." Any Christian with their head screwed on knows that. Do not take this book as an endorsement for you to guzzle down a few 40s of Schlitz every day. Let us move on to another of our four views: *prohibition.*

Position 2 - Prohibition

The next school of thought regarding alcohol is *prohibition.* Prohibitionists believe that all alcohol use is a sin, or that alcohol itself is evil. It is a full-blown, extreme dualistic concept that superstitiously attributes demonic powers to a food. Except for a few ascetic wing nuts, every Christian drank wine and beer until the late 1800s.

It is one thing to argue alcohol is evil. But prohibitionists even attempt to rewrite history in saying strong drink *was never used* in the early

---

[3] Some references include: Deut. 21:20; Ecc. 10:17; Matt. 24:29; Luke 12:45; 21:34; Rom. 13:13; 1 Cor. 5:11; Eph. 5:18; and 1 Peter 4:3.

[4] Some references include: Gen. 19:32-35, Prov. 4:17, Rev. 17:2, Prov. 20:1, and Prov. 21:17.

church. Pure idiocy. To argue early Christians used grape juice and not real vino is laughable. In fact, Paul is clear on the matter. "When you meet together, it is not the Lord's supper that you eat. For in eating, each one goes ahead with his own meal, and one is hungry and another is drunk" (1 Cor. 11:20-21). Who was getting drunk off Oceanspray? They used wine. Paul never said to consume water instead of Pinot Noir to avoid possible abuse. In fact, the real problem Paul was addressing was selfishness, not alcohol. Overindulgence is the issue.

Prohibition has found traction in the modern-day church ever since the temperance movement of the 1800s (part of the *holiness movement* in which Christian revival was associated with shutting down all tap houses). In the old days, when a big name revivalist like Sam Jones or Charles Finney would come to town, his job was not considered done until saloons were closed and casks of perfectly fine barley pop were busted open or flushed down the river. Methodists were huge on temperance, but their founder John Wesley was not so absurd. Although he disavowed hard liquor, he famously said, "Wine is one of the noblest cordials in nature."[5] Wesley even influenced Arthur Guinness to become one of the most philanthropic Christian businessmen of the world, developing a healthy, nutritious, black Irish beer that acted as a "meal in a pint" for the poor working class who could not afford food, but got their vitamins in a glass.

While the temperance movement's initial thrust was to curb abuse and advocate moderation, it quickly devolved into a legalistic crusade that demanded complete abstinence. Pushed mostly by old, prudish, fuddy-duddy church ladies – they eventually got enough politicians in their pockets to ratify the 18th Amendment to the U.S. Constitution – banning alcoholic beverages in America for 13 years. We still have the "sin tax" on alcohol and tobacco today. A Cohiba cigar costs $30 a stick, but a bag of sugar (which can also kill you) runs about $2. Hypocrisy.

The perverted notion that holiness equals teetotaling has remained to this day in many denominations. It is the lackluster concept that the only way to avoid excess is to forbid drinking altogether. I would not say the doctrine of prohibition is *as* demonic as abortion, but it runs pretty close.

---

[5] John Wesley, *The Works of the Rev. John Wesley in Ten Volumes, Vol. III* (New York: J&J Harper, 1827), 332.

Ironically, during the push for prohibition, beer makers even used John Wesley in advertisements to appeal to the church's slipping sense of sanity.

139

Wouldn't you want to just keep drinking?

My biggest problem with prohibition is not that it caused the rise of Al Capone, the rum runners and the development of organized crime – which evolved into gangland violence, Columbian drug cartels, massacres, murders, rapes and abortions by the millions (*thank you* religion, for drawing hard lines where lines do not exist). No, that is not my biggest problem. My *biggest* beef with prohibition is that it paints God out to be a dry-as-a-ship's-biscuit, pious, prudish pap of a joyless taskmaster … when in reality, God is the life of the party!

He is the wine itself. *God is a drinker.*

His character has been radically impugned. God is hammered drunk on His love for you (Song. 7:9). God is a celebrant. He is pure joy. Pure fun. Pure exhilaration. The true God of the scriptures has been maligned by our legalisms, twisted projections and idolatrous images of Him as a humorless, feelingless, party-quenching force of doom and gloom. Who wants to hang around that guy? We are created for cheer and mirth in this life. Alcohol is an allotted enjoyment for our hours off, as a signpost pointing to the joys of heaven. While the party in this world has common sense limitations, C.S. Lewis says our earthly revelry is the best metaphor for the next life:

> It is only in our "hours off," only in our moments of permitted festivity, that we find an analogy. Dance and game are frivolous, unimportant down here for "down here" is not their natural place. Here, they are a moment's rest from the life we are placed here to live. But in this world everything is upside down. That which, if it could be prolonged here, would be a truancy, is likest that which in a better country is the End of Ends. Joy is the serious business of heaven.[6]

Prohibitions do not remedy the situation of alcoholism or drug abuse. Pleasure and excess are not to be *removed* from our life; rather they are to be found at a higher level by turning to God (the source of all delight, though some attempt to idolatrously replace Him with substances). Man has attempted to fill a void only God is intended to fit. Thus we are told, "Do not be (continually) drunk with wine, because that will ruin your life. Instead, be (continually) filled with the Holy Spirit" (Eph. 5:18). This verse does not exclude the enjoyment of natural wine, but our ultimate fulfillment comes from the Lord.

Reasons for addiction could be many. It may be rooted in bad parenting examples or a false sense of God's disapproval of us. Like any negative habitual pattern, it is bolstered by an identity crisis, not recognizing the truth of our freedom from sin. Of course, physical and psychological bonds to the substance can also take place. But ultimately, only His tangible Holy Spirit alone can fulfill the itch we try to scratch.

Finding God as our supreme satisfaction does not mean we should thus *prohibit* all drink in order to protect ourselves from potential abuse. Martin Luther sarcastically wrote, "Men can go wrong with wine and

---

[6] C.S. Lewis, *Letters to Malcolm: Chiefly on Prayer*, (San Diego: Harvest, 1964), 92-93.

women. Shall we prohibit and abolish women?"[7] This cuts to the heart of the matter. Prohibition does not prevent abuse. Just the opposite.

Prohibition Makes Sin Increase

Simply stated, we do not reject God's gifts because of the potential of overindulgence. Luther continues, "pagans worship the sun, moon and stars, shall we pluck them out of the sky?"[8] Just because someone idolizes the drink does not mean we outlaw it out altogether. That is the knee-jerk reaction that robs our liberty. Not only in the church but even politically in every culture, when blanket rules are instituted to guard against a few bad apples, personal liberties continue to erode and power is given to a ruling class. In fact, many great saints have argued that a rejection of creation is actually an indirect rejection of the Creator. This is largely why prohibition is such a hellish doctrine.

Religion takes a good thing, asserts ungodly regulations against it, and by doing so provokes sinful rebellion against those regulations. A man not prone to drink too much will often do so if you tell him *all drinking is off limits*. So you end up with two extremes – rejection of the gift (prohibition), or overindulgence (drunkenness). By attributing superstitious dimensions to food (fermented barley) and prohibiting alcohol altogether, this paradoxically causes people to abuse it. Paul tells us in Romans 5:20 that the law causes sin to increase. How much more do our manmade legalisms do this very thing!

It does not take much of a Bible study to realize prohibition is a heretical train of thought. There is not a single Bible verse against booze. Just the opposite in fact ... it is a gift of God given to *cheer* our hearts.

God makes grass grow for the cattle, and plants for man to cultivate – bringing forth food from the earth: wine that cheers the heart of man ... (Ps. 104:14-15).

If you do not know there is a difference between getting cheered and hammered drunk, I would recommend you never keep any Tylenol around the house either – because you could not tell the difference between taking two to feel better versus swallowing the whole bottle.

---

[7] Martin Luther, Fourth Sermon at Wittenburg, March 13, 1522

[8] Ibid.

During prohibition in America, bootleggers had to produce a higher concentration of firewater in smaller amounts so they could smuggle it. Quality and flavor standards went out the window – it just needed to get you cock-eyed. The horrible taste led to the advent of fruity, mixed drinks to cover the nastiness. Before that, people could enjoy *good* scotch or bourbon neat without tangerines and sugary syrups. By the time prohibition ended, all the mom and pop craft beer brewers were also out of business, and the big conglomerates like Budweiser swooped in to provide cheap, mass-produced beer to the thirsty throngs. Forget quality, this piss water just needed to be strong enough to get you wobbly after ten cans.

The reason the United States has been plagued with crap beer since the 1920s is because of religious devils. It has only been in the last decade or two that an appreciation for good, craft beer has been redis-covered in America (what I call true revival). Martin Luther would have agreed with me. The avid critic, Luther approved of an Augsburg beer law saying, "The selling of bad beer is a crime against Christian love."

American Jesus

As a kid from the American Bible Belt, where prohibition still reigns in the church, I can say after all my subsequent world travels that no-where on the globe have I seen more hypocrisy, binge drinking and mental roadblocks over alcohol than in that part of the country. With a grid for moderation being absent in the church, alcohol is wrongly deemed "illicit" as well as our accompanying God-given appetite for it. Regulation against the right use of God's gifts only causes man to per-vert their usage all the more. Southern Christianity is schizo. Meet a Christian there who realizes you are okay with a drink, and he as-sumes you will sit down and drink a whole case with him. It is bizarre.

Ironically, most Bible Belt Christians in America would not want to out-law guns, religion or free speech even though all three can similarly be abused. But on Sunday morning, Baptists will openly advocate a ban on all tipple (despite the fact they were secretly getting hammered at a tailgate party the night before). They worship the Bible, but do not read it. If they did, they would follow the command to "Go, eat your food with gladness, and drink your wine with a joyful heart" (Ecc. 9:7), rather than sneaking it in the dark to excess with a duplicitous heart.

The American church's proclivity toward prohibition is a shame and an embarrassment. No other nation has exported so much dry, spartan, missionary austerity to poor developing countries in the name of Jesus – hurling the filth of this ascetic heresy to the likes of Africa, South America and beyond, where a poor fellow could literally be excommunicated for having a cold beer on a hot day thanks to Uncle Sam's twisted influence. Every other nation with a Christian heritage as rich as ours has actually cracked their Bibles enough to know alcohol is God's gift to mankind.

I once knew of a Youth With a Mission student from America who was visiting a sister base in Europe. Like most evangelical outreaches, YWAM is dry in America. A kid is literally kicked out if ever caught having grog during his discipleship course. But this student was about to encounter a sudden crisis of faith. Imagine his surprise, after settling in to the overseas dorm when he first visited the refrigerator: Lo and behold, *in Europe, YWAM kept the fridge rammed full of cases of beer!*

They were a bit more enlightened than their Yankee compatriots.

Ironically, one of my favorite things about visiting Muslim countries in the Middle East is finding the liquor stores. *Only* Christians run them. And with the exception of backsliding Muslims, only Christians frequent them! Everyone there knows the Christians get away with a happier life. Never have I walked into a package store that felt more like church than in the Arabic world! A little spot of light in a religious landscape.

I love my country; but as an American preacher I bear the reproach whenever I visit a nation with healthy, balanced views on spirituality and alcohol. Perhaps my favorite place to go is the United Kingdom, where no one bats an eyelash at finishing a conference worship session, walking to the lobby bar for a pint during the break with half the congregation, then returning for the next lecture. In fact, I have done revival meetings *in the pubs*, while everyone sucks down a pint with the sermon! They are surprised to see me hydrating along with them, as they assume *all* American Christians are backward in this area.

When we planted a church in California some years back, I am pretty sure that every elder meeting we ever conducted was convened over a couple beers at a local tap house. Thank God I now live in the beer mecca of North America – Portland, Oregon in the Pacific Northwest. The extra carbs earn me a few extra pounds, but I am a happier man.

My Addiction

With the prohibition movement, the gospel quickly shifted away from being the good news of Jesus Christ to a focus on personal sinfulness and non-biblical moralism. This is what sent me into a downward spiral early in my own life. Some people have been so raked through the coals by alcohol abuse (themselves or someone they love), it seems much safer to avoid freedom in moderation and turn instead to regulations. *Regulations we can control.* It just seems easier and safer to say all booze is a no-no. *Why take the risk?*

"Well John," some may quip, "It's easy for you to say all this. … Tell it to someone who has an addiction! Explain it to someone who grew up with an alcoholic parent!"

No problem. *I've had both.* Personal addiction *and* alcoholic parents.

Prohibition only made it all worse.

As a young kid, I remember like it was yesterday. One balmy Georgia summer I traveled away from home for the annual summer vacation Bible school. Hosted through some regional Pentecostal network of churches, this camp was run by a strict *holiness* denomination (a distant grandchild of the temperance movement). Our affiliation, the Church of God, apart from having quite a cocky name (*we alone are God's church!)* had an obsession with preaching *against* random stuff. Men cannot have long hair; no skirts above the ankle; no casual dress on Sunday mornings; no fuggin swear words or you are going to hell, etc., etc.

Now all this did was make problems worse. The old pale hags said ladies should not wear makeup or cut their hair, so the young women would cake on the mascara half an inch thick with enough hairspray to stand up their perms like the Eiffel Tower. You were not allowed to smoke, so everyone choked down a pack as soon as they walked out of the church building where God was not looking. You were not allowed to do anything. So what was the stellar fruit of these random, obscure little regulations? Divorces. Suicide attempts. Poverty. Drug addictions. I saw it all firsthand.

Well, a few years before my old legalistic pastor (a husband and father of two) turned into a gay, atheist hairdresser in Atlanta, he used to take me to this summer VBS camp. There guest speakers viciously exhorted us about the dangers of hellfire if we did not uphold the moral standard of these shouting, spitting, hillbilly exegetes. On one particular night of one particular summer, I was provoked to great fear and anxiety over the condition of my eternal soul (as was the case during most sermons). But this night we were cajoled into doing something about it. Every kid was told to come forward to the altar (one of their favorite moves – the *altar call*) and swear a solemn vow to God that we would never use alcohol or tobacco for our entire life.

Quite a momentous decision for a pre-pubescent kid still watching ALF and playing Atari. For that particular hillbilly preacher, I am sure the goal of the night was to see a couple hundred warm bodies at the front of the church. He would feel better about himself, have a testimony to share of reforming the youth, then forget about it in a few weeks.

Not me. *I didn't forget.* That vow paved a course of addiction and depression for years. I had bound myself to the law.

Fast forward to another lazy summer day. I was at my grandmother's lake cabin when I took my first cigarette from her pack of menthols. I was not halfway to the filter when already I began to question whether my eternal soul could be redeemed. *I had broken a vow to GOD.* There was strong, voluminous theology for losing one's salvation in the *Church of God.* Anyone in their right mind should know that humble, crucified, servant-saviour Jesus throws 12-year-old boys into hell for having a cigarette. But it was not just the smoke ... *it was the vow!*

In no time flat, I was out at my grandparents' farm, camping deep in the woods around a fire when my older cousin surfaced a bottle of cheap brandy from his knapsack. I had already broken the smoking end of the vow, but the no-drinking rule was still in effect. My torn conscience only fueled my curiosity. By the end of the night the trees were spinning around me. I was smashed. Drinking, smoking, but never forgetting the vow.

MONEY. SEX. BEER. GOD.

From preteen into teenage years, the guilt of not living up to the standard of Pentecostal VBS holiness pushed me to invent an altar ego in which I would try my best to forget that God even existed or saw what I was doing. I had already broken the vow, so if I was going to hell, I may as well enjoy the ride there. In the meantime, I would regularly ask forgiveness, but I did not think it worked or applied if you had directly broken a promise to God Himself. Best thing to do is ignore the whole idea of Him altogether. The crushing guilt and fear was too much.

By the time I could drive, I smoked a pack of Marlboros a day and would get trashed with my friends anytime I could escape the house. It was likely the grace of God that my old humpty car did not work more often and that I was too young, nerdy and white in south Georgia to have better drug dealer connections. I had my first DUI at age 17. The same year I got high as a kite and arrested for vandalism; drunkenly ran my car off a truck loading dock (that's right, I drove right off a four-foot vertical wall, standing my car on its nose); slammed drunk into a telephone pole; and not to mention I got liquored up every single night I worked at a local sandwich shop by trading hoagies for sop under the table to the guys running the package shop next door. All of this before I was out of high school. I was working hard on my testimony.

By the time I hit college, I was smoking two packs of menthols a day (grandma's favorite), drinking to the point of total blackout, wondering how I ended up back in my room the next day. I would sleep through midterm exams, stopped going to class, and at times would consume up to 36 beers – an entire case – in a single day. By the time I was 18, I would find blood in the toilet and sometimes land in fistfights or jail for public intoxication. I would wake in the morning with no awareness of what happened the night before, with all of my money missing. I went from being the beloved party animal (voted "Class Clown" in high school), to being hated by everyone in my dormitory (always drunk, pissing in the communal water fountain or just being a nuisance).

Even in my dilapidated moral state, I knew I had to pull back from the booze just to survive. So in my immature sense of rationale, I decided just to switch to marijuana. At least I would be more chill with no blackouts. While I was never addicted to hard drugs, the marijuana was a quick segue to recreationally using LSD, nitrous oxide, painkillers or anything else I could get my hands on. Even then I was a bright enough boy not to try heroine, crack or methamphetamines. I knew my propensity toward addiction. But I smoked reefer from the time I woke up until the time I went to bed. I was constantly doped up, lazy and depressed. I would lie, cheat or steal – whatever it took to fuel my addiction. I had to be high on something all the time.

Now this is the part where I am supposed to tell you I had a radical encounter with Jesus in the middle of an acid trip, got instantly delivered, filled with the Holy Ghost and realized that God's presence was the very thing I had been looking for all those years.

Yes. That is exactly what happened.

But the point of my testimony is not to say, "God can deliver you as well!" *He can.* He already has if you have eyes to see it. And the point of sharing my story is not to encourage you to "say no to drugs." The point is to "just say no" to religious legalism and prohibition – to show like clockwork how its progression (with all the guilt, fear and ungodly abstinence) always incites and fuels sin, overindulgence and ultimately the lie we can exist and be satisfied apart from God's presence.

As stated in our introduction, the yeast of Herod (worldliness) and the yeast of the Pharisees (religion) always feed off of one another and produce one another. Not until I had a real encounter with the Lord, who was nothing like the fearful idolatrous *G.O.D., Inc.* of my youth, did I ever realize I was absolved from the law and swallowed up in His unconditional grace. That also meant complete liberty from silly, childish preteen vows that never had any substance at all. In his treatise *The Judgment of Martin Luther on Monastic Vows*, the great reformer assured monks and nuns they could break their monastic vows without sin, because vows were a vain, illegitimate attempt to win salvation.

So many people are sadly locked into psychological conundrums over irrelevant temporal prohibitions – what to eat, what to drink, what to wear – things that have absolutely no significance in the scope of eternal value. And these human legalisms are all supposedly endorsed by an ungodly trinity: fire-breathing Zeus, his depressed suicidal son, and the spirit of fear. My suppression of natural desires only caused them to become enflamed in a perverse way, in which I ironically turned away from Mr. Happy in order to pursue an elusive lie of fulfillment in sin. Actually, Mr. Happy never minded me having a drink. Drinks were His idea. Had I involved Him in the whole process, I probably would not have ended up in the grocery store freezer sucking nitrous out of fresh Reddi Wip cans everyday or faking skateboarding accidents at the clinic to get codeine. But then again, God the great iconoclast, had to destroy my idolatrous *Church of God* image of Him and allow me to see the full extent of what legalism and Gnosticism does to a man. Had I never experienced the dark side of religion, I would not have the insights of grace that I have been given today. My idol of substances had to be replaced by an intoxication on Him. But furthermore, my idolatrous, legalistic image of Him was the very thing that had driven me to the substances.

Position 3 – Abstention

If you will remember, we started our chapter addressing the four major views that churchgoers have regarding alcohol. Let us return to that list, moving on from prohibition to discuss the next opinion that perhaps the largest segment of Christians hold today:

Abstention.

But before I define it … I am sure many are already asking, "Why even bring any of this up? Aren't you causing unnecessary division by writing a book promoting booze?"

That is a laced question only a Christian would spew from his pie hole. For starters, I am not *promoting* booze in the sense that I am telling you to go drink. I am not your juice referee and could honestly care less if you drink or not (just stay away from my expensive scotch). And as for the "division" issue, I will agree that alcohol is a divisive topic in church circles. In fact, there is a time and place to keep your opinions to yourself (*I have also found that the gospel is divisive in church – should we shut up on that?*). We dance on enough eggshells in the church. Nevertheless, I will address the division issue soon. By now, hopefully you recognize there is *some need* for discussion, because without a balanced approach, there has been lots of *imbalance*.

If you think I should just keep quiet on adult beverages, there is a chance you are probably already an *abstentionist*. Abstention is a demonic view on booze that is likely the most popular stance among Christians on planet earth.

"Did you just demonize a large segment of Christians?"

"Nope. Just their demonic idea. But the Apostle Paul did the demonizing, not me."

So what is it? **Abstention, by definition, is the idea that – although alcohol is not a sin – *we should abstain from it, so as not to cause our brother to stumble.***

Let me say for starters that a lot of Christians would do well to stumble into a good stiff drink. It might just wipe that self-righteous, stagnant, pull-away-to-the-homeschool-bread-baking-circle-to-shun-the-world-and-watch-Little-House-on-the-Prairie look of attrition off your face and cheer you up a bit.

Holier Than Jesus

Perhaps you have heard, when it comes to drinking, that Christians are *called to a higher standard?* In some things, perhaps … but not here. In our pious arrogance, so many have presumed to hold a higher moral standard than Jesus.

> *The Son of Man came eating and drinking, and they say, "Here is a glutton and a drunkard, a friend of tax collectors and sinners." But wisdom is proved right by her actions* (Matt. 11:19).

Now in saying Jesus "came drinking" Matthew does not refer to water. Everyone drinks water. Jesus dipped His beak into the rotgut. Like it or not, that is how your Saviour rolls. But perhaps according to your "higher moral standards" Jesus was not setting a good example? The guy intentionally and scandalously created booze as His first miracle.

Again, I am not saying you *have to drink.* There is no spirituality based on it one way or another! If you have a medical condition, leave it alone! If you do not like the taste of it, leave it alone! Who cares?

Maybe you just do not feel like having a beer … Fine. *Who cares?*

In fact, if you attend AA, please do not go on a bender tonight with the flimsy excuse that "John Crowder told me to go drink." *I did not!* If you have had trouble with the bottle, then stay off it for a while until you learn some balance (but let me add that Alcoholics Anonymous theology is not ultimately going to fix you. Do not identify yourself as a lifelong alcoholic. Identify yourself as a son of God. Addiction has no place in you. Do not be in denial if you have been hitting the bottle too hard – confess it so you are not deluded – but overall recognize you have been completely liberated from that old sinful nature! Find your ultimate addiction in the presence of God).

In my communion services, I never offer the "grape juice option" any more than I would use Kool-Aid or Nestle Iced Tea. I use wine – the biblical sacrament. We do not use peanut butter if we are out of pinot noir (in such case I would just commune with Jesus and sip nothing). If you are going to do the sacrament, then use wine. He prescribed it for a reason (in the sacrament of marriage, you do not just use a horse if you cannot find an eligible woman). How many times have I heard someone say, "Well I can't do communion that way because I'm an alcoholic"? That is the fundamental reason for your alcoholism wise guy – you have believed a lie about yourself. Identify yourself as a sinner and what do you expect? Of course you are going to sin. AA helped you admit you had a problem – pulled you out of your delusion. But only the gospel fixes that problem by declaring you are a saint. Grace has made you addiction free.

There are dozens of reasons you may stay off the drink. Get out of the "should" or "should not" mentality. You are still being superstitious. These are personal decisions, and there is freedom.

The problem of abstention is when we *forbid ourselves or others* from drinking in the name of love, because we do not want to *cause offense* in people's lives. Perhaps you heard it said that you need to uphold a "good Christian witness." What witness? That God does not want you to have any fun? Absurd. The very last way you should *witness* to a nonbeliever is by avoiding the canned heat.

Unbelievers are offended by your teetotaling, not your moderate drinking. So who are you afraid to offend? *The religious people?* Rest assured, Jesus offended them all the time. That is about the only way you can deal with religion.

Causing Offense

I love people. But offenses are going to happen. I do not go around intentionally trying to offend people all the time. But every now and then I do prod the hornet's nest a bit if the situation calls for it. I was recently in Jakarta, where an Indonesian megachurch pastor had warned his flock against me for my "extreme" preaching on grace. One night at dinner my local friends alerted me that this very pastor happened to be sitting in the very same restaurant we had entered. I decided to make him uncomfortable by going over and giving him a hearty handshake of love ... but not without bringing along a bottle of beer in the other hand just to watch his reaction. Since it was Indonesia, I knew American Pentecostalism had taught them drink was evil.

Sometimes if I know it will irritate someone's religious attitude, I may crack a cold one. But I am sensitive to the situation. Other times, I may have dinner with a different pastor (who may also have a hang-up with malty beverages), but I will avoid a brew for the sake of fellowship. In general we do not *try* to offend. Sometimes it is the only way to wake people up. I have compassion if I know someone's conscience is torn over it, but I can be brazen if the person is a legalistic prick.

Gauge the scenario. Paul's instruction about avoiding offense over food or drink is a common sense precept that must be considered in a case-by-case situation. He is not categorically telling you to forsake your freedom and return to the law. Some Christians are so hyper-cautious they will not even have a drink in the quiet of their own home.

In Romans 14, Paul clarifies that we should be sensitive toward weak-faithed people who think certain foods are unclean. If it is wrong to their own conscience, then it is wrong for them to do because they would be acting despite their inner conflict. Bear with them, and do not criticize them, because God loves them – they belong to Him, not you. Do not judge them as individuals, even though it is right to reject their ridiculous ideas about abstention just as Paul did.

Paul is adamant in teaching that no food or wine drinking is wrong in itself. The point Paul is hammering is that we should not judge/criticize the individual person with whom we disagree, and avoid unnecessary offense because "the Kingdom of God is not a matter of food or drink, but of righteousness, peace and joy in the Holy Spirit" (Rom. 14:17).

152

Pick your battles. Food is a trifling matter. So there are plenty of times I will not drink around a person for sake of not causing unnecessary division. But Romans 14 is not the whole counsel of God! It applies to certain scenarios. How much unbiblical regulation gets hoisted on people in the name of "not stumbling?"

I also try not to drink around an alcoholic who idolizes his cup (in 1 Cor. 8 when Paul cautions against stumbling people over food, he is specifically talking about food consecrated to idols. The issue he is addressing is idolatry. The food is not demonic itself – it is safe to eat. But he says not to eat if it would cause your weak-in-the-faith friend to slip back into idolatry). That does not mean I must avoid all pubs because an alcoholic may be sitting in one of them. At the end of the day, this is all just a matter of common sense – something most Christians seem to lack. In fact it sometimes helps to let an alcoholic see someone living in moderation, whose joy runs deeper than the cup.

Nevertheless, Paul is not saying to forfeit your freedom in this area – that is abstention. He is just saying to use it wisely and do not stir up unwarranted storms. For the sake of fellowship, I may not drink in front of certain religious people. But let me also add that if they *do not drink*, I doubt the fellowship will ever go very far. Not because I do not like them, or that I am judging them or that we are not brothers. It is just hard to fully connect with someone at a deep, natural friendship level who embraces religious Gnostic tendencies in their spirituality. If they are misguidedly pitting food against God, rest assured they will pit your friendship against God.

Here is a proverb you can take to the bank: *never fully trust a pastor who will not have a beer with you.*

While leaders in the church should not be "enslaved to *much wine*," I would likewise never trust a leader who does not tip back a glass of *some wine* every now and then. If you do not have a grid for moderation, then you lack balance and are prone to hoist your asceticism onto others or snap and go overboard at some point.

Does Reverend Bob have a medical condition, or perhaps not like the taste? Maybe ... but if that is what Rev. Bob told you, I would like to inform you that most guys in ministry have ulterior motives for abstaining rather than the flavor (a religious fear, man-pleasing, performance orientation or outright banking their spirituality on food). With ministers in particular, this can be a telltale sign of Gnosticism and/or legalism in his worldview. Again, he may be a great guy – and I will even be his friend. But if such a man claims to be of the cloth, then in the capacity of a *minister* I will only trust him as far as I can throw him. The drink itself is irrelevant – it is just a litmus test of an underlying mindset, attitude and corrupted belief system to which I refuse to submit. But hey, maybe I am just deluded for reading scripture!

Doctrines of Demons

Sound harsh? Paul is quite caustic about it all. Let us look at one of our key verses on Gnosticism I tackled earlier in our *Sex* section:

Now the Spirit expressly says that in latter times some will depart from the faith, giving heed to deceiving spirits and doctrines of demons, speaking lies in hypocrisy, having their own conscience seared with a hot iron (1 Tim. 4:1-2, NKJV[9])

Heresy hunters assume *doctrines of demons* refer to teaching about miracles, or grace, or anything happy and enjoyable in the Christian life. But Paul explicitly tells us what these *doctrines of demons* actually are! He continues with the next verse:

*They forbid people to marry and **order them to abstain from certain foods**, which God created to be received with thanksgiving by those who believe and who know the truth. For everything God created is good, and **nothing is to be rejected** if it is received with thanksgiving, because it is consecrated by the word of God and prayer* (1 Tim. 4:3-5).

Abstention is a doctrine of demons. Although it does not categorically say alcohol is evil, it is still a rejection and abstaining from foodstuffs for spiritual reasons. In fact it rejects something meant to be enjoyed with thanksgiving to bring glory to God.

So whether you eat or drink or whatever you do, do it all for the glory of God (1 Cor. 10:31).

---

[9] *New King James Version* (Thomas Nelson Publishers, 1982).

154

The great Baptist preacher Charles Spurgeon, who was both a drinker and a cigar aficionado, once employed this verse beautifully. Most Baptists today vilify both alcohol and tobacco and often ignore that their great saint enjoyed both. Once in 1874 Spurgeon had the famous holiness preacher Billy Sunday speak as a guest in his pulpit. After Sunday delivered an hour-long rant against the evils of tobacco, he sat down and Spurgeon returned to the stage.

Spurgeon thanked *Mr. Pentecost* for sharing his convictions on the matter, but assured everyone that he still intended on "smoking a cigar before retiring to bed" that night. Spurgeon said he found ten commandments, not eleven or twelve, adding, "If anybody can show me in the Bible the command, 'Thou shalt not smoke,' I am ready to keep it." He said Mr. Pentecost was free to live by his own conscience, and Spurgeon would live by his. Then Spurgeon famously said he would continue to smoke cigars "to the glory of God."[10]

Position 4 - Moderation

Is it possible there is an alternate view on alcohol we could embrace? What if we considered a crazy, radical concept called *moderation!*

This is the fourth and final view on booze we will address. It is the biblical, balanced and incarnational perspective. Moderationists rightly believe that drinking is not sinful and that Christian conscience should guide each person.

But how can we trust the Spirit to guide Christians without laws?!?

With all this talk of drinking you probably think I am an absolute tosspot! I enjoy the occasional IPA, a dram of smoky scotch or a finely aged red wine; but I am not constantly sucking it back. If it were not for my high propensity to retain lard on my waist, I would probably have a bit more. Nevertheless, I see such imbalance over this issue; some sensible discernment is needed in the church. Alcohol becomes quite the *non-issue* when you cease to idolize it or superstitiously vilify it.

---

[10] *Christian World,* on September 25, 1874 via *The Spurgeon Archive*
http://www.spurgeon.org/misc/cigars.htm

Alcohol has a clear purpose from God. As stated, the gift of alcohol is to *cheer the heart of man* (Ps. 104:15).

> *But the vine said to them, "Should I cease my new wine, which cheers both God and men ... ?"* (Judg. 9:13, NKJV)

There is a difference between getting cheered and blacked out in your own vomit on the bathroom floor. Also, let me add that it is not a sin to have a few extra on the occasional celebratory occasion. Nor should you sit and count your brother's drinks for him, "Oops that's two and a half! You've reached your limit." Chill out. Scripture is concerned about you not being a *drunkard* – continually swilling it back like a hog at the trough, getting regularly hammered. Have some class.

There is a balance in life in which fear is no longer involved ... not worried that you are going to go overboard. Maturity means you just know when to cut it off without having to over think it in some bizarre, religious, irrational way. I cannot remember the last time I *worried* I might drink too much; and I surely cannot remember the last time I sat down intending to do so.

What About Marijuana?

In discussing alcohol, a related question is easily answered that often pops up: *what about marijuana?* Well it is an amazing God-given substance if you suffer a legitimate medical condition in which you are willing to trade in your coherence, ambition and intellect in exchange for relief from agonizing pain. But to suggest you can use marijuana moderately, you lie to yourself and you know it.

Even in the prehistoric days when I attended college, the common argument among potheads was that grass is somehow *healthier* for you than beer. With beer, you can have a few and be cheered without crossing the line of inebriation. With reefer, it is pretty impossible to burn even a tiny bud without instantly getting blazed every time. If you are a pothead, I would encourage you to drop the justification and just stop it. Makes you lazy, depressed, insecure, confused, disoriented and a deadbeat selfish parent and under-contributing member of society. Should I say more? You say, "Well God made it!" Yep, He also made corncobs so people can wipe their rear ends in the Third World, but we do not smoke or eat those. God gives us natural-world remedies for a proper use. If you do not have cancer, kick the habit. You will have a better life. So will your kids, who deserve a sober parent.

Addiction is straight up idolatry. The Bible clearly instructs us to be intoxicated on heaven but sober from the things of this world. I have nothing to gain by encouraging people to pop a cork of the bubbly – your decision to drink alcohol is between you and the Lord. Alcohol consumption is not worth a schism; but neither should we be pushed around by religious restrictions. The Lord never said wine was bad in itself; He only discourages drunkenness (in the natural) while encouraging it in the Spirit. Alcohol is good. Only *excess* is the problem. There are many verses touting the benefit of alcohol if used in moderation. The early church father John Chrysostom writes, "Wine has been given us for cheerfulness, not for drunkenness."[11] There is a difference. Here is a helpful, interesting quote from the apocryphal book of Sirach (Ecclesiasticus):

Wine is as good as life to a man, if it be drunk moderately: what life is then to a man that is without wine? For it was made to make men glad. Wine measurably drunk and in season bringeth gladness of the heart, and cheerfulness of the mind: But wine drunken with excess maketh bitterness of the mind, with brawling and quarrelling. Drunkenness increaseth the rage of a fool till he offend: it diminisheth strength, and maketh wounds. Rebuke not thy neighbour at the wine, and despise him not in his mirth: give him no despiteful words, and press not upon him with urging him [to drink] (Sirach 31:27-31).

This ancient Jewish narrative sums up the biblical view. Choose moderation. In addition, do not get mad at someone drinking, nor encourage his drunkenness! Leave him alone. On a personal one-on-one level, your position on alcohol should really be kept in the closet in most cases. As Paul said in Romans 14:22, *"...whatever you believe about these things keep between yourself and God."* So why do I bring

---

[11] John Chrysostom, "Saint Chrysostom: Homilies on Galatians, Ephesians, Philippians, Colossians, Thessalonians, Timothy, Titus, and Philemon," *A Select Library of the Nicene and Post-Nicene Fathers of the Christian Church*, ed. Philip Schaff, Homily XIX, Vol. XIII (Grand Rapids: William B. Eerdmans Publishing, Co.).

it up? There are two main reasons. From a teaching perspective, we *do* need instruction to protect us from the life-wrecking extremes of Gnosticism. Secondly, God is not focused on natural wine, but He *is* a drinker. If you do not learn to become inebriated on the New Covenant, you *will* become intoxicated on the things of the world.

There is a threshold of moderation for those who drink natural wine. But there is something innate within the core of every person that craves a drink without limit. Something that thirsts for a sea of endlessness. Jesus is the drink that lasts forever.

Wet Church History

Alcohol has been a part of the worshipping community from the dawn of time. It played significantly into God-ordained Jewish feasts and sacred rituals. Sukkot, the feast of booths, was a celebration directly connected to harvest and the pressing of the wine grapes. An eight-day, kosher Oktoberfest if you will. In fact, there was even a *liquor offering* instituted if someone was geographically prohibited from reaching the appointed place assigned to bring his tithe. If someone lived too far away, they were instructed to spend their tithe on a massive party … which included buying the *hard stuff!*

> Use the silver to buy whatever you want: cattle, sheep, goats, wine, liquor – whatever you choose. Then you and your family will eat and enjoy yourselves there in the presence of the Lord your God (Deut. 14:26, GWT[12]).

In fact, every book of the Old Testament mentions wine, with the exception of Jonah. During the temperance movement, dry activists hired scholars to rewrite the Bible and erase the mention of wine from all the Greek classics in school textbooks.

While dualistic heresies of extreme asceticism infiltrated the early church, alcohol still played a major role in daily living for the bulk of believers during the entire Christian era. The famous theologian and doctor of the church, St. Thomas Aquinas, believed absolute abstinence from drink was detrimental. "If a man deliberately abstains from wine to such an extent that he does serious harm to his nature, he will

---

[12] *God's Word Translation* (Holiday, FL: Green Key Books, 1995, 2003).

158

not be free from blame," he said.[13] Ironically, Aquinas said the state of drunkenness itself was not sinful if one found himself accidentally there after too much social lubricant. Just do not knowingly expose yourself to intoxication through willing overconsumption.

In the third century, St. Cyprian compared the use of alcohol to the joys of salvation:

> ... and in the same way, that by that common wine the mind is dissolved and the soul relaxed, and all sadness is laid aside, so, when the blood of the Lord and the cup of salvation have been drunk, the memory of the old man is laid aside, and there arises an oblivion of the former worldly conversation, and the sorrowful and sad breast which before was oppressed by tormenting sins is eased by the joy of the Divine Mercy.[14]

Simply stated, *everyone* drank beer or wine except a few fringy ascetic loons. Especially into the Middle Ages, water was highly unsafe to drink. Having no concept of sanitation, people would draw water from sources that were polluted by sewage, especially in areas with no fresh running springs. Beer was a matter of survival.

Historically, the church was the largest producer of wine, operating vast vineyards. And of course, the church has long been in the business of brewing beer. At times, church abbeys were charged with producing beer for surrounding communities for explicit public health needs in the Middle Ages. Monastic orders such as the Cistercians, Trappists, Carthusians, Carmelites, Benedictines and others have a rich history of brewing – and our Catholic brothers still make copious amounts of it today to support their orders. I love to contribute to the great cause of mother church by grabbing myself a Belgian abbey ale.

Monks were allotted up to *four liters of beer per day* for their own personal consumption. About 700 years ago, German monks from the city of Einbeck developed a malty, strong beer now known as *bock*. They continued to up the alcohol content to make a stronger variant known as the *doppelbock* (double bock). By the seventeenth century, the

---

[13] Thomas Aquinas, *Summa Theologica*, II.II Question 150, Article 1.

[14] Cyprian of Carthage, *Epistles of Cyprian of Carthage*, Epistle 62 http://www.newadvent.org/fathers/050662.htm (accessed Feb. 11, 2016).

monks had begun using the beer to sustain them through the annual Lenten fast leading up to Easter. At one point, the nutritious brew, often dubbed "liquid bread," was the *only* thing they would consume during Lent … literally taking a *46-day beer fast!*

A spurious legend says the doppelbocks were so tasty, the monks wondered if the drink conformed to the sad, penitent spirit of Lent. They decided to consult the pope on the matter. They set off on a long journey to Rome, but weather conditions caused their batch of beer to spoil. Upon tasting the beer, the pope was disgusted, quickly affirming that the beer was a perfect choice for the self-abasing Lenten season.

One such imbibing German monk turned reformer was Martin Luther.

Drinking with Luther

Martin Luther was given a barrel of Einbeck beer for his wedding day, when he broke his monastic vows and married wife Katherine – a former nun who was trained as a master brewer. Not only did he enjoy barley pops, but Luther set the precedent with Katie for clerical marriage. A good marriage should be enjoyed, he said. "We are permitted to laugh and have fun with and embrace our wives, whether they are naked or clothed," said Luther, just as Isaac fondled Rebecca (Gen. 26:8). Luther's face was on the label of the first Einbeck beer to ever be imported to American in 1880.[15]

While many Christian Bible schools and colleges today vet applicants with alcohol related questions on their applications, they have set up a wall that would exclude most of the greatest saints and ministers throughout church history.

"Do they seriously envision St. Paul or Calvin or Luther opening bottles of Welch's grape juice in the sacristy before the service?" writes Robert Capon, "Luther at least would turn over in his grave."[16]

Every reformer enjoyed booze – John Knox, Huldrych Zwingli, John Calvin. In fact, as a pastor, John Calvin's annual salary package in-

---

[15] Jim West, *Drinking With Calvin and Luther! A History of Alcohol in the Church* (Lincoln, CA: Oakdown, 2003), 31.

[16] Capon, *Supper of the Lamb*, 89.

160

cluded upwards of 250 gallons of wine. Calvin remarked, "Nowhere are we forbidden to laugh, or to be satisfied with food ... or to be delighted with music, or to drink wine."[17] Among the reformers, Luther was hands down the most vocal proponent of beer. The phrase *wine, women and song* is attributed to him, "he who loves not wine, women and song remains a fool his whole life long."[18] He also famously quipped, "It is better to think of church in the ale-house than to think of the ale-house in church."

Supposedly Luther discovered the groundbreaking truth of salvation "by grace, through faith" while sitting at the toilet. Although Protestants hail Luther as a hero, most have never actually read him. Otherwise he would still be condemned as a heretic today. His writings are full of fart jokes, cussing like a sailor, sharp sarcastic mocking of religionists and ... of course ... praise of good beer. He wrote:

> *If our Lord God can pardon me for having crucified and martyred Him ... He can also approve of my occasional taking a drink in his honor. God grant it, no matter how the world may interpret it!*[19]

Luther once joked, "Tomorrow I have to lecture on the drunkenness of Noah (Gen. 9:20-27), so I should drink enough this evening to be able to talk about that wickedness as one who knows by experience."[20] He is widely credited with saying, "Whoever drinks beer, he is quick to sleep; whoever sleeps long, does not sin; whoever does not sin, enters heaven! Thus, let us drink beer!"

Ironically, the above statement rang with a bit of truth. Did you know why most church services are held at 10 a.m. or 11 a.m. on Sunday mornings? This tradition goes back to Luther. Regularly sitting up late, discussing theology and drinking beer with his buddies on Saturday nights, Luther gradually began moving the 6 a.m. Sunday morning

---

[17] John Calvin, Commentary on Psalm 104.

[18] A possible variant from one of Luther's Table Talks, but written by Johann Heinrich Voss in 1777. See Heinrich Boemer & William Koepchen, *Luther in Light of Recent Research* (Christian Herald: 1916), 212.

[19] Eric Gritsch, *The Wit of Martin Luther* (Minneapolis: Fortress Press, 2006), 119.

[20] Ibid.

mass forward hour by hour ... eventually setting the time as late as possible for it to still be called a *Sunday morning* mass. If not for Luther's love of beer, you would never sleep in on Sunday mornings.

Gospel of Laughter

Luther's humor underlies and discloses a theology of freedom that is perhaps one of his greatest legacies. It was anchored in an awareness of his own limitations and an ability to laugh at himself and not make grandiose speculations about God or his own spirituality that were beyond him. His organic appreciation of the natural life, juxtapose to the hyper-spiritual fears of his former days in the monastic cloister, was a fruit of the gospel. His humility to no longer take himself or religious works too seriously also gave him a light, carefree approach toward the devil. "I resist the devil," said Luther, "and often it is with a fart that I chase him away."

Luther was very cheeky in his polemics. After feeling liberated from an improper fear of God, he also became very loose in his communication with adversaries. Signing his correspondence "Friar Martin Eleutherius" (the liberated one), Luther freely employed mockery and provoking language. The titles of some of his exchanges, for instance, were:

> - *To the Goat in Leipzig*
> - *Concerning the Answer of the Goat in Leipzig*
> - *Answer to the Hyper-Christian, Hyper-Spiritual and Hyper Learned Goat Emser in Leipzig – Including Some Thoughts Regarding His Companion, the Fool Murner*

In his tracts against the papacy, Luther employed an artist to develop satirical caricatures. One cartoon pictured a she-devil whose rectum gave birth to the pope and the cardinals. Another pictured the pope riding a pig, with a handful of manure, among several others along the same humorous theme. Addressing the pope as "Most Hellish Father" or "Holy Madam Pope Paula III," it was not uncommon for Luther to use this type of language:

> *Gently, dear Pauli, dear donkey, don't dance around! Oh, dearest little ass, don't dance around - dearest, dearest little donkey, don't do it. For the ice is very solidly frozen this year because there was no wind - you might fall and break a leg. If*

a fart should escape you while you were falling, the whole world would laugh at you and say, "Ugh, the devil! How the ass has befouled himself!"[21]

Understand that I love my catholic brothers – and in fact, I once considered Luther's language a fruit of bitterness. What I had missed was his playful sarcasm. His love of humor, beer and his wife spoke volumes of Luther's grasp of a joyous, earthy, incarnational spirituality resting on Christ's finished work. "Sadness is an instrument of the devil whereby he gets much accomplished," said Luther[22], noting elsewhere, "Sadness is hereditary to us, and the devil is the spirit of sadness, but God is the spirit of joy, who saves us."[23]

"You have as much laughter as you have faith," said Luther. "The gospel is nothing less than laughter and joy."[24] Only through the lens of humor does one understand Luther. He never wanted to split from the church, but rather wanted the Roman Catholic church *reformed.*

Railing against the practice of indulgences, in which people paid sums of money to have their sins absolved along with superstitiously collecting relics, Luther anonymously printed a humorous pamphlet announcing some special, recently discovered relics coming on tour. These included: two feathers and an egg from the Holy Spirit; a pound of wind that roared by Elijah in the cave at Mount Horeb; three flames from the burning bush at Sinai; five strings from David's harp; and three locks of Absalom's hair which were caught in the oak and left him hanging. Whoever paid to see them would receive ten years of past sins forgiven, as well as ten more years of future sins in advance.

Drink the Devil Away

I can picture Luther sitting around late with his buddies drinking pints and laughing over his latest little booklets. For Luther, joylessness was incompatible with Christianity. He vehemently rejected the somber,

---

[21] Martin Luther, *Against the Roman Papacy, an Institution of the Devil,* 1545.

[22] Gritsch, *The Wit of Martin Luther,* 117.

[23] Dr. Werner Thiede, "The Reformer's Liberated Laughter." http://www.luther2017.de/en/martin-luther (accessed Feb. 11, 2016).

[24] Charles Haddon Spurgeon. "Commentary on Psalms 126." *Spurgeon's Verse Expositions of the Bible* http://www.biblestudytools.com

cowling, hypocritical face of religion – he was a man of music and mirth and celebration. He did not tolerate religious condemnation, and even sarcastically writes to a friend in Wittenberg that he should occasionally "sin against the devil":

> Be strong and cheerful and cast out those monstrous thoughts. Whenever the devil harasses you thus, seek the company of men, or drink more, or joke and talk nonsense, or do some other merry thing. Sometimes we must drink more, sport, recreate ourselves, aye, and even sin a little to spite the devil, so that we leave him no place for troubling our consciences with trifles. We are conquered if we try too conscientiously not to sin at all. So when the devil says to you, "Do not drink," answer him, "I will drink, and right freely, just because you tell me not to." One must always do what Satan forbids. What other cause do you think that I have for drinking so much strong drink, talking so freely and making merry so often, except that I wish to mock and harass the devil who is wont to mock and harass me. Would that I could contrive some great sin to spite the devil, that he might understand that I would not even then acknowledge it and that I was conscious of no sin whatever. We, whom the devil thus seeks to annoy, should remove the whole Decalogue from our hearts and minds.[25]

Despite his fondness of wine and beer, Luther was by no means a drunkard, nor did he seriously endorse sin as his critics would sometimes slanderously accuse him. Calvin and Luther both preached against drunkenness as an evil. Luther spoke against excess in *Soberness and Moderation against Gluttony and Drunkenness:*

> We ought to give thanks to God for providing us with food and drink and then besides, liberating us from the papacy, and feeding us with food and drink. If you are tired and downhearted, take a drink; but this does not mean being a pig and doing nothing but gorging and swilling.[26]

---

[25] West, *Drinking With Calvin and Luther!*, 34.

[26] Martin Luther, *Soberness and Moderation against Gluttony and Drunkenness* (I Peter 4:7-11), May 18, 1539.

Luther was against overindulgence, but also fully understood festivity and a hearty enjoyment of what the Lord provides. "It is possible to tolerate a little elevation, when a man takes a drink or two too much after working hard and when he is feeling low. This must be called a frolic. But to sit day and night, pouring it in and pouring it out again, is piggish," he said. "You should be moderate and sober; this means that we should not be drunken, though we may be exhilarated."[27]

Calvin likewise said that drinking should be moderate, "lest men forget themselves, drown their senses, and destroy their strength."[28] But Calvin also understood that, "It is permissible to use wine not only for necessity, but also to make us merry."

Calvin noted in his commentary on Psalm 104:15, "Nature would certainly be satisfied with water to drink; and therefore the addition of wine is owing to God's superabundant liberality." Calvin encouraged moderation, but also noted that "in making merry" those who drink wine "feel a livelier gratitude to God." Calvin cautioned, "If a man knows that he has a weak head and that he cannot carry three glasses of wine without being overcome, and then drinks indiscreetly, is he not a hog?"[29] For Calvin, moderation was found when it was God-centered eating and drinking, "and for that cause it is said *Thou shalt eat in the presence of thy God.*"[30]

Drinking Past the Law

Luther constantly praised his wife Katie's beer, especially expressing his fondness for it when traveling afar, when he was forced to drink bad beer, which he said would often give him diarrhea. "I keep thinking what good wine and beer I have at home, as well as a beautiful wife," he wrote her, "you would do well to send me over my whole cellar of wine and a bottle of thy beer."

Writing to the theological dean of Wittenberg about a party in 1535, he notes that Katie was brewing "malt liquor, as they call it. My Lord Katie

---

[27] Martin Luther, Sermon from Wittenburg, May 18, 1539.

[28] West, *Drinking With Calvin and Luther!*, 53.

[29] Ibid., 54.

[30] Ibid., 59.

has brewed seven kegs in which she put thirty-two bushels of malt, hoping to gratify my palate. She trusts that the beer will be good, but you and the rest will find that out by testing it. ..."[31] At his own home, Luther supposedly had a mug with three rings on it. The rings on the tankard represented the Ten Commandments, the Apostle's Creed and the Lord's Prayer. He was said to drink all the way to the Lord's Prayer, but was amused when his friend could not make it past the law.

"I'm like a ripe stool," he once wrote to Katie, laughing even in the face of his impending death, "and the world's like a gigantic anus, and we're about to let go of each other."[32]

Today the definition of a *Protestant* would be foreign to the likes of Luther, Calvin or Zwingli. With no scripture *at all* condemning drinking, but only urging self-control, the *cult of abstinence* today preaches empty moralisms: that the Christian's duty is to stay off the bottle entirely – the magical fix to guard against alcoholism. But the reformers were preaching the grace of the gospel in the face of tyrannical, abusive religion and legalism. Luther said, "But while I sat and drank beer with Phillip and Amsdorf, God dealt the papacy a mighty blow."[33]

As the Reformation spread throughout Europe, and the shifting religious demographics changed over the next hundred years, one group fled persecution to America. The *Puritans* were not the dry, dour abstainers one might think. The Mayflower was loaded down with more than 7,500 barrels of wine and beer – more booze than water. Another ship, the Arabella, left for America in 1630 with 10,500 gallons of beer; 10,000 gallons of wine and only 3,500 gallons of fresh water.[34]

Why the Temperance Movement?

If moderate consumption of alcohol has always been embraced by mother church (apart from a few nutjobs) how did the tides turn against it? Why do nearly 300 million Pentecostals worldwide today think it is evil, and even more evangelicals avoid it just to be "on the safe side"?

---

[31] Ibid., 37.

[32] Gritsch, *The Wit of Martin Luther,* 5.

[33] Martin Luther, Second Sermon at Wittenburg, March 11, 1522

[34] Richard J. Hooker, *Food and Drink in America: A History* (Indianapolis: Bobbs-Merrill, 1981).

The temperance movement began in the early 1800s, largely as a re-action to the high rates of alcoholism in society. Earliest temperance societies were more true to their name: "temperance" by definition means *moderation*. They were initially against *drunkenness*, allowing responsible use of booze. In fact, the movement was originally aimed at distilled liquor, but members continued to drink wine and beer. Yet by the 1840s, the legalism had cemented into a crusade, and all tem-perance societies advocated teetotalism against *all* forms of alcohol.

The church has a long, sordid love affair with moralism as an elixir to society's problems. The church decided to help its fellow man by turn-ing off the tap altogether. There is no doubt that the culture of the eighteenth century was sinking into a pit of substance abuse at the time. But it helps to understand the sociological reason for the rampant problem.

The first endemic spread of alcoholism on a mass societal level sprang up in the eighteenth century during the industrial revolution. This was not because rum is demonic. It is because people are not created to live their lives as utilitarian cogs on an assembly line. During this time, vast numbers of people from rural communities moved to urban slums to fill factories as unskilled labor. The inherent controls and rural life-style norms regarding alcohol were lost. Simultaneously, new technol-ogy and industrial production of alcohol made stronger drink cheaper and more readily available. A culture where children grew up alongside their parents, learning the family trade, was gutted. Fathers and sons were separated. In a single generation, the family unit disintegrated.

In England, an experimental method of distilling 60 percent gin with juniper berries entered wide-scale production. From 1700 to 1735, gin production increased ten times over to 5 million gallons, with the black market generating another 50 million gallons.[35] With no cultural or his-toric context for regulating consumption, gin became an outlet for the over-worked masses toiling for long hours and living in destitution. Al-cohol became an easy escape from a horrible utilitarian life.

There was not a strict divorce between church and society in those days. Far from it. Temperance began as a public health initiative and

---

[35] "A Pint Sized History of Alcohol." http://www.drugaidcymru.com (accessed Jan. 31, 2016).

social reform – but quickly picked up steam as a spiritual, revival agenda in the pews. The movement grew by aligning with other side-lined causes of the day like suffrage (women's voting) and abolition (the anti-slavery movement). A skewed societal narrative was developing that all drinkers were equivalent to misogynists and slavers. As the holiness movement further evolved, alcohol was folded into a long list of random banned activities deemed as *sins* without a shred of biblical reasoning. To commit one of them was to commit all of them:

> *Alcohol, tobacco, the theatre, the cinema, foolish talking, jesting, using slang, dancing, the ballroom, the circus, wearing makeup, lotteries, playing cards, spitting, eating pork, eating oysters, gambling, profanity, medical doctors, reading papers, whistling or holding diversions on Sunday.*

I love most of this stuff! Many of these prohibitions would carry over into the Pentecostal and charismatic traditions. Petty legalisms never quite make any sense. Who was the first Amish person to decide that buttons and tractors were a sin? Doesn't really matter, because after a couple of generations, the creeds have been enshrined.

The Joy of Life

Religion essentially seeks to extract the *joie de vivre*. Life is a celebration to be lived in God. Take wine and all creaturely enjoyments out of the mix, and you have a radical misunderstanding of God's very nature. By rejecting the joy of His creation, one has dishonored the Creator Himself. "The Christian religion is not about the soul; it is about man, body and all, and about the world of things with which he was created, and in which he is redeemed. Don't knock materiality. God invented it," writes Capon on our dualisms.[36] "Why do we marry, why take friends and lovers? Why give ourselves to music, painting, chemistry or cooking? Out of simple delight in the resident goodness of creation, of course; but out of more than that, too. Half earth's gorgeousness lies hidden in the glimpsed city it longs to become."[37]

---

[36] Fr. Robert Capon, *Bed and Board: Plain Talk About Marriage* (Simon and Schuster, 1965).

[37] Fr. Robert Capon, *Supper of the Lamb: A Culinary Reflection* (New York: The Modern Library, 1967), 189.

In his classic way, Capon explains the divine party out of which creation emerged, and to which our creaturely joys prophetically point:

*Let me tell you why God made the world. One afternoon, be-
fore anything was made, God the Father, God the Son, and
God the Holy Spirit sat around in the unity of their Godhead
discussing one of the Father's fixations. From all eternity, it
seems, He had had this thing about being. He would keep
thinking up all kinds of unnecessary things – new ways of being and new kinds of beings to be. And as they talked, God the
Son suddenly said, "Really, this is absolutely great stuff. Why
don't I go out and mix us up a batch?" And God the Holy Spirit
said, "Terrific! I'll help you." So they all pitched in, and after
supper that night, the Son and the Holy Spirit put on this tremendous show of being for the Father. It was full of water and
light and frogs; pine cones kept dropping all over the place,
and crazy fish swam around in the wineglasses. There were
mushrooms and mastodons, grapes and geese, tornadoes and
tigers – and men and women everywhere to taste them, to
juggle them, to join them, and to love them. And God the Father looked at the whole wild party and said, "Wonderful! Just
what I had in mind! Tov! Tov! Tov!" And all God the Son and
God the Holy Spirit could think of to say was the same thing:
"Tov! Tov! Tov!" So they shouted together "Tov meod!" and
they laughed for ages and ages, saying things like how great it
was for beings to be, and how clever of the Father to think of
the idea, and how kind of the Son to go to all that trouble putting it together, and how considerate of the Spirit to spend so
much time directing and choreographing. And for ever and
ever they told old jokes, and the Father and the Son drank
their wine in unitate Spiritus Sancti, and they all threw ripe olives and pickled mushrooms at each other per omnia saecula
saeculorum, Amen.*

*It is, I grant you, a crass analogy; but crass analogies are the
safest. Everybody knows that God is not three old men throwing olives at each other. Not everyone, I'm afraid, is equally
clear that God is not a cosmic force or a principle of being or
any other dish of celestial blancmange we might choose to call
Him. Accordingly, I give you the central truth that creation is*

the result of a Trinitarian bash, and leave the details of the analogy to sort themselves out as best they can.[38]

Fermentation is a Prophecy

C.S. Lewis points out that *fermentation* itself is a prophecy pointing to the continual agency and presence of God in creation:

God creates the vine and teaches it to draw up water by its roots and, with the aid of the sun, to turn that water into juice which will ferment and take on certain qualities. Thus every year, from Noah's time till ours, God turns water into wine. That, men fail to see. Either like the pagans they refer the process to some finite spirit, Bacchus or Dionysus: or else, like the moderns, they attribute real and ultimate causality to the chemical and other material phenomena which are all that our senses can discover in it. But when Christ at Cana makes water into wine, the mask is off. ... The miracle has only half its effect if it only convinces us that Christ is God: it will have its full effect whenever we see a vineyard or drink a glass of wine we remember that here works He who sat at the wedding party in Cana.[39]

Capon describes wine as "water in excelsis." Further echoing Lewis, Capon shows that wine itself is proof of God's continual work in His ongoing sustenance of creation.

In a general way we concede that God made the world out of joy: He didn't need it; He just thought it was a good thing. But if you confine His activity in creation to the beginning only, you lose most of the joy in the subsequent shuffle of history. Sure, it was good back then, you say, but since then, we've been eating leftovers. How much better a world it becomes when you see Him creating at all times and at every time; when you see that the preserving of the old in being is just as much creation as the bringing of the new out of nothing. Each thing, at every moment, becomes the delight of His hand, the apple of His eye. The bloom of yeast lies upon the grapeskins year af-

---

[38] Ibid., 84-85.

[39] C.S. Lewis, "Miracles," *God in the Dock* (Eerdmans: 1970).

ter year because He likes it; $C_6H_{12}O_6=2C_2H_5OH+2CO_2$ is a dependable process because, every September, He says, "That was nice; do it again." Let us pause and drink to that.[40]

Fun with Fasting

With all this talk of drinking, you may like to pair your fine glass of Bordeaux with a little morsel to eat as well. But even if I convince a religionist to relax his stance on the bottle, I may never convince him that God wants him to *eat* as well.

In my earlier book *Mystical Union* I have given an extensive treatment on the subject of fasting (one of the favorite divination tools of the charismatic world to curry divine favor). I would be remiss in this book on Gnostic dualism not to address it again to some degree. Gnostics love asceticism. And what better way to harm yourself to the glory of God than to starve yourself?

The zealous fervor of those *hungry for more of God* often transmits to abusing and emaciating their physical bodies in order to gain spiritual benefit. Fasting is the classic discipline of Gnosticism. We presume like the bewitched Galatians that Christ has not already given us *everything* God has to offer as a gift; so we must act to attain what Christ could not complete on behalf of our own spirituality.

More than any other discipline, fasting affirms our idea that God is against physical pleasure. Fasting is one of the primary practices of charismatic *voo-doo do-do (doing* something in an attempt to *get what you already have … working for the gift).* Self-abasing speakers who boast in their self-denial from the fork and spoon mesmerize countless sheep. The resurgence in fasting has grown to a fevered pitch in charismatic circles since the trend was rediscovered in the 1950s Pentecostal healing revival. But our Catholic and Orthodox brothers have always enjoyed implementing this abusive ritual on the flock, without the bells and whistles of promised gifts of healing and superpowers.

It has always been easy to manipulate crowds with guilt. And tales of fasting are easy ways to elevate your spirituality over others, by making them feel lazy, less spiritual and incompetent in comparison to you.

---

[40] Capon, *Supper of the Lamb: A Culinary Reflection,* 85.

MONEY. SEX. BEER. GOD.

I have determined to be mesmerized by nothing but the cross. As Paul stated, "I resolved to know *nothing* while I was with you except Jesus Christ and Him crucified" (1 Cor. 2:2, NIV).

The grueling outward observance of fasting simply appeals to our inherent notion that pain equals gain. Fasting does not draw you closer to God. Jesus brought you into complete union with God.

There is not one single New Testament commandment to fast.

Some may quote Matthew 17:21, where Jesus supposedly says that certain demons come out only through "prayer and fasting." The problem is that verse *does not exist* in the oldest extant manuscripts. That is why almost every modern translation does not even include it!

The same conversation is found in another synoptic gospel account (in Mark 9:29). But in the Book of Mark, Jesus says nothing about fasting. He merely says some demons only come out by *prayer*. The disciples must have seen many delivered *without even praying* for them! We never read of Jesus give the disciples an exorcism class before He sends them out. It is quite possible (just as Peter's shadow healed the sick) that when Andrew and Bartholomew walked into town, their very shadows caused the demons to flee.

"But Jesus, why didn't this kind come out?"
"Because sometimes folks need to know what's going on. You need to say ... *'Come out!'*"

However it worked, it is by Christ's power – not our diet regimen – that we are liberated. If you want to hang on to a verse that does not really exist (Matt. 17:21), that is totally fine with me. But please at least define fasting the way that the scripture defines fasting. Even in the Old Covenant, the Lord says the *true* fast He desires has nothing to do with your Big Mac. It has everything to do with generosity, loving others, thinking outside ourselves and being generous to the poor (Isa. 58). It deals with the issues of the heart, not irrelevant outward observances like pizza or calamari consumption.

Well if Jesus fasted for 40 days, you better believe that I need to fast for 40 days!

172

Look, Jesus did a lot of stuff I cannot do (like die for the sins of the world). He did not take any disciples into the wilderness with Him when He fasted. *His fast was part of His substitutionary act.*

How Long is That Day?

Even in the Old Covenant era, God did not want His people beating up their physical bodies in order to gain spiritual benefit like the pagan nations around them – like the Molech and Baal worshippers. The Jewish people had a God-ordained *feasting* culture. Every holy observance was a feast with food and wine. There was only *one day* a year that God's people were commanded to fast – the *Day of Atonement.* We know that Christ has now atoned for the sins of the world, and that day has become the greatest feast of all! The New Covenant never says to keep the fast. It says to keep the *feast* (1 Cor. 5:8). Christianity is not a fast; it is a festival.

Even today, Muslims, Buddhists, Hindus and Greek-pagan-influenced Christians put far, far more focus on fasting than our Jewish brothers. See how the Pharisees griped about Jesus' followers' celebratory lives:

> Their next complaint was that Jesus' disciples were feasting instead of fasting. "John the Baptist's disciples are constantly going without food, and praying," they declared, "and so do the disciples of the Pharisees. Why are yours wining and dining?" (Luke 5:33, TLB[41])

Jesus returns their question with one of His own, "Do happy men fast?" (Luke 5:34) He said it was impossible for His disciples to fast because the Bridegroom was with them.

> But the time will come when the Bridegroom will be taken from them, and **on that day** they will fast (Mark 2:20, NIV).

So often we read this passage as if Jesus refers to an "upcoming age" – a future coming dispensation when we will begin abstaining. As if fasting "on that day" means: *In the coming era ... when it shall come to pass ... in the long days ahead.*

---

[41] *The Living Bible* (Wheaton: Tyndale House Publishers, 1971, 1979).

Jesus is not saying everyone will fast after He goes to heaven. In all of the best manuscripts, Jesus' statement "on that day" is *singular*. Jesus is speaking about *one single day* – the Day of Atonement. How long did that day last? For how long would He would be taken away? No more than 40 hours. From Friday evening until Sunday morning. Would you want to eat the day your best buddy dies? His disciples were too busy running to save their own skin anyway.

Trust me that the Bridegroom is closer to you right here, right now than He was to Peter, James and John when He said that. He said it is better that He should go, because He now dwells *within* us by the Spirit. You are now one with the Bridegroom. Flesh of His flesh. Bone of His bone. He who is in Christ is one Spirit with the Lord! Why are you starving yourself to get closer to your Siamese twin?

Commentator Adam Clarke points out that the early church only fasted once per year, for 40 hours, as a remembrance of the time Christ was in the grave. But later, religious ding dongs came along and turned the 40-hour fast into a 40-day fast (calling it Lent) as an attempt to repeat Christ's finished work in the desert.

"This fast is pretended to be kept by many, in the present day, in commemoration of our Lord's *forty* days' fast in the wilderness; but it does not appear that, in the purest ages of the *primitive Church*, genuine Christians ever pretended that their ... fast was kept for the above purpose. Their fast was kept merely to commemorate the *time* during which Jesus Christ lay under the power of death, which was about forty hours," writes Clarke. "They put days in the place of hours; and this absurdity continues in some Christian Churches to the present day."[42]

Some may ask, "Well didn't the apostles fast after the cross in the Book of Acts?" Indeed they did, a handful of times. And it was always for the exact same reason. It was never to become more holy, never to get filled with Smith Wigglesworth power and never to twist God's arm to end abortion (as if He is the big abortionist in the sky). The only reason they ever fasted was to clear their heads and focus before they ordained a new leader. I can honestly say that, of all the people I ever ordained, I am only glad I did it a few of those times in retrospect. You

---

[42] Clarke, *Commentary on the Whole Bible*, Excerpt from Matt. 9.

174

risk endorsing someone who will lose the plot of the gospel. This is why ordination "the laying on of hands" should not be done flippantly.

Even for the apostles, their prayer and fasting formulas for ordination did not always work. After Judas killed himself, they figured, "Well, we should replace him." So after all their prayers and petitions, they eventually *rolled a dice!* They cast a lot and chose Matthias. Did you ever hear a peep about Matthias again after that (no hard feelings, Matthias!)? Maybe God had his own replacement pick up his sleeve. Paul says in Galatians 1 that he was not an apostle appointed by man – he was not an apostle by the roll of the dice! He received this gospel revelation directly from Jesus Christ Himself and never asked any of the big boys' permission in Jerusalem before he started preaching it!

Studied Neglect of the Body

Fasting is unfortunately employed as tool of divination to win God's favor. And while Jesus' emphasis on fasting was not to forbid it, one could easily argue that He downplayed it and never encouraged it.

When you practice some appetite-denying discipline to better concentrate on God, don't make a production out of it. It might turn you into a small-time celebrity but it won't make you a saint (Matt. 6:16, MSG[43]).

If your self-esteem and faith are so weak you must beat yourself up to earn approval, kindly do not ruin everyone else's fun: at least cheer up!

When you fast don't be like the hypocrites who go out all depressed. Their glum self-denial they hope you will applaud. Truthfully, they already have their reward. But when you are fasting keep it secret for the Lord ... (Matt. 6:16-18, ECK[44]).

If you know of any particular minister's fasting routines, do not be impressed. The fact he told you about them just invalidated his fasts. He should have kept quiet.

---

[43] Eugene Peterson, *The Message* (Colorado Springs: NavPress Publishing Group, 2005 ed.).

[44] Lindsey Eck, *The Sermon on the Mount*, (Passage adaptation accessible at http://www.corneroak.com/sermon_lyrics.html).

"But John, this minister is very humble ... He was just talking about his fast to *teach us*."
No, he was strutting his little peacock feathers, showing off to you.

"Wait John, he's not like that. He's a very humble man."
That's exactly how you play the fasting card! Fasting has been played with false humility for 2000 years.

This is exactly what Paul is dealing with in his letter to the Colossians who were dealing with these exact same Gnostic influences. Paul says, "In view of these tremendous facts (that you shared in Christ's death and life), don't let anyone worry you by criticizing what you eat or drink" (Col. 2:16, PHI[45]). He goes on to address all the latest charismatic trends – special holy days, moon patterns, supposed angelic encounters – whatever the latest pop Gnostic topic at hand that was supposed to make them more spiritual or more anointed. And he says these confused charismatic preachers had "forgotten the Head" which is Christ – the sole source and consummation of all our spirituality. He goes on to hammer home the vain, false humility of those preaching asceticism:

> *So if, through your faith in Christ, you are dead to the principles of this world's life, why, as if you were still part and parcel of this world-wide system, do you take the slightest notice of these purely human prohibitions – "Don't touch this," "Don't taste that" and "Don't handle the other?" "This," "that" and "the other" will all pass away after use! I know that these regulations **look wise** with their **self-inspired efforts** at worship (**willpower worship** [KJV]), their **policy of self-humbling**, and their **studied neglect of the body**. But in actual practice **they do honour, not to God, but to man's own pride** (Col. 2:20-23, PHI).*

Maybe you know of some intergalactic superhero of a minister who claims to have come into great magical powers after a 40-day fast. Well I can tell you about a million others who just got sick and hungry. So often, they simply confuse what God gave them as a gift by attributing it to their own self-denial. Instead of thanking God for His gifts, they point to their own routines as steps and formulas of how to "get what

---

[45] J.B. Phillips, *The New Testament in Modern English* (New York: The Macmillan Co., 1962).

they have." It is easier to sell formulas on the book table than to admit you got what you got as a gift. *Everything was a gift.*

The Taco Bell Challenge

Some years ago, we launched what I call the Taco Bell Challenge. It is an open invitation that works like this: I invite you to go and fast for 40 days. Meanwhile, I will be eating grilled stuffed chicken burritos. At the end of 40 days, we will see who can work the most miracles.

John that sounds very arrogant.

I totally agree. How arrogant to think you can go work up a bunch of miracles with your fasting!

Ultimately, fasting is a heart issue. I am not against it – I actually live a fasted lifestyle. I fast *frowns, depression, evil, religion* and *boring meetings!* Every one of these fasts is a billion times better than a food fast. The Lord does not care about your caramel custard – He is concerned with the condition of your heart (I do not mean your cholesterol level).

Unfortunately these days, massive prayer and fasting cults are in vogue. They are endorsed by all the right people and cater to the church's inherent sense of lack, fear and insecurity. They serve up 30-plus-hour, doom-and-gloom teaching sets on their odd interpretations of the Book of Revelation (when Jesus returns and we help Him slaughter people). They have 20-plus-hour teaching sets on random books like Lamentations (that should cheer you up). And yet they do not have *one single* teaching available on the Pauline epistles? Do you think the gospel of grace should fit in there somewhere? But the Good News invalidates every ministry aimed at self-improvement. Religion thrives on distance, delay and unfinished business.

Busted at the Quickie Mart

A friend who currently works with our Cana New Wine Seminary, was previously a leader in such a prayer and fasting group (he eats just fine now). Back when he was in that camp, he remembered a time when they were deep into a 40-day fast. They were on day 17, when at 5 a.m. he finally broke. He and his roommates snapped and rushed down to the local Quickie Mart to buy a fistful of frozen taquitos. After gobbling down the fast food, they started to walk back out of the gas station ... and what did they see?

Lo and behold ... a lone, solitary car was sitting in the parking lot.

They looked at the car and were aghast to discover *sitting inside was the head honcho "prophetic" guy who calls ALL of the 40-day fasts.*

"Oh no," they thought as their hearts sank. "The Lord surely sent him here to bust us!"

But as they took a closer look into the car window, what did they see?

They guy was weeping.

... and he was eating a powered sugar jelly doughnut.

Once these young guys had outed the cheating, bigwig minister – with powdered sugar all in his mustache – he finally confessed something quite profound. "Out of all these 40-day fasts I have ever called over the years, I have never finished a single one of them," he said. Can you fathom the hypocrisy? This is a guy who built his *whole ministry* on shaming others into starving themselves.

"Well, we should have grace on the guy," you may say. I fully agree. On the surface it is not a big deal ... some preachers get busted snorting coke off a hooker's butt. This guy is like, "Hey, I'm just hungry ... I'll settle for a doughnut!"

But do you notice a big, big problem here? *Here is a guy who is heaping burdens on others that he himself cannot even carry.* And we think that is okay? It is okay to keep trucking along preaching this demonic self-abasement, while my friend Tony saw firsthand the fallout of countless teenagers under his influence who thought God was disappointed or literally hated them because they could not go hungry more than three days? Where is the gospel in that?

Eat and Drink With a Merry Heart

Take a day off. Enjoy life. Thank God for it. Have a couple beers if you are old enough, and eat a few extra carbs and sugars every now and then. You may just be reminded that all of heaven is about the party – the celebration, the Marriage Supper of the Lamb. Kick your feet up on the table and loosen the belt. Let us begin closing the section with a final thought on a relevant parable – the party prepared for the prodigal son, once more in the provoking words of Robert Capon:

The fatted calf is actually the Christ-figure in this parable. Consider. What does a fatted calf do? It stands around in its stall with one purpose in life: to drop dead at a moment's notice in order that people can have a party. If that doesn't sound like the Lamb slain from the foundation of the world – who dies in Jesus and in all our deaths and who comes finally to the Supper of the Lamb as the pièce de résistance of his own wedding party – I don't know what does. The fatted calf proclaims that the party is what the Father's house is all about, just as Jesus the dead and risen Bridegroom proclaims that an eternal bash is what the universe is all about. Creation is not ultimately about religion, or spirituality, or morality, or reconciliation, or any other solemn subject; it's about God having a good time and just itching to share it. The solemn subjects – all the weird little bells, whistles, and exploding snappers we pay so much attention to – are there only because we are a bunch of dummies who have to be startled into having a good time. If ever once we woke up to the fact that God finally cares only about the party, then the solemn subjects would creep away like pussycats ... and the truly serious subjects would be brought on: robes, rings, shoes, wines, gold, crystal, and precious stones ("Finally! A little class in the act!").[46]

A Song for the Road

Now that we are eating, drinking and rambling off topic ... allow me to offer a final brief rabbit trail – a related addendum on the topic of *music and dance*. Music has also been in the crosshairs of Gnostic religiosity, because of the emotive sensuality it invokes. To this day, entire denominations like the Church of Christ do not even allow instruments in church! Music and dance have long been thought to inflame the *lower passions*. God is a creator, an artist, and He is fun.

---

[46] Robert Capon, *Kingdom, Grace, Judgment: Paradox, Outrage, and Vindication in the Parables of Jesus* (Wm. B. Eerdmans Publishing, 2002), 298.

MONEY. SEX. BEER. GOD.

Our Jewish roots are obviously filled with song and dance – consider the Psalms, David's ecstatic underwear dancing and his creation of musical instruments. Levites were paid to lead instrumental worship around the clock. Even Jesus is recorded as singing a hymn at the last supper (Matt. 26:30; Mark 14:26). But as Hellenistic dualism crept into the early church, leaders like Clement of Alexandria would warn that music is "evil" because the pagans used it. It was *wrong* to worship God with profane, material-world devices. Clement wrote off the entire orchestra of instruments found in the Psalms (drums, lyres, stringed instruments, cymbals, lutes, tambourines, harps etc.) by allegorizing them to represent all the parts of the body worshipping God.

By the late sixth century, Pope Gregory the Great unified a liturgical form of singing: the *Gregorian chant.* Now I love listening to chants, but would you not be bored spitless if that was the *only allowable* way to worship God? Sometimes I need some Felix Mendelssohn or Kurt Cobain. But the chant – this unaccompanied, droning, single-melody monophony – was the only permitted sacred song for roughly 400 years.

Eventually no women would be allowed to worship in song. No common people could worship. Only paid, male clergy were allowed to worship God with singing, and most often in Latin – a language that ordinary lay people did not even understand.

Nevertheless, humanity was created to create. The onslaught against music and creativity could not always be suppressed. Every fresh awakening in church history brought with it a new sound.

During the Reformation, we see that Martin Luther loved music. He differed from other reformers like John Calvin and Ulrich Zwingli who despised instrumental music in church – melting down pipe organs all over Europe. Luther played instruments, wrote songs and held a general love for art – even commissioning paintings as other reformers led revolts, vandalizing sacred art. While the Reformation was considered a step backward for art, this was not entirely the case. Luther wrote:

> *Music is a fair and lovely gift of God which has often wakened and moved me to the joy of preaching. St. Augustine was troubled in conscience whenever he caught himself delighting in music, which he took to be sinful. He was a choice spirit, and were he living today would agree with us. I have no use for*

180

cranks who despise music, because it is a gift of God. Music drives away the devil and makes people happy; they forget thereby all wrath, unchastity, arrogance, and the like. Next after theology I give to music the highest place and the greatest honor. I would not exchange what little I know of music for something great. Experience proves that next to the Word of God, only music deserves to be extolled as the mistress and governess of the feelings of the human heart. We know that to the devil music is distasteful and sufferable. My heart bubbles up and overflows in response to music, which has so often refreshed me and delivered me from dire plagues.[47]

Let us not forget classical composers like Bach, Handel and Haydn who viewed the creative expression of music as a gift of God. "The devil, the originator of sorrowful anxieties and restless troubles, flees before the sound of music almost as much as before the Word of God," said Luther. "Music is a gift and grace of God, not an invention of men. Thus it drives out the devil and makes people cheerful. Then one forgets all wrath, impurity, and other devices."

The First Great Awakening in the 1700s was marked by fresh sound as Charles Wesley composed more than 6,000 hymns. In 1882, William Booth, founder of the Salvation Army, was first credited with the phrase, "Why should the devil have all the best tunes?" Booth began to incorporate the popular bar tunes of his day into worship songs. Early pamphlets noted the Salvation Army "considers all music sacred when used with holy purpose." This was a radical step for the church.

The Sound of Awakening

Every awakening had its own innovative sound. Unfortunately today, religion has eviscerated the church of its creativity. Religion is a copy. Just as Moses received "shadows" or "copies" of heavenly realities with the law on Sinai, so has the church continued to revert to Sinai. Once the church stood as the creative art center of the community. But for the past several decades, Christian music simply copies the pop music of the day. Sure, it was an innovative idea for William Booth to baptize pop music. But today, the Christian music industry is simply obsessed with imitating true art, rather than pioneering it. Everyone

---

[47] Roland Blainton, *Here I Stand* (New York: Abingdon Press, 1950), 341.

wants to make their worship band sound like Coldplay (why not just listen to Coldplay, for God's sake?). So much of this revolves around a false divide between secular and sacred music. While I sometimes appreciate Christian music, I am more often disgusted when I hear it on the radio – the moment the radio scanner hits a Christian station, you can feel the creativity suck right out the car window. I can usually spot a Christian song by the first chord I hear (before a single lyric gives it away), because I can instantly smell the religion.

What if we got free from our dualisms between secular and sacred? We do not need to have a strained religious phrase inserted every other stanza. This is beyond just having better theology in our worship songs (which is paramount – there is a prevalent language of begging rather than celebrating grace in our songs. Musicians pull your heads out of the Psalms for a little while, and stick them into Paul's letters).

I am not saying we throw out hymns and just sing Elton John tunes. There is clearly a place for intentional worship songs. But what if we start to see that music itself – whether it has a Bible verse in it or not – can resound with the glory of God? One of the first things that struck me as a new believer was how Christian Contemporary Music (CCM) was absolutely hokey and talentless. Everyone was obviously trying so hard to be cool, yet the essence of creativity and innovative thinking did not exist there at all. I thought CCM was a joke, and I was ashamed of it. Did these Christian guys not know they had the most counter-culture message on the planet? Why were they making dorky imitations of mere secularism? Perhaps my biggest issue was the lack of authenticity. Christian music was not *real*. Forced and gimmicky. Initially I preferred chants and old hymns to CCM because at least it was original and unpretentious. Worship music has evolved greatly in the past 20 years, but it has a way to go.

Despite both the killjoys and the try-too-hards, the church actually has a rich history of creativity. Every form of modern music has its origins in the church. Every genre of rock and roll, jazz, blues, hip hop – it all stemmed out of Pentecostalism and black gospel music. Any musicologist can tell you that. Country and bluegrass stem from Scottish Presbyterian music in the Appalachians. There is no reason to continually imitate. We possess the divine Creator within us; and we should expect to pioneer new genres of music, art, science, math and cuisine (not just "Christian subculture versions"). We need less Christian artists and more artists who are Christians.

Perhaps this will happen like never before as we erase the false lines between secular and sacred. Yes God is transcendent. We need a liturgical focus of direct worship. But we must also see Him immanently in the natural order of things – incarnationally. Only then are our eyes opened to the wonder of the sacred in the everyday of life, and our spirituality can be expressed musically through the created order.

Besides a backward denomination or two in Arkansas, most Christians do not fully demonize music anymore. We do not assume anything with drums is pagan jungle music (though some circles sadly do). Nevertheless there are still fundamentalist folks who cannot listen to anything if it is not Maranatha Music. We still have these unnecessary dualisms in our head - we cannot just listen to music for what it is, and enjoy the talent with which God has blessed the artist. I am not saying we should be obsessed with sexually explicit lyrics, druggie stuff or depressed, rage-fueled lyrics. Even then, most of that kind of music lacks originality as well. It bores me. I can enjoy secular melodies without biting off the doctrine (I have had to do the same thing in church for years).

Yes, we can enjoy music without feeding off of ungodly worldviews. Everything you sing needs not be a hymn, but we should have eyes to see the glory of God even in our celebration of the natural realm. We can likewise produce God-glorifying, gospel-infused art that is not reduced to the graven image of religion or another Christian B movie. It will mean no longer copying forms and images; but really, authentically awakening to the creative image of Christ.

GOD.

The Roots of Dualistic Thinking

How can a pastor shag his secretary in the office, and an hour later offer a homily in the sanctuary? How can a Baptist get blind drunk at a tailgate party Saturday night, yet unequivocally *amen* the preacher's railing sermon against booze at 10 a.m. the next morning when his tail is in the pew? Why is God at the Wednesday night prayer group, but absent when shuffling through a stack of bills at the end of the month?

We must get to the root of our schizophrenic thinking that blinds us to God's presence. We divorce Him from areas of our real life: He exists in a place of theoretical, theological abstracts. The distant spirit in the sky whose disapproving gaze is glaring down on everything you do, but He is still somehow a *detached conceptual being*. In our sermons, discussions and seminaries we talk about Him in principle, analyzing and hypothesizing about Him as if He is not standing in the room. How many churches just teach, teach, teach irrelevant lectures ... then the congregation walks out the door, back to *life as normal* with no sense of a continuity between His presence and business as usual?

Our duplicitous thinking assumes there are a thousand darkened areas of our existence where God is not present. We do not realize that the split mindset that now pervades our Western culture is actually rooted in *pagan Greek philosophy*. So often, what is preached from our pulpits today is a version of Plato, Aristotle and Socrates ... not the Hebraic worldview presented in Jesus Christ. In fact, most of Christianity as we know it is a modified version of the ancient religion of *Neoplatonism*.

You need never have studied Plato – he has already influenced you in a thousand unbiblical, detrimental ways. His dualistic concept of a *separation between the physical and spiritual world* has vicariously entered our minds and hearts through our culture ... and unfortunately, through the church. The church was immersed in Greek/Hellenistic culture from the start. Our foundations went amiss just a few genera-tions after the first apostles. A schizophrenic wall was constructed be-tween God and the stained, fallen, physical world around us. But heaven and earth are an integrated, organic whole. The Hebrews knew

185

this. The gospel is all about *union.* Although "Saul was preaching boldly in the name of the Lord. And he spoke and disputed against the Hellenists," we sadly see that Greek/Hellenistic culture would be fully embraced by the church a short time later (Acts 9:28).

Deconstructing Plato

Plato (fifth-fourth century B.C.) is without question the author of Greek dualistic thought. In essence, his search for truth consisted of looking beyond the natural world to the unseen realm. For Plato, you could learn nothing of the truth by looking only at the physical environment. Observing a human, a tree or a horse was irrelevant. These material-world objects were mere *shadows* of unseen things that could not be understood apart from first grasping their underlying, invisible meaning. Beyond the physical, visible world (Plato considered the material world a mere illusion) lays a higher invisible dimension of reality. In this unseen dimension exists what Plato calls the *demiurge* (which Christians now call "God," but for Plato it was more of a primordial *force).*

From this demiurge came forth *ideas* (which Plato called "forms"). These *forms* may be defined as unseen principles, or invisible governing structures by which our material world is patterned in some fractured sense. Think of invisible principles that exist behind every visible thing. Behind the horse is the *idea* of a horse. Plato could never quite articulate how these unseen spiritual realities ever intersected or manifested into our tangible, physical world (he would not have used the word "spiritual" ... He is just talking about invisible concepts – *ideas).* There was never a real *connection* between ideas and reality. Plato did make an obscure, labored attempt at describing a third thing in his philosophy called "receptacles" which somehow transferred unseen ideas into our concrete, visible world (wherein the idea of a tree and the actual tree intersect). But essentially for Plato, there was a sharp division between "truth" and "perception." What we *perceive* in the natural world around us is not *truth.* Truth lies beyond the physical world ... in a realm of disconnected concepts or intangible unseen *forms.* Countless Christian thinkers have relied on Plato to define *truth* as an abstract, ineffable principle. *Truth* is a meat-and-bone incarnate Savior.

Plato divided a line between the seen and unseen that would last until now. *Ideas on one side and the real world on the other side.* The early church nearly baptized him as a saint (a pre-Christian of sorts). He is even painted all over the walls of the Vatican. The next major philosopher, Aristotle, would take major issue with Plato's "top-down" approach (Plato's teaching that the unseen must first be grasped in order to make any sense of the visible world). Aristotle instead argued a bottom-up approach: that invisible truth could only be comprehended by recognizing its blueprint in the tangible, material world around us. The only way to grasp the "idea" behind a tree or a behind a human was to study the tree or the human in order to make conclusions about what lay masked as the hidden meaning of them. The physical world, for Aristotle, had a spark of the unseen behind it, so it served as a signpost pointing us to higher invisible truths.

Granted these are rudimentary summations of Plato and Aristotle. I am admittedly no philosophy major. Never had a taste for it. But the point is not to analyze all their deductions … rather to show the underlying principle of dualism they put forward. Though these two men both took a different approach, the principle of a *separation* between the material and the unseen world was the bedrock cornerstone of their thought. Dualism would set the course of how Western humanity would think for thousands of years.

How often have you heard someone in church say, "We need to just get out of our heads a bit?" Well that is exactly the place to which we have relegated God … for us He has been reduced to *theory*. He does not intersect real life.

As a matter of fact, Greek philosophy is so important to the fabric of the church here in the Western world, that our catholic brothers are virtually required to get bachelor degrees in philosophy before they can ever begin to study the Bible in seminary. That means they are literally studying Plato, Nietzsche and Karl Marx long before they can start looking at Jesus Christ. And I am not just picking on the Catholics! Nearly every Protestant seminary is riddled with head-first Greco-rationalism. Lost in ideas, analysis, dissection and over-thinking everything rather than embracing the simple mystery of our tangible union with the Divine. The mind is great – but it gets divorced from matter.

Hello Paganism: Neoplatonism

Following Plato, later in the third century A.D., arose the tradition of metaphysical philosophy called *Neoplatonism* – a system based on

MONEY. SEX. BEER. GOD.

Platonic thought, but founded by Plotinus (204-270 A.D.) – which tried to describe how the universe fits together. This emerged as a *religion* based on Plato's dualistic concepts. In a nutshell, Neoplatonists believed that spiritual-like outer regions surrounded our physical world.

Beyond the rock and dirt of our planet lies layers of *ethos* – and far out beyond these unseen, ethereal layers was the *pure good* or *God*. This *One* is utterly detached from our world. Neoplatonism developed a concept that our world was once in a former transcendent spiritual state, but it fell down to the current physical world we now live in. *Matter*, in a sense, is a fallen degraded state from what was once pure spirituality. And of course, by a process of purification (all religions love steps to purification) exists the possibility of returning to that former exalted ethereal state. This philosophy radically influenced Christianity, Islam and Judaism.

Throughout Western church history was this prevailing myth that God is "out there" somewhere. At best there is a container mentality – physical container with spiritual substance. But your body and spirit are still *separate*. Your body is clearly nowhere close to God! Like the deists, they believed God sits out beyond the ethos separate from the physical earthly realm. He set the world in motion to run on mechanical principles; but He is not interactive, or engaged – nowhere close to it. Out in the unseen dimensions is the demiurge, ideas, concepts, intangible truths ... the inapproachable *God*.

The Soul

Just to make this a little more practical for you ... Plato has directly affected the way we think of *body, soul* and *spirit* today. Most Christians think their own human spirit is "positionally" perfect thanks to Jesus, in some abstract way. But their soul is still sinful, and their body is *extremely* wretched. This is a pagan idea. Plato ... not the gospel.

The very idea that mankind is a *tripartite* being made up of three parts (*body, soul and spirit)* is a Greek, not Hebraic idea. In fact, even in the historical church, most have simply believed we are *bipartite* (we have a visible and invisible part). Whether we have two or three parts is ab-

188

This diagram shows the dualistic worldview of Neoplatonism.

solutely irrelevant to me. Why? Because the apostles never gave one single teaching on it in the New Testament. If it had one ounce of relevance, you would figure they would have discussed it at least once.[1]

---

[1] [Notes from my book *Mystical Union: Stuff They Never Told You About the Finished Work of the Cross* (Portland: Sons of Thunder Ministries & Publications, 2010), available at www.JohnCrowder.net] There is only one scripture that could remotely indicate that man is a tripartite being, made up of three parts: spirit, soul and body.

May God Himself, the God of peace, sanctify you through and through. May your whole spirit, soul and body be kept blameless at the coming of our Lord Jesus Christ. The one who calls you is faithful and He will do it (1 Thess. 5:23-24 NIV).

Footnote continued:

Paul is not going into a big clinical dissection of the human composition here. It is simply a closing benediction at the very end of his letter. This term "spirit, soul and body" should be taken loosely as to indicate the *entire being* (i.e. "Farewell folks! God has blessed your whole being!"). In the same way, Christ spoke of loving God with all your *soul, mind, heart and strength*. He did not intend to make a strict vivisection of the human into four unique parts. He just meant to love God with your *entire being* (Luke 10:27; Matt. 22:37).

The problems with 1 Thess. 5:23-24 are many. Some translations, like the one above, insert the word "may" as if to indicate this is a request ("Lord please clean us up!"). But the word is not found in the Greek. Sounds like a prayer for something that hasn't happened yet, doesn't it? Also, the word for "sanctify" here is aorist, meaning you cannot honestly specify whether it is repeated, continuous, instantaneous, past or accomplished. In other words, this verse in no way indicates that your sanctification is an ongoing process. It could very well just say, "God sanctifies." In addition, Paul is not speaking to an individual "you" composed of three parts. He does not suggest that each part of "you" needs to be saved. He is speaking corporately to "you all" (*umas*), the same Greek word Jesus used when He said, "Come after me, and I will make you fishers of men" (Matt. 4:19). Paul is closing a letter to the corporate group.

Finally, Paul speaks of God *preserving* you. This is the real kicker that knocks the dirty soul idea out of the bucket. The word "be preserved" or *tereo* indicates that something has *already taken place* on this side of Christ's return. Perfection is not coming, but has already been given. Therefore it is preserved. You do not preserve something that you do not already have. Furthermore, Paul says it is *God* who guards over it until the end, not you.

After correcting all of these misconceptions, I feel that it actually says something along these lines:

> *And Himself, the God of peace, is the one who sets all of you apart completely. Your whole spirit, soul and body is preserved blameless until the coming of our Lord Jesus Christ. The one who calls you is faithful and He will preserve you.*

This is a verse that affirms perfection not filthiness! God did not just cover your sins; He erased *sinfulness* from you. Jesus saved *you*. Not some invisible, hidden, intangible part of you. He saved you completely. A complete sacrifice for a complete salvation.

Unfortunately, we have in this case a massive theological paradigm forming around a single verse of scripture. Whether we have three clinically delineated

---

Footnote continued:

parts, I do not really know. If the apostles thought this an important subject, they would have mentioned it once. Paul does say the word is able to "divide spirit and soul," but he says that in a poetic, allegorical sense, not a theological one (Heb. 4:12). The traditional view held by the majority of Christians world-wide – both past and present – is that man is a *bipartite* creature made of only two components: material (body/flesh) and spiritual (soul/spirit).

The danger does not come so much from building a theology on one single verse (although that is dangerous enough). The danger comes from building yet *another* theology *on top* of the theology that was built on the single verse: *Now that I believe I am three parts, I will further believe that salvation only applies to only one of those parts. My spirit is the holy part, my soul is dirty and my body is way down the ladder!*

Over time, we have built an entire system on this little verse that is like a crumbling, inverted pyramid. It is bound to fall over. What if the human personhood is far more complex than one, two, three or even a thousand parts? Just as the human body is made anatomically of innumerable parts, what if the unseen part of you is equally as intricate? Luke 17:21 says you have the entire kingdom within you. The Bridegroom calls you as beautiful as Tirzah – saying you are like an entire *City of Delight* (Song. 6:4). Zechariah speaks typologically of you, the New Jerusalem, saying you are so expansive that you are like a city without walls (Zech. 2:2-4). What if the inside of you is far bigger than the outside? The unseen realm may be vastly different than we have supposed. Adam Clarke says that a believer is a "little world in himself."

To say that one's perfection applies only to the "spirit man" while attesting that the soul is still dirty and in need of purging, presents a number of problems. Foremost, is the quandary that the spirit and soul are *still conjoined*. Even a tripartite theologian would not utterly cut off the spirit from the soul – just as to split the bone from marrow would indisputably result in the death of a man. For a man to be alive, his soul and spirit must surely be intertwined just as the soul and body are intrinsically connected. A body without a spirit is a corpse. A soul without a body is a specter. Assuming hypothetically then that our soul and spirit are two parts, but indeed interconnected, how then would light dwell within the confines of darkness? Is a spirit truly pure if it is still connected to a filthy soul? Is truth really truth when it is laced with error? How would sweet water be couched in a poisoned vessel? The demarcation of spirit, soul and body does not seem to be the intent of the Apostle Paul, else he would have focused more thoroughly and coherently on the subject. Paul was a masterful logician and would not have left such an important subject veiled, if indeed it was so important to compartmentalize the inner man.

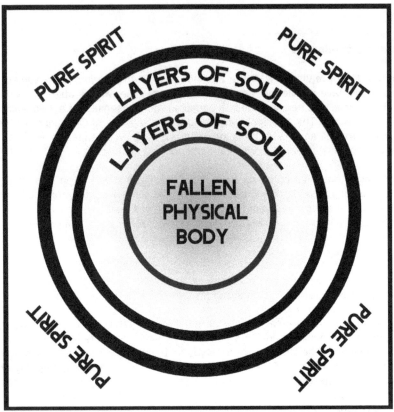

This diagram shows a commonly held modern view of body, soul and spirit in the church, influenced by Neoplatonism.

The tripartite concept (as it is taught today) is directly linked to Neoplatonic ideas. There is your fallen physical "body;" your perfect, bloodwashed intangible unseen "spirit" … and then the intermediary layers of "soul" in between the two. Many evangelicals and charismatics love to spout that your *spirit* is holy thanks to Christ's salvation, but your *soul* is still in need of continual, lifelong work. Here religion has a field day putting you on the treadmill of "sanctification" processes to clean up your soul. Inner healing and deliverance programs are all about purging the soul. Guru therapists have developed involved programs for soul cleansing, with reams of charts that diagnose all sorts of obscure imaginary "soulish" problems or demonic influences that will require extrication. In fact, the word *soulish* is even a dirty word today, is it not? Why do you think that is? The soul is essentially *unclean* for

192

most Christians – because it is the buffer between their dirty body and perfect spirit. It is like a coffee filter or something.

Christians love the term *positional* to describe their holiness. It keeps our righteousness abstract and clinically untouchable. But we have a fallen, material, sinful *body*. Somehow the *soul* is this fuzzy intermediary between the two. The middle agent that is too intertwined with our flesh to be deemed *perfect*. Remember, Neoplatonism cemented this idea of a physical world that is surrounded by layers of ethos – intangible regions – and far beyond those unseen layers is the *greater good/God*. This tiered system correlates perfectly to their Gnostic demonology as well – all sorts of powers and dark principalities must be battled and cleaned up at every level until you *arrive*. The *process* of sanctification is generally synonymous to killing off the soulish appetites (i.e. climbing the Neoplatonic layers to God).

A Holistic Holiness

People who hold to this "dirty soul/clean spirit" concept have scant Bible to back it up. It puts your "spirit" somewhere out in an unreachable realm you will never touch, taste or handle in reality. They love ideas like *imputed* righteousness – where you are, again, *technically* holy, but it will take a long time (think your whole life) to *appropriate* any of it into your soul. In empirical reality, you will always be a dirty soulish person until you die. So death will save you from sin, not Jesus Christ. The material *body* has to die.

The fact of the matter: you are in a very present, active, living union with God thanks to the incarnation, life and death of Jesus. You are completely liberated from sin. You are perfect – body, soul, spirit or whatever else you may consist of – whether you know it or not. Nothing holds you back from being the good little boy or girl that you are. You do not have to sin another day in your life!

In fact, throughout the Old and New Testament, the words "spirit" and "soul" are used *interchangeably*. It is the religious mind that has tried to carve them apart. Sanctification is not a process of lifelong soul cleansing. Christ accomplished sanctification singlehandedly. You were co-crucified with Him; you were completely severed from your old sinful nature (Rom. 6:6, Gal. 2:20, Col. 2:11, Col. 3:3, Gal. 5:24, 2 Cor. 5:14). But if the soul is just as clean as the rest of you, this has a devastating effect to our old-school notion of co-dependent priestcraft in the church and puts religious self-improvement programs out of business. It cripples the antichrist religious system of saving oneself and climbing a ladder of self-effort. It is so radically scandalous in today's Christian world to suggest someone is perfect thanks to Jesus that I would recommend for further reading my book *Mystical Union: Stuff They Never Told you About the Finished Work of the Cross*. It boggles me that the church has arrived at a position today in which the perfection of the believer and our union with Christ are considered heresies.

The Greek verb "to sanctify" does not mean to "purge and purify over a period of time." The word *hagiazo* simply means to "set apart" or to "make separate for God."[2] Thanks to Jesus, you were fully set apart for God. Sanctification is not a process. It is a *Person*.

> And because of Him you are in **Christ Jesus, who became** to us wisdom from God, righteousness and **sanctification** and redemption (1 Cor. 1:30, ESV).

He is your sanctification. Any system that tries to draw your attention away from the person of Christ and onto your own efforts is anti-gospel in nature. Of course we are *growing* and *maturing* and waking up to the truth of our perfection – learning to act like it – but we are not *becoming* holy as if Jesus' work was insufficient to accomplish that. Your union with God is not an incomplete relationship that comes progressively. Time is not the magic formula that makes you holy. Death is not the final thing that will make you holy. Jesus' sacrifice made you holy through and through. People who are adamant that we are tripartite (who knows, maybe we are?) insist we must have three parts (body, soul, spirit) as it reflects the Trinity: Father, Son and Spirit. I have no problem with that … just tell me which two parts of the Trinity are still sinful and in need of sanctification?

To say your soul is perfect thanks to the finished work of the cross is not to say every thought or feeling you have – or every action you do – is perfect or inspired by God! That is because we are still waking up by faith to the fact that – from His perspective – we really are pure. But

---

2 James Strong, *Exhaustive Concordance of the Bible* (Nashville: Abingdon, 1890), Entry G37.

the fact is still a fact. This is the identity out of which we live and find liberty. It is not just some legal, abstract "position." It is reality.

It may help us to follow the progression of how these Platonic dualisms evolved over time in the church. We need not address every tiring, detailed intricacy of every ancient philosophy that lends itself to the overall problem. A multitude of philosophical systems have developed with their own flavors of dualism. I will not bore you with the minutia of every one. Instead, I will only point out a few primary examples of certain men and ideas that have shaped *your* way of thinking (whether you knew it or not) because they molded our worldview. Perhaps this will help us *change our minds* about God's nearness and love for His creation – including the corporeal world around us.

Stoicism & Quietism

From the beginning, Platonic philosophies had a radical effect on our concept of human *emotion* and *feeling* – the unseen parts of us that are most commonly associated with the soul. Again, in dualistic Christianity the soul is considered the *unseen* part of us that is most closely associated with the *physical* body (Western Christians say your soul is comprised of the mind, will and emotions – all *tangible-world* attributes and therefore tainted ones). So emotions and feeling have been considered impure or unclean throughout much of church history.

If we revisit the era of Plato, there is another Greek figure worth mentioning: a philosopher named Zeno (490-430 B.C.), the founder *Stoicism*. To be *Stoic*, as the term is used today, is to essentially be cold and emotionless. The parallel should not be difficult to recognize here: *kill off the soulish emotions.* Stoicism has infected much of Christianity throughout the centuries and still thrives today, as the emotions are considered part of the lower, base soulish life and therefore *unspiritual.* Christianity has often been viewed as a suicide club in which we attempt to rid ourselves of any earthly passions whatsoever. To this day, just tapping your foot to a hymn on Sunday can raise eyebrows in some congregations ... *you're getting too emotional.*

Stoicism was rooted in a type of dualistic *fatalism* (fate is determined by an untouchable God, so just give up and go with the flow). For the Stoic, there is no real interaction between God/the gods with our physical earthly existence down here. We are tossed about by the whim of fate. The gods are in charge, and there is nothing we can do about it. It was a hyper version of sovereignty that tells us just to accept our lot in life. The best thing we can do is to numb down the emotions and accept whatever comes our way. If you are a plow ox, you can complain and moan about it, but you cannot change your lot in life. You will still be forced to work the field. So just stop whining and kicking against the yoke. Don't feel. Desensitize.

In the Christian world, the phrase "be content" is a way to pawn off the idea, "Accept your lot in life and stop dreaming." You cannot change anything, so just settle down and become dispassionate. Do not get too excited or upset. Do not *enjoy* too much. Sit still, shut up in church and dull down. This system of pagan belief was adopted full throttle without reservation in the Christian philosophy of *Quietism.* Quietists thought that man's perfection was found in self-annihilation, particularly through abandoning the will altogether and accepting things the way they are without any attempt at changing them. Be a drone.

How many Christians today, when they face the slightest little speed bump on the road to some goal resort to the thought, "Well, I guess God is closing that door." This quietist fatalism just wants you to passively drop over and let life kick you around.

Furthermore, the gross lumping together of all emotion with the *lower nature* lends us to reject all that is authentically human. Plato made a distinction between two parts of a man: the *reason* (the mind and its capacity for thinking) and *passion* (including the emotions). He concluded that the reason was the supreme part of our nature, which should subdue the lower parts – the feelings and emotions (for a Christian, let us substitute Plato's *reason* and *passion* for the Christian terms *spirit* and *soul.* "Your spirit man must rule your soul!"). Plato's ideas carried over to perhaps the next most influential philosopher in history, René Descartes, who believed that the emotions actually originated in the body as products of bodily organs. He bought into the same general belief of Plato, that the *reason* is our highest human mechanism. These "physical" emotional drives could overcome a person he said, and override their rational control ... the emotional life is considered suspect at best.

It is no wonder – with the improper division of *reason* and *emotion* – that the church is falsely divided between two traditions: the more theologically oriented streams (thinkers) and the more emotive, charismatic type streams (feelers). Mind and heart should not be divorced.

Devoid of Feeling

Scottish philosopher David Hume, in the eighteenth century, further resonated the ideas of René Descartes, saying that emotions had their origins in the physical body. By the time Charles Darwin came on the scene, he wrote that emotions were leftover remnants from ancient animalistic behaviors. Again, there was a higher appeal toward reason, and a call to quench the inferior, emotive "passions."

Sigmund Freud and other early psychologists followed this theme of relegating emotions to bodily origin, connected to the nervous system, which were lower and separate from the higher plane of reason.

In his book *Feel*, Christian writer Matthew Elliott points out how this negative view of emotions infiltrated New Testament scholarship. "These ideas about emotion were very much in line with what I had learned from pastors and writers and teachers in the Christian culture in which I'd grown up," writes Elliott. "Sure, preachers today are more modern than Descartes – they don't claim that emotions are generated from bodily organs or blood – yet they still view the emotions with some level of suspicion or concern." [3]

Elliott began researching the titles of some of the most popular Christian books on the market today written about emotions. The titles themselves were very revealing, echoing more of Plato than the Bible:

Deadly Emotions
Managing Your Emotions: Instead of Your Emotions Managing You
A Woman's Forbidden Emotion
Emotions: Can You Trust Them?
Those Ugly Emotions
Winning Over Your Emotions

"The most common statement I read in these books was that the 'love' Jesus commanded was not a feeling. Yet, as I read on and on into

---

[3] Matthew Elliott, *Feel: The Power of Listening to Your Heart* (Tyndale House, 2008), 15.

what had been written by theologians – hundreds of books and articles, and finally a thousand – I could never find a single argument that rested on the Bible itself that said love or joy were not feelings. Mostly it was just stated as fact," adds Elliott. "It seemed to me as if many Christian teachers and preachers today were resorting to some extraordinary word tricks to avoid the suggestion that what the Bible says about love, joy, hope and other emotions is really something we are supposed to feel." [4] How often have you heard some dry-as-a-camel's-knuckle preacher try to tell you that joy is *internal,* but that does not mean we can expect to feel it and be *happy?*

If you are in a good mood, you should let your face know about it every now and then. There is no such thing as unhappy joy.

The church has taught us that emotions and feelings are unreliable as indicators of truth, and so we are conditioned to believe they are trivial and useless, if not outright dangerous. Immanuel Kant, the stoic philosopher, taught that doing the *action of love* was important, even if the feeling of love was not present. One must focus on duty and not get caught up in emotion. The rational intention reigned supreme. This is the same, unchristian worldview that is taught as a staple from pulpits all around the world. Even staid reformer John Calvin admitted, "Duties … are not fulfilled by the mere discharge of them, though none be omitted, unless it is done from a pure feeling of love." [5]

Consider again the theology of the *deists,* which came about during the Age of Enlightenment in the seventeenth and eighteenth centuries (a time when reason and philosophy were exalted over faith). Remember from history class, America's founding fathers had roots in Deism. The "outer space" God who is *over there*; He is distant, aloof and detached from the material world. He made the world and set it into motion through mechanical laws. The Deists rejected supernatural events, miracles, incarnation, the Trinity, the inspiration of scripture – any direct interaction between God and the real world around us. They believed that *reason* based on material world observation was the only way to determine anything about God's existence. That is Aristotelian.

---

[4] Ibid., 16, 18.

[5] John Calvin, *Institutes of the Christian Religion,* translated by Henry Beveridge (Grand Rapids: Eerdmans, 1989).

Dualism in Science

Let us step outside of church for a minute and into the halls of science. This bad theology spilled over into the worldview of men like Isaac Newton. Newton's understanding of physical laws – which shaped all of science – has the inherently flawed notion of a separation between the physical and spiritual world. Helpful as they were for bringing us out of a magically superstitious and primitive mindset (and although Newton was a Christian), his thought unfortunately denies the mystical, ongoing interaction between Creator and creation.

Consider the bifurcation of the *scientific method*: on one side of the coin you have the idea/theory/concept (invisible world stuff) – and on the other side, you work it out separately in the physical observation of the laboratory (material world stuff). Idea is separate from reality. Unseen and separate from the visible. Eventually, God was written off by the sciences altogether. It became strictly about material world observation and the detached concept of *theory*. In fact, atheism has become the predominant underlying theory of science!

But even in the arena of science, we are starting to realize there is really no separation between the visible and invisible. With Albert Einstein and the subsequent advent of quantum physics, the idea of a strictly natural, observable universe run by a set of predictable mechanical laws was blown out of the water. The spirit realm and natural realm are intertwined. Scientists have begun to observe the bending of time and space, worm holes, black holes – quantum mechanical phenomena that show "reality" is unexplainable yet interconnected beyond our wildest imagination. Certain studies even show an *observer effect*, where particles react differently depending on whether or not they are being observed!

Natural laws that seemed to be "fixed" do not appear so anymore. Millions of proofs have shown an unknown but very real relation between particles in the universe. One of the most amazing discoveries is that everything in the entire universe is an entangled system that is interconnected. For instance, take two small particles that are "entangled" from the same source and observe them separately – no matter how far apart they are (put one in Times Square and the other on Saturn) – if you turn one particle, the other particle will turn simultaneously. The space between them is irrelevant – they move in unison faster than the speed of light. They are somehow united. This proven principle shows all our ideas of spatial separation could be mere *illusion*. Could it also say something of our union with God that is closer than time and space could ever fathom?

Christ holds everything together. The world was made through Him and is sustained by Him. Another interesting development conceived by Einstein is that light permeates everything and exists as the *only constant*. Light and matter are *connected*. There is no separation. What does this tell us about the True Light of the world? Einstein signaled a shift in thought from a mechanical, observable universe to a relational dynamic field structure. Time, space and matter can all bend like putty and fluctuate based on the speed of light. If time is relative – then we can literally exist in the past, present and future simultaneously. But furthermore, there is no *delay* in our union with God. We are in Him right now, whether we see it, feel it or even believe it.

Now I am no expert in this field and do not intend on giving you a science lesson – but what does this indicate about our faulty cosmological notions that God is separate from earth and matter? That God is over there, but the universe is over here? That we are grounded, but He is up in some incorporeal heaven? Heaven is in one direction, but hell is in another direction? Even the idea that hell is "separation from God" is nowhere in the scripture. Yes, there is the parable of Lazarus in which there is a "great divide" (Luke 16) but everyone on both sides is still *in Christ*. All of creation is in Him (Col. 1:17). Even those in the lake of fire in Revelation 14 are still "in the presence of the Lamb and His holy angels" (Rev. 14:10). Again, David said, "If I go to the depths of hell, there you are!" (Ps. 139:8).

The inherent interconnection between God and humanity that exists in the fabric of Jesus' identity as the God-man is seamless and more solid than reality itself. *In Him all things hold together.* Religion – the attempt to approach or set ourselves right with God on our own – is a joke. Dr. C. Baxter Kruger notes: We do not make Him part of our lives; Jesus has already made us part of His. Heaven and earth have been permanently united in the incarnation of Jesus Christ.

200

MONEY. SEX. BEER. GOD.

All things came into being by Him, and apart from Him nothing came into being that has come into being (John 1:3, NASB[6]).

Everything came spilling out of Him, and it all exists in the fabric of who He is. A long country walk. Reading in the garden. Eating out. Camping. Riding your bike. Sunbathing. Doing pottery. Cooking barbecue. Swimming. Hiking. Having a pint at the pub. Bird Watching. Board games.

He is Everywhere

I could not scratch the surface of what the incarnation means to the cosmos. It is not just that God was bound up in the humanity of Christ. But in the humanity of Christ, the entire created order was bound to God! He permeates all creation. The dividing lines of God as *here or there* have disappeared. Dualistic separations of "sacred" and "secular" dimensions of our lives are utter nonsense. Kruger writes:

> *What part of creation has come into being behind the back of Jesus? And what part of creation manages to continue to be without Him? What part of creation is not included in His relationship with His Father and the Holy Spirit? The ultimate dualistic disaster is ripping the Father, Son and Spirit apart, such that we could possibly encounter one without the other. Given the beautiful and utter oneness of the Trinity, the fact that the Son is the Creator and sustainer of all things means that He has a relationship with all creation, and in Him so do the Father and the Holy Spirit. What part of our human experience is therefore 'secular,' without Jesus, devoid of the life of the Father, Son and Spirit? Motherhood? Work? Play? Romance? Gardening, golf, teaching, doctoring, governing, loving our neighbors?[7]*

Attempting to bridge this gap on our own (between the life of the Trinity and our human existence) is the definition of religious idiocy. It is impossible to "get the Spirit into people." Only the incarnation, death and resurrection of the Son of God was capable of achieving such a mas-

---

[6] *New American Standard Bible* (La Habra, Ca.: The Lockman Foundation, 1977).

[7] C. Baxter Kruger, "Dualisms and the Holy Spirit." (June 19, 2009) http://baxterkruger.blogspot.com

sive task of uniting humanity with Holy Spirit. Unweaving you from His presence is as impossible as unweaving the Father from the Son. But we must also see that God has woven the "ordinary" business of our natural lives into the fabric of His existence. There is no separation. Kruger says, "It seems to me that we are giving ourselves far too much credit, assuming that 'ordinary' things like laughter, fellowship, caring, working, giving ourselves for others, being parents, making music, creating things are simply 'human' and have no Jesus or any Holy Spirit in them. Our dualisms have blinded us, and we don't even know it."[8]

Eastern Thought

Our Eastern brothers – such as the Eastern Orthodox Church – never embraced the dualistic perception that God was "over there" or "in the church building" or that parts of our lives somehow occur *outside* of His presence. Over the centuries Greek Platonic thought did not influence them to such a degree. For them, God holds all things together; and all things are sustained in Him. He truly exists in all and through all. The natural and spiritual life were never intended to be partitioned off from one another. Orthodox believers do not even think of a difference between *natural* and *supernatural*.

In our separation thinking, we (especially charismatics) believe we must somehow *grab hold* of the supernatural. But where is the line between miracle and the ordinary? Your eyeball is a crazy, intricate work of God. So are dolphins and dandelions and bumblebees. To the Eastern mind, everything comes from the hand of God. The fact that a tree grows out of the ground speaks of God's divine hand weaving it together. Trillions of seeds die and come alive again across planet earth every day, while scientists cannot even create life in a laboratory. His miraculous life permeates the natural order. The fact that every molecule in our bodies is held in perfect cohesion, and the synapses and neurons in our brains remember things we learned in second grade ... *all God's doing*. All the atoms in the room, car, plane, train or park in which you now sit reading this book are bound together in perfect cohesion – they do not just fly off and disperse into space dust. The Eastern mind sees the miraculous work of God in the midst of it all. But we miss God in the mundane – in the ordinary. Church people even ignore their families for some *higher* spiritual cause. Our dualisms blind

---

[8] *Ibid.*

us to the glory that envelops us in the natural order and in human relationships. To the Eastern mind, all of this is "supernatural." It is just that some unique things (like walking on water) happen more infrequently. Such perspective should infuse us with vivid inspiration in our day-to-day life because every breath is intrinsically dependent upon His divine sustenance. He is immanently infused throughout creation.

"Only miracle is plain," writes Robert Capon, "it is in the ordinary that groans with the weight of glory."[9]

Jesus is Still a Human

In the incarnation, Jesus came not only to impart His divinity but also to endorse our humanity. He values our humanity far more than we do. Interestingly, tons of Christians think the incarnation was only *temporary*. The incarnation of Jesus Christ is a permanent state of being. He has forever determined not to be God apart from humanity; in the incarnation, God has forever identified Himself with the human race. Upon His ascension into heaven, Jesus did not just become smoke in the sky – He is not an ethereal pastel Christian bookstore cupid on a cloud. Jesus Christ is still a human. The same flesh and bone that walked Nazareth. A *glorified* man, but still a real human being nonetheless.

> *This Jesus, who was taken up from you into heaven, will come in the same way as you saw Him go into heaven* (Acts 1:11, ESV).

> *There is one God, and there is one mediator between God and men, the **man** Christ Jesus* (1 Tim. 2:5, ESV).

Jesus has a meat sack, just like you and I. One day you will touch Him with His skin on. Christ's humanity was no mere shell of flesh that He rented for a temporary amount of time. God has incorporated human nature into His eternal being; and in the incarnation, humanity has been permanently brought into the Godhead. Jesus acquired an identity in the virgin conception that He will retain ad infinitum. That humanity was not discarded or dissolved away. He will always exist as a glori-

---

[9] Fr. Robert Capon, *Supper of the Lamb: A Culinary Reflection* (New York: Doubleday & Co., 1969).

fied man and almighty God simultaneously. At the ascension of Christ, He was not deified; He was glorified (i.e. He did not *become* God. He was always God, even before He became flesh. But He still retains His body in a glorified way).

Jesus did not rent out a body of flesh for a period of time, just to overcome it and teach you how to disregard your own human existence. When you die you will not become an invisible angel. The big "R-word" in Christianity is not Rapture … it is *Resurrection*. We will somehow, some way be raised from the dead with corporeal, glorified bodies. Jesus did not die to free us from matter, but to redeem it.

Your Flesh is Good

This should tell us there is absolutely nothing wrong with our flesh. To think your body is dirty is absolutely Gnostic. Part of the problem in the church is that we lack a basic definition of the word *flesh*. This is a source of confusion for many, not only because of messy Christian clichés, but because the Greek word "sarx" is used in *two separate ways* in the New Testament.

Used in one sense, *flesh* is simply your physical body. There is absolutely *nothing* wrong with your body. Your body is just sinews, muscles, and ligaments (and for some of us, copious amounts of cellulite). It is not evil. In fact it is part of creation, which God calls *good.* It is merely a physical, material vehicle that is driven by the one who owns it. It is a serious perversion even to suggest that your physical body is wicked. Your body is a temple of the Holy Spirit, bought at a high price (1 Cor. 6:19-20). Your bodily members are instruments of righteousness (Rom. 6:13).

So if our physical bodies are not evil, then why does the *flesh* get a bad rap? *Sarx* is sometimes used in an allegorical, negative sense to indicate the "lusts of the flesh." This second New Testament usage simply refers to the old *naughty self.* The "bad flesh" is not your body. It is defined as the *carnal nature with its appetites and its bodily lusts.* The term is synonymous with the *sinful nature* or the *old man.* It is the old, self-seeking existence that died with Christ – as a believer you should believe that you do not have an old *fleshly nature* anymore.

All of the ridiculous sermons you hear about battling the flesh are usually complete drivel. You died with Christ. The old is gone the new has come. It is a myth that you must "overcome your flesh." This is messy, non-gospel language.[10]

Nevertheless, in using the term *sarx*, the Gospel writers imply all that this term entails. Jesus stepped into our *broken* humanity. This is not to say He was a sinner. But to coin the term of Dr. Peter Leithart, Christ stepped into our *dilapidated* condition. He stepped into our humanity as "under the law" born of a woman and therefore "under a curse." He fully empathizes with us in every way.

Docetism's Spooky Jesus

I want to briefly return now to a Gnostic heresy we mentioned earlier called *Docetism*. It is the idea that Christ only *appeared* to be human, but that He was not really flesh (just a spirit being with no real human body). St. Jerome was not kidding when he said, "While the apostles were still surviving, while Christ's blood was still fresh in Judea, the Lord's body was asserted to be but a phantasm."[11]

One of the early Docetic heretics was a former Christian bishop named Marcion (85-160 A.D.). He argued that Jesus was a divine spirit appearing to human beings in the shape of a human form, but not a man in a true physical body. For Christ to have humbled Himself and taken on real flesh was a disgusting notion for Gnostics. For them, salvation lies in turning away from the physical world. Thus Marcion taught the sufferings of Christ were *apparent* and not real. Furthermore, they said that after the crucifixion Jesus appeared in a *spiritual* body.

Gnosticism began to spread like gangrene. In fact, Gnosticism was already present in seed form among Second Temple Jews who had likely been Hellenized with Greek thought (or possibly by Babylonian or Persian influence. Plato only cemented and popularized dualism, but anti-material worldviews preceded him) for a few hundred years before

---

[10] [Notes from my book *Mystical Union, Ibid.*] Most churchgoers are duped into believing that there is a constant war waging within the individual Christian between the Holy Spirit and the "lusts of the flesh." Because they have misread Romans 7, it is no wonder that they also misread Galatians 5.

[11] Jerome, *The Dialogue Against the Luciferians*, 23.

Christ. Jewish sects like the Essenes were into heavy asceticism. Even take a look at John the Baptist to see an example of the common assumption that piety equated rejecting all creaturely comforts. How scandalous for Jesus and His disciples to come "wining and dining" in that cultural context! But know for certain Gnosticism was not a Hebraic mindset. Wherever it originated, it clearly thrived in a worldview of Greek dualism that blanketed the Mediterranean by the first century.

As I told you, Gnosticism is now a very loose term thrown around haphazardly among theologians (a term for anything that calls the natural order *evil*). As a polemical epithet, just about every heresy was labeled "Gnosticism." Another term that was equally thrown around was *Manichaeism*. This was originally a hodgepodge religion based on the Persian prophet Mani (216–276 A.D.) that combined elements of Christianity, Gnosticism, Zoroastrianism and Neoplatonism. It held to the same dualistic belief that the physical world was fallen and evil.

Gnosticism, Manichaeism and Docetism came to represent almost the same thing. Matter was evil, and Jesus could not have been a real human. Gnostics had many more specific beliefs, including reams of intricate charts detailing layers of angelic and demonic principalities (not unlike charismatic Christians today). But we are mostly concerned with their primary bias against created matter. This formed the DNA of almost every skewed doctrine, and on this point, these heresies essentially blur together. Foundationally, they all reject the humanity of God.

Is it no wonder the early church began to see the importance of figuring out *who is Jesus?* The issue of *Christology* (the study of the nature and person of Jesus) would quickly stand out as the utmost issue of importance in the first few centuries. With every heresy attacking it, the *incarnation* must come to the forefront. If the church could nail this down, then the gospel itself would be preserved for future generations.

Christology: Who is Jesus?

The early fathers arrived at an understanding of Christology through a complex process of debate, discussion and deliberation in the first five centuries of the church. It would be flippant to blow off their conclusions as "manmade ideas" just because we watched a special on Gnosticism on the History Channel and want to give the old heresy another shot. The fathers thought Christology was the most important,

206

vital aspect of all doctrine. They may not have formed consensus on other doctrines (like atonement, sanctification or the work of the Spirit – although these are by no means small or irrelevant matters), the early church was focused more than anything on the question of *who or what Christ was*. How is He different from ordinary humans? Was He just some divine entity that appeared human? A spiritual or angelic being? An enlightened man who showed us how to be "fully realized" spiritual people? Or is He both God and man in the same person? Not just a hybrid of the two – but fully God and fully man together in one.

Is this not still the core challenge today with every New Age philosophy and cult on the planet? It all comes down to: *who is Jesus?*

Such a matter of the incarnation is quite a mystery because it presents seeming contradictions. He is both omnipotent yet impotent, omniscient yet limited in His knowledge – omnipresent yet contained within a human frame.

See the early church fathers did not think of doctrinal matters like *atonement* or *salvation* as separable concepts that could be carved away from the person of Jesus. In fact His *work* on the cross and His *person* in the incarnation were considered two aspects of one same seamless whole. His incarnation as the God man was part of His saving act that culminated at the cross and resurrection. Everything else flows from who He is. Figure out who Jesus is, and the rest of the details will ultimately fall into place.

The only other topic on which the early church spent remotely as much time or importance was defining a doctrine of the Trinity. Because it also intrinsically deals with the nature of who God is. Holy Spirit did not become incarnate. The Father did not become incarnate. Jesus is an eternal person within the Godhead. He was not just a remarkable human filled with the Spirit. The Spirit and Father both testify of Jesus being the incarnate Son of God. The Trinity is three persons of one essence ... these are foundational and eternal truths that have merited countless volumes and libraries of revelation.

The church fathers saw these two important topics, the *incarnation* and the *Trinity*, being continually challenged.[12] So Christology and the relation between Father, Son and Spirit became their primary focus. Modern critics point out the political maneuvering among church leaders in those early Christological debates – they were bitter, petty at times and many men were misunderstood or misrepresented. We cannot deny the politics (has there ever been an elder board meeting without infighting?). But a conclusion can be right even if arguments and posturing are going on in the midst of arriving at that conclusion. Even if politics and nastiness were present – it says nothing about the truth of the outcome. Although human motives may be suspect, the right result can still be reached. If we toss out the importance of who Jesus is, just because His followers are pricks at times we would be left with nothing!

Gnosticism not Another Denomination

Modern advocates claim Gnosticism was merely a branch or sect of orthodox Christianity that was unduly snubbed for political agendas – and that early Gnostic texts deserve a place in our canons of scripture.

Early Gnostics produced a lot of literature, usually under the auspices of pseudepigraphy (false authorship). Jesus' disciple Thomas did not really author the *Gospel of Thomas*, nor did Judas draft the *Gospel of Judas*, nor did Mary write the *Gospel of Mary*. Any scholar worth his salt in paperclips can tell you that. Gnostics used deviant tactics like false authorship to spread their agenda. But ever since the mid-1990s, when you walked into a Barnes and Noble bookstore, a huge section of books began appearing, suggesting that Gnosticism was a valid, misunderstood form of early Christianity.

Many people had forgotten about Gnosticism until the 1945 Nag Hammadi discovery of ancient Gnostic writings in Egypt. And of course Dan Brown's novel *The Da Vinci Code* published in 2003 has duped plenty into revisiting Gnosticism in recent days. You may have believed the hype from some conspiracy theorist video on YouTube to think that religious authorities suppressed lots of Gnostic texts that should have made it into the Bible. It was not just an authentic Christian denomination rubbed out by the powers that be. It is the very spirit of antichrist

---

[12] The largest early church heresy besides Gnosticism was *Arianism*. We will not concern ourselves with arianism here, except to say that it denied both the Trinity and a proper understanding of the incarnation.

that denies incarnation and throws salvation back upon ourselves.

Contrary to New Age, Jesus was not just a guy who taught us to realize our inner "Christ principle." We cannot pull that off. He is exclusively *the Christ,* yet mystically resident within us.

In fact, forms of Gnosticism have resurfaced throughout the past 2,000 years in various forms, up until this very day with massive cultic movements in the charismatic church focused on fasting and asceticism. Outright Gnosticism made a resurgence during the Renaissance and the Age of Enlightenment. In fact a group called the Rosicrucians were blatantly Gnostic. Nearly all secret societies trace their roots to this. It was always present in alchemy, freemasonry, New Age and all manner of mind-over-matter philosophies. Secret knowledge. Cloak and dagger stuff. It is not just present in secret societies, but also within the circles of conspiracy theory fear mongers obsessed with *exposing* these secret societies by exposing all their secrets!

At its core, the word Gnosticism means "saved by knowledge." Mind over matter. Any philosophy based on secret hidden wisdom or mysterious insights will run along that vein. I personally do not care what the illuminati is doing, whether it exists or not; and I could care less what goes on in a Mormon temple magic underwear ceremony. Reason, rationalism and knowledge can exalt themselves over empirical reality all they want. I am satisfied with the mystery of Christ in me, the hope of glory. But is it not ironic? Religionists continually bark against New Age and secret societies, but religion itself spawned this stuff! Religion is the mother of New Age. Gnosticism is the very *spirit of religion*.

Of course Christians are not buying all the Gnostic books that now fill the shelves at Barnes and Noble. Despite all the pastors that denounce the word *Gnosticism*, nevertheless the majority of them are still fighting their bodies to gain spiritual benefit. The spirit of antichrist religion replaces what Christ has done with what we ourselves must do to acquire salvation. It locks spirituality into an immaterial realm of thought, idea or theological theory while attacking humanity on all fronts to get there. Rejecting food, money, sex, music, drink and dancing – it sends you on a suicide mission to become spiritual and climb an unseen ladder. Stop trying to *become* spiritual and learn to become a *human being*. So many are trying to run a spiritual race, but they cannot even be part of the human race.

The Church Fathers on Union

Thank God that the church fathers in the first few centuries A.D. (for all their pettiness at times) laid the groundwork in showing us who Jesus was, by lending an ear to the apostles before them. In fact we must wonder if God Himself would have permitted his church to reach such a mistaken conclusion on something as vital as the person of Christ in those early ecumenical councils. Even in our darkest times, we must realize that Holy Spirit has moved in the church to pull her back from error. Trust me, mother church has believed some of the dumbest stuff over the years. But it is a low view of Providence to think God could not work through those ancient fathers to hand down to us through the ages a set of sacred texts and a basic understanding of incarnation.

The doctrine of the Trinity and the incarnation hung in the balance with the early church. There were drastic ramifications for error if they got it wrong. Today the Western church is still riddled with non-Trinitarian concepts (like the doctrine of penal substitution, in which the Father turned against the Son, destroying Him to pay off the divine bloodlust against us).[13] Many of these ideas were never embraced in the East.

While some church fathers in the West, like Augustine, would major on themes of separation from God, other large voices in the East would serve as a beacon pointing us to *union*. Union over separation must prevail. This is the essence of the gospel. Men like Athanasius and Irenaeus were such voices. A disciple of Polycarp, who was himself a direct pupil of the apostle John, Irenaeus gives us an early glimpse into the meaning of the incarnation like none other. In his writings you see a depiction of a Father whose absolute goal in the incarnation was never about appeasing His wrath toward man, but to share the life of the Trinity with our broken humanity, adopting us into the divine family.

> *...the Son of God being made the Son of man, that through Him we may receive the adoption – humanity sustaining, and*

---

[13] For more on navigating our misunderstandings of the atonement regarding penal substitution, particularly the modern Western concept that Jesus was dying to avert God's wrath and twist the Father's arm to love us, see my book *Cosmos Reborn: Happy Theology on the New Creation* (Portland: Sons of Thunder Ministries & Publications, 2013), available at www.JohnCrowder.net.

receiving, and embracing the Son of God.[14]

For [God] promised, that in the last times He would pour Him [the Spirit] upon [His] servants and handmaids, that they might prophesy; wherefore He did also descend upon the Son of God, made the Son of man, becoming accustomed in fellowship with Him to dwell in the human race, to rest with human beings, and to dwell in the workmanship of God, working the will of the Father in them, and renewing them from their old habits into the newness of Christ.[15]

Therefore, as I have already said, He caused man (human nature) to cleave to and to become one with God. For unless man had overcome the enemy of man, the enemy would not have been legitimately vanquished. And again: unless it had been God who had freely given salvation, we could never have possessed it securely. And unless man had been joined to God, he could never have become a partaker of incorruptibility. For it was incumbent upon the Mediator between God and men, by His relationship to both, to bring both into friendship and concord, and present man to God, while He revealed God to man. For, in what way, could we be partakers of the adoption of sons, unless we had received from Him through the Son that fellowship, which refers to Himself, unless His Word, having been made flesh, had entered into communion with us? Wherefore also He passed through every stage of life, restoring to all communion with God.[16]

Chalcedonian Christology

God's desire to become one with the human race is most clearly revealed in Jesus Christ. The early church – perhaps as a *reaction* to facing the heresies we have discussed – found it more and more paramount to clarify the nature of who Jesus is as the God-man. Therefore the council of Chalcedon in 451 A.D. eventually summed up for us the most basic and foundational understanding of Christology. The Chalcedonian council stated that:

---

[14] Irenaeus, *Against the Heresies*, III.16.3

[15] *Against the Heresies*, III.17.1

[16] *Against the Heresies*, III.18.7

- Christ is one person
- He has two natures: one divine and one human
- These two natures are distinct and have their own integrity:
  they are not mixed together or confused like a demigod.

Now granted there is still some mystery in this – because it is not all fully defined, nor could it be. Also depending on your metaphysical worldview, people can look at these statements all sorts of ways. I mean what is a *nature?* (What is the nature of a man, or a dog or a tree?) And if you really want to get existential – then what is a *person?*

But essentially, we can say that Christ has *one* of whatever goes with the *person* and *two* of whatever goes with the *natures.* Now this is a mystery to ponder. Only when we realize who He is, only then can we begin to sort out anything whatsoever about His work. Because a certain sort of saving work requires a certain type of person. Christ had to work salvation from both sides – repairing the divine-human relationship both from the side of God and from the side of humanity. Only God and man together as one unified person could seamlessly accomplish a union between both sides. The question is not "What will you do with Jesus?" but "What did Jesus do to you?" His work was only a byproduct of His being.

From the Definition of Chalcedon we read:

> Following, then, the holy fathers, we unite in teaching all men to confess the one and only Son, our Lord Jesus Christ. This selfsame one is perfect both in deity and in humanness; this selfsame one is also actually God and actually man, with a rational soul and a body. He is of the same reality as God as far as his deity is concerned and of the same reality as we ourselves as far as his humanness is concerned; thus like us in all respects, sin only excepted. Before time began He was begotten of the Father, in respect of his deity, and now in these "last days," for us and behalf of our salvation, this selfsame one was born of Mary the virgin, who is God-bearer in respect of his humanness.
>
> We also teach that we apprehend this one and only Christ – Son, Lord, only-begotten — in two natures; and we do this without confusing the two natures, without transmuting one na-

ture into the other, without dividing them into two separate categories, without contrasting them according to area or function. The distinctiveness of each nature is not nullified by the union. Instead, the "properties" of each nature are conserved and both natures concur in one "person" and in one reality. They are not divided or cut into two persons, but are together the one and only and only-begotten Word of God, the Lord Jesus Christ. Thus have the prophets of old testified; thus the Lord Jesus Christ Himself taught us; thus the Symbol of Fathers has handed down to us.

Jesus was not ashamed to condescend and take on our human flesh. Nor is He ashamed to call us brothers. As the perfect and full manifestation of the other-giving love of God, He fully embraced our broken existence into Himself.

Maintaining the Mystery

It is important to know the church fathers in the Council of Chalcedon were not so much attempting to explain away the mystery of the incarnation (which itself cannot be fully articulated), as much as they were drawing some important parameters to protect our understanding from early heresies. Dr. Oliver Crisp notes that Chalcedon's description of the *hypostatic union* (the union of God and man in Jesus) is "minimalistic because the definition says as little as doctrinally possible about the hypostatic union, while making it clear that certain ways of thinking about the person of Christ are off-limits, or unorthodox."[17] Crisp references Richard Sturch in saying, "It has long been recognized that the main purpose of most of the early Councils was not so much to lay down an orthodox line as to rule out lines which were *not* orthodox."[18] Thomas F. Torrance explains:

The place of the mystery of Christ in our understanding can only be stated and guarded in negative terms. The mystery is that in Jesus Christ true God and true man are united in one person – that is the doctrine of the hypostatic union. But we

---

[17] Oliver D. Crisp, "Desiderata for Models of the Hypostatic Union," *Christology Ancient and Modern* (Grand Rapids: Zondervan, 2013), 27.

[18] Richard Sturch, *The Word and the Christ: An Essay in Analytic Christology* (Oxford: Oxford University Press, 1991), 214.

*must mark out, on either side of that mystery, what it is by say-
ing what it is not. In this way we allow the mystery to declare
itself to us, and to keep on declaring itself to us without hinder-
ing the depth or breadth of its self-disclosure by positive manmade definitions of what it actually is. This is the Chalcedonian
doctrine of Christ. In this statement we say that God and man
are united in Jesus Christ, divine and human nature in one
person, in such a way that (a) there is no impairing or diminishing either deity or humanity in the union; and (b) there is neither separation of the natures nor confusion between them.*[19]

Now I may be the only preacher you have known to back up beer
drinking, love making and money spending with Chalcedonian Christology. But God knows we need a solid theological foundation so religion stops spoiling our party. God has embraced our material world!

Gnostic dualism flourished like mushrooms in the theology of numerous early sects, as it still does in the Western church today – but do
not think the very church fathers opposing Gnosticism were not also
influenced by it. Western church fathers, primarily Augustine (whom I
mentioned above), would adopt Plato and in effect blend two oppo-
sites: *separation and union.* In his work *The Two Cities*, Augustine con-
trasts Rome (the new Babylon) symbolizing all that is worldly, with Jerusalem (the heavenly city) to symbolize the community of Christians.
The present world consists of a mixture of the two. He hammered out
the first concept of *original sin*, from the fall of Adam, noting that the
present, temporal world will perish. But this should be contrasted with
the Orthodox Christians of the East who never fully embraced Western
dualisms or the full depravity of an original sin doctrine. For the Orthodox, humanity is fallen but still bears the image of God undistorted
within themselves. There is still a spark of *original innocence.* Christ is
our truest nature and original identity, not fallen Adam.

So Many Early *isms*

Most early Christological heresies revolved around this struggle to
rightly connect God with a humanity that must (in the Gnostic mind)
clearly be evil. While there is no need to memorize the following, allow

---

[19] Thomas F. Torrance, *Incarnation: The Person and Life of Christ*, edited by
Robert T. Walker (Downers Grove: InterVarsity Press., 1998), 83.

me to bat cleanup and mention a few more early dualistic heresies just to show the huge scope of the problem:

Apollinarianism argued that Jesus assumed a human nature, but not a human soul. Instead his divine nature took the place of the soul. This idea diminished the full humanity of Christ and was rightly condemned. It was similar to Docetism (where Christ was not a real human, but just a *spirit being*).

Nestorianism (inappropriately named after Bishop Nestorius, who did not actually hold this view) claimed that Jesus had two natures, but that He also had *two persons*: one human and one divine. It separated the person of Jesus, rather than unifying Him (confusing, I know).

Eutychianism is the view that Christ's human nature was absorbed into His divine nature. Like a co-mingled demigod. A blended, half-caffeinated latte.

It is not necessary to explore in detail every heretical *-ism* that sought to contort the incarnation, but there were numerous others (Monophysitism, Miaphysitism, Dyophysitism, etc.). As appreciative as we must be of the timeless benefit of the church fathers' parameters on Christology, we must also remember that these early debates could also get a bit anal retentive, splitting hairs in their definitions and overly focused on the heresy hunting. Sure, it was necessary – but these councils were also a sign of their times. An inordinate obsession with a philosophical mapping of the metaphysical being of Christ could also get a bit clinical at times and miss the mystery of the whole marriage of heaven and earth that He is.

Similarly in the Nicene Creed, theologians made a painstaking and exhaustive attempt to clarify the technical term *homoousios* (that Jesus is the same "substance" or "essence" as the Father – consisting of the same, equal "God stuff"). Why were they so focused on that word? Well it is *hugely* important. But they needed to clarify it because *the Gnostics were already throwing the term around inappropriately.*

This theological language seems draining and irrelevant to many. But prior to these clinical definitions, church fathers like Athanasius had used much more colorful, biblical imagery to describe Christ (not just abstract metaphysical terms). The Son is the "radiance" of the Father's glory (Heb. 1:3). The Son is the stream flowing from the Father's "fountain of living waters" (Jer. 2:13). And Jesus is the Word and Wisdom of the Father (John 1:1-3; Prov. 8).[20]

Christologies often emphasize the polarity of divinity and humanity in the incarnation, when in actuality it is their very union in Jesus which constitutes the highest theme of the gospel. Yes let us distinguish His two unmixed, unconfused natures. But the fact that they are forever bound together in the hypostasic union (the union of the one Person Jesus) is of paramount importance. Surely we can better appreciate this mystical union by clarifying the two seemingly contradictory parts. Yet theologians have a way of overcomplicating matters by clinically dissecting what is united in order to put it back together again like a Lego set. In our analysis let us not put more weight on the contradiction than we do the unity of the parts. The fact that God has united Himself to humanity shatters our notions of separation.

More Philosophical Confusion

The separation between mind and matter evolved in later centuries through philosophers like Immanuel Kant (1724-1804) into an *epistemological* dualism. *Epistemology* is the science of *knowing*. It is concerned with *how do we know things?* (How do you know God speaks? How can you know anything about God? Etc.). Philosophy is highly vested in this field. For Immanuel Kant, there was a disjunction between the human knower and the thing or reality which an observer seeks to know. A separation between the actual, red, leather-interior Ferrari and your human awareness that the Ferrari even exists. Following the Scottish Enlightenment philosopher, David Hume (1711-1776), there was a major divide between your *perceptions* and what is objectively "real" because the only way we could observe the mechanical world was by our own human mind and senses. And could those senses be trusted? They were too subjective.

In other words – does anything really exist, or is it all one big Matrix of a head-trip? (you need loads of LSD to get anything out of philosophy).

---

[20] Peter J. Leithart, "We Saw His Glory: Implications of the Sanctuary Christology in John's Gospel," *Christology Ancient and Modern* (Grand Rapids: Zondervan, 2013), 115.

Hume pioneered *skepticism*, in that true knowledge is completely unattainable, because all our observations of the world around us are run through our faulty human senses – putting subjective human experience at the center of reality. Hume essentially pioneered atheism because the idea that we could conceive of an intangible God through our human senses was nonsensical. For such philosophers, to call something "reality" was to impose our own "artificial" perceptions upon the things we are observing.

By the nineteenth century, theologians were desperately trying to run with these trends in philosophy. And this brought the birth of modern *liberal theology*, which embraced skepticism, exalted the mind of man over everything, and wrote off nearly every biblical narrative as nonfactual. But this was not a new trend. Just dualism resurfacing once more. Separating mind/idea from fact/reality.

Much of this was built on earlier French philosopher René Descartes' famous statement: *I think therefore I am.* This was a critical turning point in philosophy that has remained for hundreds of years. An extreme inward turn toward the self. The highest form of self-aggrandizing, where a person's thought becomes the ultimate standard of truth, of right and wrong – of reality itself.

Your mind does not dictate reality. But this concept has been playing out in Western theology ever since. Suddenly the solid events of the recorded scriptures could not be trusted. The human mind and reasoning became the standard by which we gauge spirituality.

It is no coincidence that most theologians seem to measure their spirituality by an accumulation of mental data. I will not say philosophy is inherently evil, but it surely has its limits at apprehending truth. And Western theology trends much closer to the deceiving sophistry Paul cautions against (Col. 2:4) than to raw childlike faith and mystery.

When Theology and Reality Divorced

By the nineteenth century, everything was up for questioning; it was all up for grabs in the world of theology. Theologians started tossing out the virgin birth, the resurrection – everything essential to the gospel. The founder of modern liberal theology, Friedrich Schleiermacher (1768-1834), did not seem too bothered about the factuality of the gospel events in scripture. Ironically, what was essential to him was the mere "feeling" of religion – his own subjective "sense and taste for the infinite." *I think, therefore God is.* Faith in Christ had been radically reduced to his own inner head-trip and goose bump. Reality was not as important as your own personal subjective *perspective* of reality (touchy-feely subjectivity is something charismatics usually get blamed for – not theologians!).

Suddenly thought/theory/theology began to develop on an entirely separate course from the factual/concrete/real world stories depicted in the Gospels.

Now most conservative Christian theologians would not go down the route of throwing out the factual events of scripture. But there is still a subtle dualism when we elevate our thoughts and ideas about God over the raw experience of Him in daily life. Not every theologian bought off on liberalism, but our tendency to replace God with abstract "thoughts about God" became rampant.

We are not saved by figuring out God and surely not by knowing some nifty stuff about Him. We are saved by Jesus Himself. At the end of the day, you can never even *know* God on your own anyway! Remember when Jesus scandalously told the religious elite that *none of them* knew God?

> *No one knows the Son except the Father, and no one knows the Father except the Son and those to whom the Son chooses to re-veal Him* (Matt. 11:27, NIV).

What a way to invalidate all the professionally religious guys! *No one knows the Father* ... this statement taken alone is quite daunting. But the greatest news on the planet is that Jesus in His humanity is the *Knower.* And Jesus in His divinity He is the *Known God.* The Known becomes the Knower. Jesus knows the Father *for us* – and *as us* – so we can know the Father through Him. And because of Him, one day we shall *fully know*, even as we are *fully known* (1 Cor. 13:12). Want to know what God looks like? He looks like Jesus. In the flesh. Not some abstract Platonic force in the sky. What would happen if we left the figments of our imagination behind and started to worship a more Christlike God?

218

Our epistemology (our *knowing* of God) can never be divorced from the concrete man Jesus Christ. God cannot be figured out through Bible study – this runs deeper than the mind. And right beliefs surely do not climb us into His presence. "Of His doing you are in Christ" (1 Cor. 1:30). No human willpower, decision or vote was involved.

Neither can He be logically deduced by sitting on a rock in the woods observing the natural world around us (the Aristotelian error of nineteenth century *natural theology)*, though it is true He does sing beautifully through creation. Jesus alone is the image of the invisible God.

Connecting the Dots

So where are we today? We are faced with a theological landscape of liberalism that demythologizes any miraculous/supernatural event in the Bible. A landscape that says the actual facts of scripture cannot be trusted (or they are stripped of any sacred weight, reduced only to an inspirational storybook of "man's thoughts about God").

I could never in one broad stroke dismiss 200 years of liberal theology as contributing *nothing* to our understanding about God. All of the textual critiques of scripture that emerged over this time have contributed to a robust discussion and library of knowledge that is vastly important. However, the over-analytical, non-mystical approach of modern theology has been riddled with the cumulative effect of centuries of dualism. The preeminent theologian Thomas F. Torrance was brilliant in highlighting connections between Greek dualism of the early centuries, to the rediscovery of Aristotle in the Renaissance, its reemergence in Newton during the scientific revolution and its blossoming into outright atheism through the Enlightenment philosophers. He shows that right down to the nineteenth century liberal theologians the vain attempts at demythologizing anything supernatural in the biblical texts all resulted from their existing predisposition toward dualistic thinking.

What we are up against in the demand for demythologisation is a revolt against actual human history in its physical and concrete particularity. The gospel can no more be stripped of its physical event character than the Logos can be stripped of the flesh He assumed in the incarnation. But the whole problem is a false one, resting on a false alternative, the dichotomy between a realm of ideas and a realm of events. The only way to

*solve the problem is to get behind it and to cut away the false
starting point, to get back to the biblical way of thought in
which idea and event are thought of in a unity, and only as dis-
tinctions within a unity.[21]*

Torrance says the philosophical and cultural perspectives of Greece
were the starting point for the early Christological controversies as well
as the "unconscious canons of thought" behind the Enlightenment and
later liberal theologies.

*When the Christian Church spread out from its centre in
Judaea into the Mediterranean world its preaching and teaching of the gospel came up against a radical dualism of body
and mind that pervaded every aspect of Graeco-Roman civili-
zation, bifurcating human experience and affecting fundamental habits of mind in religion, philosophy and science alike. The
Platonic separation between the sensible world and the intelligible world, hardened by Aristotle, governed the disjunction
between action and reflection, event and idea, becoming and
being, the material and the spiritual, the visible and the invisible, the temporal and the eternal, and was built by Ptolemy
into a scientific cosmology that was to dominate European
thought for more than a millennium. The combined effect of
this all-pervading dualism was to shut God out of the world of
empirical actuality in space and time.[22]*

Christ bridges the gap between the unseen and our tangible world of
time and space. He bridges the faulty Kantian notion of a gap between
the knower and the known by knowing the Father for us. The unknown
God became visible. "So the Word became human and made His
home among us. He was full of unfailing love and faithfulness. And we
have seen His glory, the glory of the Father's one and only Son" (John
1:14, NLT[23]). Jesus did more than merely *reveal* the Father. He single-
handedly brought us into a complete mystical union with God.

---

[21] Torrance, *Incarnation: The Person and Life of Christ*, 295.

[22] Thomas F. Torrance, *The Trinitarian Faith* (London: T & T Clark, 1991), 47.

[23] *New Living Translation* (Wheaton: Tyndale House Publishers, 1996, 2004, 2007).

Salvation by Gnosis?

The bulk of our discussion on Gnosticism has dealt with its low view of nature. But there is another essential aspect to the heresy that is worth noting (and which we have already begun to breach).

As stated, the meaning of the term *Gnosticism* is "salvation by knowledge" (*gnosis* meaning *knowledge*). I have mentioned that the thrust of the heresy was to pursue a type of hidden wisdom or enlightenment. By learning or uncovering information, spiritual secrets, etc. one climbs a ladder of spirituality. Mysteries reserved for the elite. In this it is not dissimilar to the kabbalistic mystery cult of Judaism. In fact, any non-Christological vein of mysticism is always Gnostic by nature.

I have long made the argument that both theologians and modern charismatics are especially prone to Gnosticism in their own respective ways when it comes to "salvation by knowledge." I will explain …

There is a not-so-subtle vein that runs deep within theo-academia that spiritual growth consists primarily of an accumulation of knowledge and facts. I know plenty of intellectuals who gauge their spirituality by their exegetical skills or by how many theological terms they have memorized. If you can discuss dynamic monarchianism, supralapsarianism and redaction criticism with them, then you are surely an enlightened one. These are the guys who write books nobody reads and criticize everyone they deem uneducated enough to be real Christians. Granted you may consider that to be mere snobbery. But in their heart of hearts many are operating out of an insecurity to prove themselves and subconsciously feel they are made more spiritual by an amassing of doctrinal facts. One sees this primarily in non-charismatic circles (as charismatics are not particularly known for their stellar theologians). For such academics, the Christian life is not one of personal devotion as much as it is a call to study and *know more*.

We are not saved by our theological acumen. One could be mentally comatose in a vegetative state and still be saved. Your brain does not save you. Jesus Christ did. Of course theology and rightly knowing about God are *hugely important*. How we think affects how we live, the quality of our marriages, jobs, families, etc. In fact, theology is a form of repentance (Greek: *metanoia* = change your mind)! Rightly learning about God – primarily recognizing His goodness and grace – is para-

221

mount to seeing the kingdom manifest in our lives. But as important as theology is – we have to keep it on a short leash. Ultimately, theology must stop at the door of faith. Our minds do not control or contain God, but must surely be shaped by Him. In the end, as we stand before the ineffable, all we are left with is the Mystery of Christ. We will never have all the answers. The Good News is that the Answer has us.

This subtle version of "salvation by gnosis" has turned many churches into a classroom rather than a wholesome, authentic family or community. As the old adage goes, we may know *about* God without really *knowing God*. The latter is *true* gnosis to which we are called. Let us move toward an intimate knowing of God, as well as our neighbor.

Intellectual pursuit need not be divorced from personal devotion, but it is never a substitute for it. Teresa of Avila says that in one intimate experience of divine ecstasy, "what the poor soul has not been able to collect in perhaps twenty years of exhausting intellectual effort, the heavenly Gardener gives it in a moment."[24] We are created for the real presence of God, not just ideas about Him. Grace is not a doctrine; He is a Person.

So yes there are those obsessed with getting their doctrine right, while vacating God in their normal, everyday life. But in the charismatic world, Gnosticism flourishes in another package – more akin to its earliest form. Not in the pursuit of books, but of *secret knowledge* in the sense of visions, locutions and direct divine revelation.

Charismatic Superstition

I am all for visions and God speaking to us today. But we do not get our doctrine from our subjective imaginative experiences. We do not disconnect from the real world. There are countless charismatics who do not know an ounce of biblical Christology, but they are engrossed with teachings on bizarre, hidden, super-spiritual superstitions. They can never seem to have a comfortable conversation about normal stuff like kids, the dog or the latest game on ESPN. They are engrossed with conspiracy theories on the illuminati, nephilim and promoting all manner of intangible means of ascent into the glory. Some are always

---

[24] Teresa of Avila, *The Life of Saint Teresa of Avila by Herself* (London: Penguin Group, 1957 ed.), 117.

222

focused on secret demonic influences on their own lives or others (spirits of leviathan, jezebel, etc.). And if they can just figure out the "hidden keys" to get deliverance or some type of inner healing from it, then all their problems will be solved. Christ and Him crucified is too simple an answer to their problems … it always has to be superstitious and overcomplicated.

Original second century Gnostic doctrines were chock full of strange cosmological ideas about angels, principalities, demons and levels into heaven. In the same way, many charismatics today are overly concerned about underlying spiritual influences in the unseen world that must somehow be dealt with to achieve higher dimensions of spirituality. Obsessed with angels and demons, they cannot rest in the reality that we are seated with Christ above every stronghold. Paranoia is rampant. The Apostle Paul comes out guns blazing against Gnosticism in the book of Colossians and Ephesians – clarifying that Christ is the Head over all principality and power … and these guys who were rattling off visions about the "spiritual world" with all its layers of invisible forces were spouting imaginary nonsense (all pushing their ritualistic fasting routines and formulas). First and foremost Paul said they had forgotten the Head and the simplicity of their victory in Him.

This Gnosticism starts subtly in charismatic circles with the seemingly benign desire to have "more of God." But such a request belies the fact that we already have *all of God* thanks to our union with Christ (Col. 2:9-10). If I have a sense that I lack Him in some way (separation/dualism), then I am prone to start doing ignorant, self-defeating nonsense to "get him." There is the outright ascetic stuff (fasting, etc.). But there is also a bustling market of self-appointed teachers on the circuit who provide something much better: *divine insight directly from God*. The charismatic obsession with self-proclaimed experts who have the inside prophetic track with God gives the consumer hope that contact with the Big Guy may be possible through the new guru. *"Finally, the secret that will fix my problems!"* While insecurities do not allow them to rest in their own personal *union with God* themselves, they bite off any bizarre new spin these fortune tellers sell them.

And the weirder the more believable.

MONEY. SEX. BEER. GOD.

The New Gnostics

I once had a friend, a young guy who was legitimately gifted by God. I helped him get meetings in the early days, and he had been connected with a large, respectable charismatic ministry on the West Coast. He eventually gained a sizeable platform in the charismatic world by being featured in documentary films working physical healings on the streets, etc. I appreciated his gifts but also his genuine sweetness.

But soon the Gnostic tendency toward "understanding the deeper things" pushed him further and further into outright delusion. All of life became about visions ... not empirical reality. He began to live in a fantasyland of imagination, to the point of perhaps full-blown schizophrenia. He fancied himself as possessing so much "inside revelation" from God, that the illuminati wanted him taken out. He literally started thinking the CIA was after him. He even had the coercive power of making others think their imaginations were real to the point my best buddy at the time was literally convinced the guy had taken him on an interplanetary trip to the Sun and that his face transfigured into a lion.

Birds of a feather flock together. Soon the kid from the documentary was connected with another new Gnostic from New Zealand. The New Zealander really had the inside scoop on the hidden things of God. He taught serpent-seed theology: that Eve literally had sex with the serpent and that much of "humanity" are secretly reptilians in disguise (mostly those in power like the Queen of England or Beyoncé). Unfortunately, I am not making this up. The Kiwi teaches that Adam was made of gold dust, and that the reason gold is valuable is because if we eat it, it causes us to transfigure and be closer to God (that is sane, right?). He teaches that we are to go "into the spirit" and battle dragons, literally killing demons by burning them to death, and make ourselves teleport from place to place (all of this happens in his imagination mind you – but he conveys his testimonies to listeners as actual fact). He even taught the brilliant idea that you should fast from reading your Bible, because you become too dependent on it. You should rely more on your imagination of course! Everything was about new odd formulas of "cleaning your soul gates" and battling imaginary principalities. Needless to say the guy is light on his Christology. But he gives lip service to the Lord. If you employ a strict regimen of "praying the blood" every day like a magical incantation, he says it is quite effective.

224

MONEY. SEX. BEER. GOD.

Unbelievably, countless charismatics lap this stuff up.

Obviously we should give latitude for some theological differences in the church. The problem here is not one of biblical interpretation, but basing everything on subjective imaginary experiences. Clearly church history and the scriptures have a rich history of bizarre miracles. So the "weird" factor is not necessarily an indicator of trouble when God is glorified in an environment of grace. The issue is an under-emphasis on Christ's finished work and an overemphasis on the believer's role in defeating boogeymen and detaching themselves from the real world around them (a good example is when the fellow claims he does not need to exercise because he has the *spirit of might* ... But the guy is no Hulk Hogan). When people walk away from the meetings feeling *less spiritual* than these shamen, the gospel has not been preached.

Well by the time my old friend (from the CIA's Most Wanted List) bumped into this New Zealander, things went from crazy to batshit crazy. His interplanetary travels started taking him to Mars (which he discovered is apparently the home of satan), before he realized he was called to intergalactic relations with alien races. He transformed his Christian ministry into some interplanetary diplomacy thing, and talks about projecting his spirit into the galactic core (occasionally giving a high-five to Jesus as his spirit-guide who showed him how to transfigure into a fully-realized space cadet). He even thinks he is currently in high-level discussions with NASA agents in his mind (hand on the Bible, I am really not making this stuff up).

This would be funny, but sadly enough the guy has checked himself out from the real world like a VHS tape from Blockbuster. And that is exactly what *salvation by gnosis* does – gets you trapped in a looney world of imaginary powers and principalities and angelic forces which (even if they exist) Christ has already seated us high above, and to which we need not pay much attention. But folks will still flock to these meetings; because they need some sort of panacea they think the gospel alone is incapable of providing.

True Gnosis

We need a gnosis of the gospel. A knowledge that Jesus did it all, weaving us completely into the life of God. Charismatics who get heavily into Gnosticism cease to be real people anymore. The more weird

225

and unnatural, the more spiritual they think they become. Trust me, I am all for crazy manifestations and unusual miracles (after all, I am the guy forever infamous for bizarre YouTube clips I will never live down). Yet the goal is not to *try* to be abnormal so as to be spiritual. I also love seer gifts, visions and believe in personal revelation from God. He speaks to us. But in the charismatic world, Gnosticism thrives in the lives of people who cannot just be normal. You cannot have an ordinary chat about weather or sit for a cold drink together at the bar. It always has to be about some angel they saw, or how miracle oil appeared on their palms. They live in a world of disconnect. Lives that are not incarnational. Yes I thoroughly appreciate the supernatural dynamics of our faith! I see more healings than most – even bizarre stuff like weight loss miracles, blind eyes opening, etc. Often when charismatics approach me for a one-on-one sit down, they expect me to prophesy their future or levitate in front of them, because of this very embrace of the supernatural I have strongly advocated over the years. But when I crack open a beer and talk about a movie or a recent UFC cage fight I just watched, they walk away scratching their heads because I knocked the wind of super-spirituality out of their sails.

Is Holy Spirit with you when you go shopping, or to a secular concert, or when you mop the floor or make love to your wife? How about having a chat with your kids on the way to school? So many are looking for *revival* – an "outpouring" of the Holy Ghost to come down from the sky. I am done with all of that. I do not want revival. I want *reality*. The church is technically looking for an *inpouring* (God coming from an external place), but what He gave us was a true *outpouring* … that out of our bellies would flow rivers of living water! Their idea of revival starts with God "up there" somewhere, coming for a visit. He has been here all along. I am not looking for an encounter of a lifetime. I am living a lifetime of encounter. Yes, He is transcendent and above us. But He is also immanent and latent within our natural lives. I am no longer striving to access bizarre miracles like walking through walls – as much as I love the phenomenal. I am just overawed with ecstasy to realize His hand keeps my physical heart beating at 65 bpm and that He sends hummingbirds to my porch while I enjoy a cigar in the sun.

If we are trying to bring heaven to earth, I have news for you. Jesus said (quite often) that the kingdom of God is already *at hand*. Where is God right now? Knock knock! He has been here all along. The incarnation changed everything. In Christ, He assumed the whole cosmos into the divine life. Even unbelievers "live and move and have their being in Him" Paul tells the pagans in Acts 17:28. This is true whether we have the eyes of faith to see it or not. What if we simply woke up?

There are no *unbaptized* parts of our lives that are out of His range. Drop the double-minded polarity. It never occurred in the mind of God that creation would be something separate from Him. As soon as we wall God off from certain areas, we jump to a place of insanity – a religious schizophrenia. Delusional separation anxiety. *He does not exist in this area of addiction, my finances, my health, my dysfunctional family relationships.* Before you know it, we are locked into this false pagan mindset that is based entirely on a lie. We start forming personality disorders founded only upon smoke and mirrors.

God was always here – and is shining right now in the midst of the darkness. Even the darkness is as light to Him. Plato and Aristotle could see a dualistic split between light and darkness. Good and evil. Right and wrong. But the apostle John throws us a brain scrambler in the first chapter of his Gospel when he tells us that the light is shining *in* the darkness! (John 1:5). There is nowhere you can hide from the inescapable love of God.

ABOUT THE AUTHOR

 John Crowder loves to push the envelope and provoke God's people to extreme joy. He is a father and is recognized internationally as an author, speaker and advocate of supernatural Christianity. John is on the forefront of a fresh renewal movement marked by the message of grace, ecstatic experience, miracles and a recovery of the foundational preaching of the finished work of the cross. John and his wife Lily have four children based in Portland, Ore. As founders of Sons of Thunder Ministries and Publications, they speak at schools and conference events around the world. SOT hosts mass evangelism events and operate multiple homes for orphan children in developing nations. They have a background in church planting and currently oversee *Cana New Wine Seminary* in Portland, Ore. Along with his bi-annual magazine, *The Ecstatic*, John has written thousands of articles during his journalism career. He has authored seven books:

Money.Sex.Beer.God.
Chosen for Paradise
Cosmos Reborn
Mystical Union
The Ecstasy of Loving God
Seven Spirits Burning
The New Mystics

John's weekly video teachings on *The Jesus Trip* have garnered more than a million views. John and Lily have a heart to see the Kingdom of God manifest creatively in every sector of society. Their vision is to equip the Church and reach the world by clearly communicating the finished work of the cross. Creative miracles and unusual signs and wonders mark John's ministry.

CONNECT WITH US
SONSOFTHUNDER

There are many ways to stay connected with us!

Visit us online at:
www.TheNewMystics.com

Find out about conferences, mission trips, schools, teaching resources, John's itinerary and more.

Email us at: info@thenewmystics.org
Call us toll-free: 1-877-343-3245

Write us at:
P.O. Box 40
Marylhurst, OR 97036

Find us on Social Networks:
Facebook: www.facebook.com/revjohncrowder
Twitter: www.twitter.com/thenewmystics
YouTube: www.youtube.com/sonsofthunderpub
Linkedin: www.linkedin.com/in/johnwcrowder
Google Plus: www.google.com/+JohnCrowder
Instagram: www.instagram.com/thenewmystics

Visit our Mission Page: www.TheNewMystics.com/Missions
Find a trip you can join and see updates on our orphanages!

MONTHLY WEB CONFERENCE

Discover our live monthly Web seminar: *The Inner Sanctum*

THENEWMYSTICS.TV

The Inner Sanctum continues to be a fun connection point for gospel drinkers all around the globe who want to stay plugged in with finished-work theology in an atmosphere of joy and impartation. Members now have access to dozens of hours of archived shows, making it the most comprehensive place to view Sons of Thunder teachings. And each month, John Crowder and guests engage one-on-one with viewers for live teaching and Q&A sessions.

Our Inner Sanctum Web broadcast provides a user-friendly format and we continue to add more interactive features. The Inner Sanctum is also a social media platform where members create a personal profile, share pictures and chat with friends 24-hours a day, even when the show is not live.

Find out about membership for yourself, your church or a home group by visiting **www.TheNewMystics.TV**

THE ECSTATIC MAGAZINE

We produce our bi-annual magazine *The Ecstatic* as a way to bring a cohesive voice to the growing interest in authentic, mystical Christianity – a mysticism rooted in the grace message of Christ's cross – not in dead works, asceticism or external disciplines. In a practical sense, *The Ecstatic* serves as an information gateway to the ministry of John & Lily Crowder. But moreover, it is a first fruit in publishing toward bridging several important themes that are converging at the moment: finished work theology, the miraculous, divine satisfaction and daily human existence in the incarnational life. All of these concepts are intrinsically woven together with contributions from modern writers and ancient voices. A new grace-based, Christ-centered mysticism is on the rise. It is bridging many streams. Relevant is its cultural approach. Radical is its charismatic fervor. Reformative is its theology of grace. These are guiding values of this publication and our own lives. It is a theological journal whose frequency is joy unspeakable.

Subscribe to John Crowder's magazine, *The Ecstatic,* for free:
www.TheNewMystics.com/Ecstatic

FREE VIDEOS: THE JESUS TRIP

Subscribe to *The Jesus Trip* ... a weekly video teaching from John Crowder. You can join simply by visiting our web site: **www.TheNewMystics.com**. On our homepage, type in your email address and sign up for our weekly newsletter. You will receive new video links every time they become available.

Or visit: **www.TheNewMystics.com/TheJesusTrip**

Have an iPhone? Get The New Mystics App for videos on the go

DIGITAL DOWNLOAD STORE

Visit our online *Digital Download Store* to get instant audio teachings on many topics from John Crowder at: **www.JohnCrowder.Net**

DIGITAL DOWNLOAD STORE

Visit our online *Digital Download Store* to get instant audio teachings on many topics from John Crowder at: **www.JohnCrowder.Net**

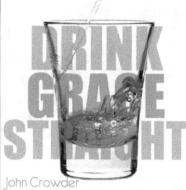

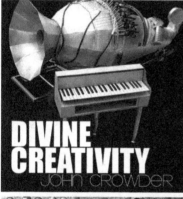

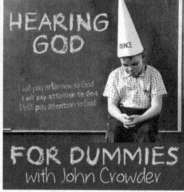

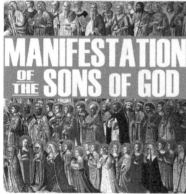

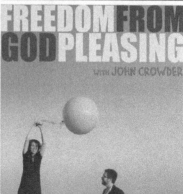

MORE BOOKS BY JOHN CROWDER

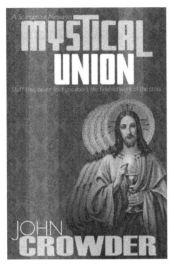

Mystical Union
A Scandalous Message!

When you think of the cross, do you think of *fun*? Get ready for the gospel as you've never heard it. With clear revelatory truths on the New Creation and the scandalous joys of the cross, Mystical Union is one of John's most revolutionary, life-changing works. The happy gospel of grace is about uninterrupted union with the Divine. This book lays out our most core beliefs. It promises to wreck your theology and cheer you up with undeniable biblical truths on the free gift of perfection.

$19.95 + Shipping (Hardback)

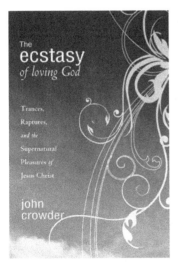

The Ecstasy of Loving God
Trances, raptures & the supernatural pleasures of Jesus Christ

God has destined you to live in the joyful radiance of Himself, just as Adam was called to live in the realm of Eden. Ecstasy, or "extasis," is the Greek term for trance, and is linked with a pleasurable, God-given state of out-of body experience recorded throughout the sciptures and the Church age. In this book, John takes us on a journey from past to present to introduce us to a lifestyle of a deep practice of God's presence.

$15.95 + Shipping

MORE BOOKS BY JOHN CROWDER

Cosmos Reborn
Happy Theology on New Creation
Take a grace-centered look at regeneration, the new creation and the new birth. Christ cured the human condition. John's new book explores the universal scope of the cross - if one died for all, then all died! "For God was in Christ reconciling the cosmos to Himself." He has woven humanity into His divinity! Dispel the myth of a dark, schizophrenic god of religion. This book makes a scandalous case that the Father of Jesus Christ is in a good mood. Get a religious detox – a dose of happy theology – liberating good news!

$19.95 + Shipping (Hardback)

Chosen For Paradise
The Inclusion of Humanity in the Saving Act of Jesus Christ
Do we choose God or does He choose us? Must our striving human willpower conjure up our own salvation? Or does God predestine some for bliss and others for destruction? John cheers up theology's biggest problem with his shortest book ever. "Election" is not considered a fun topic. But this book revisits our perspective on the volatile chapters of Romans 9-11. See that God is not choosing one person over another. He chose Christ to represent all of humanity!

$14.95 + Shipping

ORDER AT WWW.JOHNCROWDER.NET
OR CALL TOLL-FREE 1-877-343-3245

MORE BOOKS BY JOHN CROWDER

Seven Spirits Burning
The Sevenfold Spirit of God
John's long-awaited book, *Seven Spirits Burning,* is an extensive, biblical plunge into the nature and operation of the sevenfold Spirit of God. This book unpackages a deep theological and Christocentric understanding of the seven Spirits. John has taught for years on the seven Spirits, but not until now has he released this detailed compilation of his study and experience. This book could possibly be the *magnum opus* of anything written to date on the Spirit's sevenfold nature. Engage the depths of your union with God.
$19.95 + Shipping (Hardback)

The New Mystics
The supernatural generation
Two thousand years of miracle workers and pioneers crammed into one generation. The fiery bowls of heaven are being poured out through an extreme body of spiritual forerunners. Are you called to walk among them? *The New Mystics* contains more than 70 photos, illustrations, and biographies of men and women whose lives demonstrated the phenomenal throughout the ages. Let their stories inspire you to join their ranks as part of this supernatural generation.
$15.95 + Shipping

CANA SEMINARY

Cana is where the water of the word is transformed into the wine of contemplative experience. Students, pastors and lay leaders who want a grace immersion are invited either to enroll in our two-year online course, or join us live for one summer of intensive theological training and hands on impartation in an atmosphere of joy unspeakable in Portland, Ore.

John Crowder hosts this unique seminary for wild-eyed wonder junkies to be deeply established in the revelation of the gospel of grace. Cana offers a unique marriage of life-transforming, happy theology woven seamlessly with an intoxicating practice of the presence of God. Where else will you find doctorate level theologians and mystical ecstatics on the same platform? Cana is a drunken seminary. A theological circus of fun geared to saturate students with the Living Word - in the wine of the New Covenant. More than a ministry school ... Cana is a *Message School*.

www.Cana.Co

PARTNER WITH US